1993

Power, Publicity, and the Abuse of Libel Law

Power, Publicity, and the Abuse of Libel Law

DONALD M. GILLMOR

New York   Oxford
OXFORD UNIVERSITY PRESS
1992

Oxford University Press

Oxford   New York   Toronto
Delhi   Bombay   Calcutta   Madras   Karachi
Petaling Jaya   Singapore   Hong Kong   Tokyo
Nairobi   Dar es Salaam   Cape Town
Melbourne   Auckland

and associated companies in
Berlin   Ibadan

Copyright © 1992 by Donald M. Gillmor

Published by Oxford University Press, Inc.,
200 Madison Avenue, New York, New York 10016

Oxford is a registered trademark of Oxford University Press

Library of Congress Cataloging-in-Publication Data
Gillmor, Donald M.
Power, publicity, and the abuse of libel law / Donald M. Gillmor.
p. cm.   Includes bibliographical references and index.
ISBN 0-19-507192-1
1. Libel and slander—United States.   2. Process—United States.
3. Press law—United States.   4. Publicity.   I. Title.
KF1266.G55   1992
345.73'0256—dc20
[347.305256]   91-26698

9 8 7 6 5 4 3 2 1

Printed in the United States of America
on acid-free paper

To my grandsons, Stephen, Kevin, and Geoffrey,
for touching me with immortality

Contents

Preface

Abuse of process is the alarm sounded in this book, abuse of the libel laws by the rich and famous, the politically powerful, the annointed of our society. Libel litigation has become a devastatingly effective weapon for silencing those who dare to challenge the morality of power, privilege, and prestige. Plaintiff and defendant battle in a confined judicial arena; public discourse is circumvented. Lawyers ultimately are the only winners in these kinds of libel suits. The most skillful among them join the priesthood of a field of civil law so complex that few noviates are inducted. Those outside the magic circle of comprehension are doomed to bring losing suits and, if they are judges, to misinstruct jurors on the bewildering rules of libel litigation. A systematic study of reported libel cases involving the media between 1982 and 1988 suggests the futility of highly public plaintiffs bringing libel suits.

This is also a book about an arrogant and self-righteous press that idealizes a free flow of information but has yet to learn how to provide space and time for reply to those it savages. Some media targets have instant access to major means of mass communication and, therefore, need not be indulged. Others do not, and will be able to respond only if editors and news directors demonstrate an interest in accommodating public discourse on issues of political or cultural significance. It does matter that a governor's family life is bizarrely unconventional; or that a doyen of popular culture has violated a widely shared moral canon. A reply to a press exposure of human misjudgment will engage the community's attention; a libel suit will exclude it. A sensational court proceeding, then, is often substituted for dialogue.

It is also contended in this work that defamatory charges swirling around controversial issues of public importance, regardless of their subject matter, do not exceed the limits of tolerance that an unqualified First Amendment demands. Those who interpret the First Amendment to construct a theory of freedom of expression are too often prepared to contract or constrict freedom of speech and press in the interest of other values. Counterspeech, I will argue as did Justice Louis Brandeis, is a more constitutionally sensitive solution to the problem of defamatory attack.

I have used—more likely misused—history to suggest that our press has become tepid and hesitant where the bigger issues of abuse of power are concerned. Two hundred years ago when criminal and seditious libel laws were in force mainstream editors took chances that few would take today. The expense, uncertainty, and stress of a ten-year libel suit today seems to have a more sobering and inhibiting effect on editorial courage than the certainty, in the past, of a heavy fine and/or imprisonment as criminal sanctions. Punishment for sedition, the bane of a free society, has come back disguised as benign civil litigation. It is anything but benign.

Any misinterpretations of history or the First Amendment theories of others are due to my own ineptitude and should not be blamed on those whose works I consulted or those who were kind enough to read the manuscript in its earlier drafts and advise changes.

While the idea for what many will consider a radical and hopelessly naive appeal to both lawyers and journalists has occupied my mind for a long time, no part of it had been put to paper before the opportunity came to apply for a Fellowship at the Freedom Forum Media Studies Center at Columbia University. My application having been accepted by a generous admissions committee, I duly became a senior fellow in a company of young, experienced and incredibly stimulating professionals, academics, and elder statesmen from both camps.

My gratitude first goes to the Center's executive director, Everette E. Dennis, who is not only a constellation of ideas but a faithful friend and co-editor. His encouragement was unflagging. The hospitality of Everette and Emily Smith will not soon be forgotten. Jane Coleman, associate director of the Center, made the transition from Minneapolis to New York painless. It was good to be reunited with John Pavlik, the Center's research director, and, like Everette, a Minnesota alumnus. John and Mark Thalhimer, technology studies coordinator, did for me what I couldn't have done for myself—the analysis of data from a study of 614 libel cases.

That study could not have been undertaken or completed without the energy, legal knowledge, and commitment of Columbia law student Melanie Grant. No research assistant has ever worked harder. We taught one another a good deal in the process of what for me was a lovely and I hope lasting friendship.

Special thanks to my colleague, Hazel Dicken-Garcia, for valuable historical bibliographic materials and suggestions. She is not to blame for any misinterpretations on my part. And to David Demers for his prodigious skill in data analysis.

My thanks also to Professor Vincent Blasi of the Columbia University School of Law who, by giving me permission to sit in his First Amendment theory class, provided me with the opportunity to see a great teacher in action. It also made me feel comfortable in the School of Law by which I was designated a visiting scholar.

Program assistants, Lisa DeLisle and Paul Eisenberg, kept the fellows' wing of the Center free from the ravages of the outside world. Lisa, under whose care I came, possessed the gift of being able to turn a workplace into an island of calm and serenity. Shirley Gazsi, associate director/communication manager, kept me connected to the outside world by making sure that I got a few telephone queries. Wendy Boyd, systems coordinator, got me going on a strange computer and then fought it in my behalf for months when it proved to hate footnotes. My thanks also to David Stebenne, Craig Fisher-LaMay, Beth Hoffman, Elizabeth Manus, Jeanne Sahadi, Judith Ulrich, Donna Van Cott, Hunt Williams, Sujoya Roy, and Deborah Rogers whose amiable presence and assistance helped make the fellowship a memorable experience.

My lasting appreciation also to Senior Fellow Leo Bogart, eminent communications scholar, whose enthusiasm got my manuscript its first reading by a prospective publisher; to Senior Fellow Lawrence Grossman, former president of NBC and PBS News, whose lasting skepticism about my thesis made me work harder than I might have done; to Joann Byrd, executive editor of the Everett (Washington) *Herald*, whose sensible concept of newsroom ethics won me over; and to Brandy Ayers, Joyce Barnathan, Wolfgang and Lia Donsbach-Nikopoulou, Joe and Marylou Quinlan, John Phillip Santos, Beverly Shepard, Robert Snyder, and Mary Ellen Zuckerman for their various acts of kindness and the intellectual excitement they generated.

My appreciation also to Minnesota colleague Al Tims, whose computer skills know no bounds, for getting me through the initial nightmares of a new computer program back home and for bailing me out when I messed everything up. And to my friends and staff associates Kathleen Paul, Karen Stohl, and Mary Achartz for marching me through to final drafts, and for much more.

Most important to whatever modest success this project may have were those colleagues who read the entire manuscript in its early draft—Everette Dennis and Minnesota colleague William Huntzicker through academic eyes, and Senior Fellow and former publisher John McMillan with the pencil of a skilled editor. John and Carolyn McMillan, new friends, treated us to a weekend of peace and quiet outside of New York City as did Roger and Barbara Myers of Columbia Teachers College, friends of 30 years, who introduced us to Storm King's marvelous outdoor art gallery.

Finally my deepest appreciation and love to Sophie, my partner and friend of four and a half decades, who walked the streets and museum corridors of New York alone until I could join her on weekends, who entertained our many guests, and who was so brave about the dirt, danger, and decibel level of the greatest city on earth.

Minneapolis   D.M.G.
September 1991

Power, Publicity, and the Abuse of Libel Law

Introduction

> [I]f all printers were determined not to print anything till they were sure it would offend nobody, there would be very little printed.
>
> BENJAMIN FRANKLIN[1]

"Nineteen-seventy-four was the worst year of our lives," writes author Susan Sheehan, speaking for herself and her husband Neil Sheehan.

"Marcus Aurelius Arnheiter, the ex-captain of the U.S.S. Vance, had sued Neil, Random House, and others for libel shortly after the book's publication (*The Arnheiter Affair*). A suit had been expected, because Arnheiter had a record of suing and losing but Neil, Random House, and the publisher's lawyers could not have imagined the costs in money and misery of the several libel suits that Arnheiter proceeded to file on this occasion. In late 1973, one of the lawyers directed Neil to write a memo cataloguing his entire research files. Neil spent most of 1974 writing a 343-page memorandum and organizing a 14-foot-high stack of books—research material for the lawyers."[2]

It would be five more years before the U.S. Supreme Court would bring an end to these suits.

This should not happen, and it is the purpose of this work to argue on historical, legal, and empirical grounds for substantial structural changes in the law of libel that might keep the admirals, generals, police chiefs, senators, governors, and city council chairpersons at bay so that the public in the future would not be deprived of a year of a Neil Sheehan's or any other journalist's ouput.

America has had a feisty press from the beginning. Courts, following federal and state constitutions, have been prepared to interpret laws in such a way as to give that press relatively free rein, a freedom that startles outsiders and many Americans as well. In spite of serious setbacks, particularly in times of presumed danger to the constitutional system itself or to a self-appointed moral authority, there has been a continual expansion of freedom of expression. Constitutional interpretation, at least to the end of the 1980s, and common sense have combined to nourish speech and press rather than starve it.

A society that punishes seditious libel as a crime, wrote Professor Harry Kalven, Jr. in one of his seminal essays, is not a free society no matter what are its other characteristics. Seditious or criminal libel is criticism of government or its officials or commentary on public affairs that is perceived as being a threat to public peace and good order or to the authority of the state. It is the hereditary enemy of free speech.

Before the nineteenth century, truth or accuracy was no defense against a charge of seditious libel. Because subversive truth was more dangerous than subversive lies, tyrants of times past believed that the greater the truth the greater the libel. In the United States, however, the right to complain bitterly and without restraint about how we are governed became a basic right.

Yet the crime of sedition lingered. It lingered in state and federal laws punishing radical political speech and speech that was thought to create a danger to peace and public order. In the 1960s Alabama state officials sought to punish the *New York Times* for publishing a partially inaccurate civil rights advertisement. Not until 1964, when the U.S. Supreme Court ruled in this case, *New York Times* v. *Sullivan*, did the Court seek to lay to rest the crime of sedition. The ruling allowed government authorities to win damages in libel suits only when they could prove with convincing clarity that a libel was published with *actual malice*, that is, with prior knowledge that it was false or with reckless disregard as to whether it was false or not. Eventually public figures would come to be held to the same standard, and, for a brief time, even private persons, if they became involved in public issues.

New York Times was to lead to a dizzying progression of libel cases in which the finer points of libel law would be squeezed through a ringer of revision and reinterpretation. The Court would vacillate between basing its libel decisions on the content of an offending publication or on the social status of a plaintiff. Media lawyers themselves would proclaim that no part of the fabric of American law was more dazzlingly complex than libel. Some proclaim it even more complex than tax law. Perhaps the many psychosocial dimensions of reputation makes this inevitable. Textbooks on libel become obsolete before they are published. As a mass communication law textbook writer for more than twenty years, this has been my experience.[3]

Libel's complexity created a vacuum in comprehension that sustained sedition, but in a new form: the civil libel suit in which an outraged public official, suing in his or her own name, or an offended public figure, asks for astronomical sums of money to compensate for damage claimed done to reputations by negative media exposure. Sedition in civil guise.

Soon these suits, rarely won by public person plaintiffs, notably public officials and celebrities, would constitute one-third of all libel cases. Defendants in most of these cases are newspapers and newspaper employees, although a $58 million judgment was made by a jury in 1991 against a Dallas television station, WFAA-TV. And they are the big cases, the cases that get the most publicity and sometimes occupy court dockets for decades.

Nonmedia defendants seeking to petition their governments for a redress of grievances or attempting to challenge public policy by participating in the political process would also feel the sting of monumental libel claims by public officials, real estate developers, and powerful pressure groups. Libel suits would become a way of winning in court what could not be won through the voting booth or at the bar of public opinion.

In a society with a revolutionary heritage it is painful to see free expression attacked from every angle and defended with doubt and dispiritedness. But that was the reality of America in the year of the bicentennial of the Bill of Rights. Many kinds of literary, artistic, scientific, and political expression, those forms that even to a conservative Supreme Court are thought to have a redeeming social value, are being condemned by zealots of every stripe. Libel law is a powerful weapon for shutting up those with whom you disagree. Little is left, it would seem, of Louis Brandeis' memorable prescription for a free society:

"If there be time to expose through discussion the falsehoods and the fallacies, to avert the evil by the process of education," he wrote in a 1927 concurring opinion, "the remedy to be applied is *more speech not enforced silence* [emphasis added]."

Legal scholars in large number have also deserted the Brandeisian maxim by proposing legal theories that are contractionist, that is, designed to sacrifice one form of speech to shore up another. Because no individual right can be absolute in a civilized society, principled measures, to be sure, have to be taken to ensure that rights may coexist. But the measures proposed are often unnecessarily extreme. Harm from various forms of speech is assumed without any seeming awareness of existing social scientific evidence. Or theories are spun from trivial cases involving unsavory epithets or symbolic kinds of speech such as flag burning, draft card burning, and obscene gestures. Free expression cannot survive long in so stifling an atmosphere.

Courts divide plaintiffs into public and private persons. Public plaintiffs are further divided into public officials and public figures. Public officials are those persons elected or appointed to public office. Public figures are subdivided into voluntary and involuntary categories, although the latter is rare. They are further subdivided into vortex or limited purpose public figures and pervasive or all-purpose public figures. A special but seldom used form of the all-purpose public figure some courts call the public personality (celebrity), a Madonna, a Michael Jackson, or Jordan or a Magic Johnson. Anyone not fitting into one of these preconstructed boxes would be classfied a private person. Unfortunately for defendants and their insurance companies, the courts, without explanation, are classifying more and more public people as private. It is the public official and the celebrity who primarily concern this study. They are the policymakers, the agenda and trend setters, the power and the glitter.

A close study of 614 libel cases involving the media in the period 1982 to 1988 was undertaken to assess the effects libel suits might have on the character of political and social discourse. The results were startling. First, the courts appeared to have no systematic way of deciding how to categorize plaintiffs, and plaintiff category is important under the *New York Times* rules. A plaintiff who was a public official in one jurisdiction would not be in another. A public figure by one judge's definition would be a private person by another's. The courts chose to put practically no one in a category of public figure that judges themselves had developed—the "persuasive public personality" or what I am calling the "celebrity." We found forty-four plaintiffs who by our reckoning fit the category. Courts were prone to call plaintiffs "private persons" when they were clearly public persons. Private plaintiffs have only to prove "negligence" by a preponderance of the evidence to collect damages, and states are relatively free to make negligence mean whatever they want it to mean. There also seemed to be little consistency in how courts determined whether a publication was true or false and whether it had caused injury. Most of the defamatory references were to the public lives of plaintiffs.

Actual malice, that is, knowing falsehood or reckless disregard as to truth or falsity on the part of a publisher, was found in only nine percent of the 340 cases in which the question was addressed. And only 19 of 381 plaintiffs the courts called "public" were able to prove actual malice sufficiently to win money damages. In only 28 of 164 cases involving public officials did plaintiffs win jury verdicts. Of forty-four celebrity plaintiffs identified by the authors in the study, only eleven won jury verdicts. When the appeals process had concluded, only ten public officials and six celebrities—some of them institutional celebrities—had prevailed in the eight-year period studied. The average damages award was slightly in excess of $500,000. The few eventual "winners" were two gubernatorial candidates, two law enforcement officers, a judge, a judicial candidate, a former U.S. attorney, a borough council president, a regulatory board member, and a television star.

These figures suggest a certain futility about libel suits involving public people, the two categories of public official and celebrity, particularly. Plaintiffs in the final analysis have very little to gain, defendants much to lose in libel litigation. Taxpayers cover expenses incurred by the judicial system in return for brief moments of maudlin entertainment. Only attorneys, it would appear, benefit from the process. And the process is out of control.

It is for this reason that I propose a remedy that only the U.S. Supreme Court can apply to a situation that is having a grievous effect on the public dialogue:

Public officials at policy-making levels and celebrities (those

whom courts have called "pervasive public figures" or "public
personalities") shall have *no* remedy in libel law. For such persons
to claim legal remedy subverts the underlying purpose of the *New
York Times* doctrine by reviving, at least where public officials are
concerned, the crime of sedition in the guise of a civil libel suit
subjecting the press, large and small, strong and weak, responsible
and irresponsible, to a danger not fully anticipated in Justice Brennan's opinion for the Court in the 1964 landmark case. Only a
structural change of this magnitude will, in the final analysis, preserve the historical purposes of the First Amendment.

In return for immunity from "official" and "celebrity" libel suits,
publishers, editors, and news directors would voluntarily make
available time or space for a reply in the words of the person
feeling himself or herself to have been wronged, without screening
or filtering through ombudsmen, readers' representatives, or readers' advocates. Public officials and celebrities would then speak
with their own voices, within reasonable word limits and with
editing by communication organizations only to correct embarrassing lapses in language or to avoid compounding libel or
invasion-of-privacy problems. Thereby, outright errors or mis-
taken impressions carried in initial news reports could be corrected
or disputed. Responses to news reports could be carried in a special
location in the news section, responses to editorial or opinion
material on the op-ed page. News and editorial page executives
would, of course, make their own decisions as to when replies were
warranted by the qualities of the original publication and the topic
of disagreement. Replies would never be mandatory nor would
there or could there be any sanctions for noncompliance.

Through this self-regulatory form of accountability a media system that is often arrogant, self-congratulatory, and deaf to the pain
of those it covers would honor its frequently claimed commitment
to Justice Brandeis' "more speech" principle. And it would be a
small trade-off for the power the media now exert under the protective umbrella of the First Amendment.

This proposal does not emerge from a benign view of the mass
media or the people who make them work. They are an individ-
ualistic lot, skeptical, sometimes cynical, difficult to persuade, and,
fortunately perhaps, impossible to organize. Compassion and sensitivity are not always their strong suits. Seldom do they have time

for contemplation. Still there are impressive people in the news-rooms of America. What is of more concern are the processes over which journalists have no control: the accelerating concentration of ownership and power in the mass media that may in time lead to a homogenization of content and a singleness of perspective that no application of the First Amendment can remedy.

But these are questions for another study. Libel laws in the hands of politicians, public employees, and the "stars" remain weapons that have the same deadly effects on editorial courage, content diversity, and political participation as the seemingly inevitable economic processes of a postindustrial capitalist system. These effects bear down especially hard on the smaller newspapers and the disappearing family-owned dailies. Nevertheless, a privilege of reply is not too high a price for the press to pay for a public discourse that it claims to cherish and that is at the core of the idea of democracy.

1

A Proposal to Modify the Law of Libel

John Mortimer's irrepressibly literate barrister, Rumpole of the Bailey, in one of his infrequent forays down from the desolate plateau of criminal law into the fertile valley of civil litigation, looks with relish toward a libel case.

His chambers clerk, Henry, he says,

> "...spoke with almost religious awe when he handed me my brief in *Nettleship* v. *The Daily Beacon and anon*. Not only was a highly satisfactory fee marked on the front but refreshers, that is the sum required to keep a barrister on his feet and talking, had been agreed at no less than five hundred pounds a day."
>
> "You can make the case last, can't you Mr. Rumpole?" Henry asked with understandable concern.
>
> "Make it last?" I reassured him. "I can make it stretch on till the trump of doom! We have serious and lengthy allegations, Henry. Allegations that will take days and days, with any luck. For the first time in a long career at the Bar I begin to see..."
>
> "See what, Mr. Rumpole?"
>
> "A way of providing for my old age."[4]

Not to disparage those American attorneys who preside over the fairest and most accessible legal system in the world. Or the media bar, first and last line of defense for freedom of speech and press in America. But rather to suggest that these same lawyers may be the only beneficiaries of a libel law system that is in a state of terminal fibrillation. All other participants, it would seem—plaintiff, defendant, the public, and the overburdened court structure itself—lose in the end. Perhaps it could be said that, with few exceptions, only lawyers win libel suits.

The Iowa Study

There is evidence to suggest that many plaintiffs sue with no expectation of winning money damages, but they sue anyway. While libel insurers and attorneys are skeptical of these findings, believing as they do that generally money awards alone drive libel cases, the Iowa Libel Study demonstrated that some plaintiffs see themselves as "winners" by the very act of suing, even though they know in advance that the odds against a legal verdict in their favor are high indeed.[5]

One libel scholar wrote of plaintiffs, "To them, the libel suit represents an official engagement of the judicial system on their behalf and the act of suing represents a legitimation of their claims of falsehood. . . . [M]ost plaintiffs appear to pursue and achieve objectives through a libel suit that bears strikingly little relationship to the objectives set by the legal system . . . ascertainment of fault and imposition of money damages. . . ."[6]

Libel seldom creates any real economic loss to a plaintiff, especially if the plaintiff is a public person.[7] Instead he or she may be rewarded with valuable publicity or with more cautious coverage in the future. Fifty percent of losing plaintiffs in the Iowa study were satisfied either that the media, in lieu of money damages, had been suitably punished by a long and expensive suit or that they had managed to deflect additional bad publicity or had gained good publicity. Money damages clearly were not the primary purpose.

But what about the other 50 percent? Is it not possible that through a lawsuit these plaintiffs raise the sensitivity of reporters and editors to the consequences that may flow from overly aggressive news reporting? Do litigious public people create a chilling effect on the media that cuts down on the flow of information important to the public? The evidence is not all in, but public people are aware of the fearful effects that even the threat of a libel suit can have.

For private persons and those whom the courts call voluntary or involuntary limited purpose public figures, the benefits of emotional relief, vindication of reputation, and the possibilities of money damages may justify the social costs of libel suits. But the legal system bends under the weight of public officials and celebrities launching foredoomed libel suits against the very media upon whom they depend for fame and fortune. By the very act of suing, public people keep themselves in the public eye.

I propose that some citizens be denied remedies in libel law. Social, cultural, and political policymakers, the agenda setters, those fixed in the social structure, and some of those plaintiffs designated by the courts as public officials or pervasive public figures (celebrities), should be made libel proof. That the media, the major and minor organs of public opinion, newspapers, magazines, television, and radio, whatever their faults, thereby be immunized against these kinds of lawsuits by the highly visible and influential among us. That where possible these most public of potential plaintiffs use the media for response and rebuttal, and that will often be possible in the ordinary course of events. Where it is not, I further propose that the media demonstrate a commitment to public discourse by making their facilities available to those they have wronged when the facts, the harm done, and the issue of contention warrant.

Public officials have enjoyed access to the channels of communication since Gutenberg and an absolute privilege against libel suits in America since 1959, if their defamatory utterances occur as a part of their official duties.[8] As early as 1801, John Thomson, a highly literate New Yorker about whom little is known, made a reasoned argument for the proposition that because members of Congress enjoy an absolute privilege to debate without qualification, their sovereign, the People, ought to enjoy the same privilege.[9]

"There are many cases scattered through the records of the courts," Frederic Hudson, managing editor of the *New York Herald,* wrote in his capable 1873 history of American journalism, "where journalists in the United States, without malice, and in the performance of their duty, have made mistakes and have been prompt to publish suitable corrections, yet they have been prosecuted, and sometimes mulcted in heavy damages in time and money by the peculiar views and feelings of judges and jurors before whom the cases were brought."

In language with a rather harsh Victorian veneer, Hudson added, "[S]uits are instituted by worthless characters, and upon the merest pretext, for the purpose of extorting black-mail, and there are plenty of lawyers who are always ready to aid the rascals. Sometimes timid people are disposed to make a compromise rather than submit to the annoyance of a defense. Very often libel suits are instituted from mere malice, and when there is no libel at all, because, under the present law, the prosecutor can punish the defendant by causing him heavy costs, even though the suit goes against him in the end."[10]

The rhetoric, while a bit loud, does sound a contemporary note. It is the cost of defending, not the risk of paying damages, that unnerves today's prospective libel defendant. Cost is connected to complexity. A libel suit begins with the questions: Is it defamation? Was the plaintiff identified? Has there been a publication? Is what was published true? Was the plaintiff injured? (Falsity and injury must be proved by the plaintiff.) Is the plaintiff a public or a private person? Was there fault on the part of defendant—the reporter, the editor, the publisher?

The constitutional or First Amendment defense against libel created by the U.S. Supreme Court in the great landmark 1964 case of *New York Times* v. *Sullivan*,[11] and gradually extended by its progeny to plaintiffs other than public officials,[12] revolutionized libel law. It shifted the burden of proof from defendant to public-person plaintiff either to demonstrate with "convincing clarity," "knowing falsehood" (something equivalent to a deliberate lie), or a "reckless disregard for truth or falsity" (gross negligence) on the part of the offending media. Later, "serious doubts as to the truth of . . . publication" would become an acceptable variant of the test.[13]

Private-person plaintiffs, that is those persons who hold no public office or enjoy no social notoriety, would under the new rules, said the Court, be required to prove "negligence," a lower level of fault, by at least a "preponderance of the evidence," and the states could develop their own definitions or versions of "negligence." "Convincing clarity" is a standard of proof higher than that required in most civil suits; "preponderance of the evidence" is a standard below "convincing clarity."

Before 1964, truth or privilege were the only primary defenses in libel, and the burden of proof was on the publisher. Truth had to be proven in every particular to constitute a defense to a libel claim. If privilege was the defense, a publisher had to show that the offending information was taken from a public governmental record and reprinted with some degree of accuracy or that it was fair comment and criticism of a government official or a performer seeking public approval. There were secondary defenses, such as consent of the plaintiff, lack of identification because the plaintiff was part of a group too large to afford individual identification, the statute of limitations had run, or the libel was committed when a broadcaster was subject to the equal opportunity provision of the Federal Communication Act. And there were factors, such as retraction, correction, and the use of usually reliable sources, to mitigate or lessen the damages in a suit lost by the press.

Regretfully, the Court labeled the two-in-one test of fault of *New York Times* "actual malice." The definition of actual malice soon became tangled and confused with the older concept of common law malice, traditionally defined as spite, ill will, hostility, or revengefulness, and necessary in some jurisdictions to support an award of punitive or exemplary damages (damages assessed by the court as punishment of the publisher so as to set an example to others). Those definitions do not apply to actual malice. Some courts still haven't figured out the difference. The Supreme Court in *New York Times* made actual malice a federal standard that had to be met by any public official seeking to punish the media by means of a libel suit. And the U.S. Supreme Court has since ruled that actual malice must also be demonstrated before an award of punitive or exemplary damages can be made to any plaintiff— public person or private person. State courts do not always comply with Supreme Court directives. In no other tort action, it should be noted, with the possible exception of fraud, are the motives of the defendant relevant.

And so while *New York Times* v. *Sullivan* was good news for the press, actual malice, unintentionally it seems, would become bad news for the First Amendment.

The staggering complexity of libel was demonstrated in a 1979 case decided by the U.S. Supreme Court. In *Herbert* v. *Lando*,[14] the Court extended the pretrial discovery process so that plaintiffs, in suits against the press, could take as much time as necessary and use all legal means at their disposal to uncover actual malice by exploring every twist of the editorial process including a defendant's "state of mind." This required opening up the editorial process to public scrutiny (something the press within limits might be well advised to do voluntarily); it also meant that the raw notes, memos, and recorded conversations of journalists, once they had been destroyed as a matter of newsroom policy, could no longer contribute to an historical record or help to correct errors in that record.

Anthony Herbert, a maverick former army colonel, had become by his own exertions a Vietnam War "super-hero" and in the public mind a critic of the military. A skeptical "60 Minutes" producer cast doubts on both those images of Herbert. Defendant's deposition in the case required twenty-six sessions and stretched over a year. The nearly 3,000 pages of transcripts and 240 exhibits included reporters' notes, network memoranda, drafts of scripts, unused film, and videotapes of interviews. Since the case, libel suits have become painfully more expensive, time-consuming, and incursive for defendants who may be serving a legitimate public interest. Prolonged discovery periods have greatly increased the costs of libel suits.

If the "actual malice" test was intended to discourage public officials and celebrities from suing except under extreme provocation, it failed. There are proportionately more libel suits now than ever before, a sizable segment of them brought by public officials. If seditious libel, punishable criticism of government or its agents, was laid to rest by *New York Times*, as some in the scholarly community concluded, it may be premature to perform its requiem.[15]

In spite of high risks of failure, public-person plaintiffs are encouraged by *Herbert* v. *Lando* to be tenacious in pursuit of the psychological phantom of actual malice, if they can satisfy the threshold requirement of proving falsity—the proving of a negative incidentally—and can establish that a defamatory publication points to them so as to cause at least imagined injury.

A Cynical Public

The public is already cynical, perhaps, about the increasingly concentrated power of the major media relative to other institutions,

suspicious of their fairness, and distressed by their wolf-pack methods of news gathering or what David Shaw of the *Los Angeles
Times* and others call "media feeding frenzies"[16] (and reinforced
in the public mind by repeated depictions of herd journalism in
television and movie dramatization).

In a broad review and analysis of public attitudes toward the
news media over a 50-year period, Professor D. Charles Whitney
of the University of Illinois concluded that the public does "care
about the way in which journalists do their jobs, and the manner
in which they interact with private citizens in particular."[17] A 1984
credibility study by the American Society of Newspaper Editors
(ASNE), for example, found that 75 percent of those surveyed
believe "reporters are only concerned about getting a good story
and don't worry much about hurting people."[18]

While public attitudes toward the press are complex and variable
over time, jurors drawn from the public seem quite prepared to
find at least "reckless disregard" in much of what the media do—
powerful corporations shredding the reputations of comparatively
defenseless individuals for profit.[19] And jurors have been reaching
verdicts against media defendants at an alarming rate and awarding
huge sums in money damages.

Plaintiffs prevail in something like three out of five libel trials,
and punitive damages are levied in the same proportion of cases.
On appeal, however, when the constitutional defense of libel law
is applied, plaintiffs in suits against the media succeed in less than
10 percent of cases.[20]

This disparity between trial and appeals court judgments may
be partly explained by the fact that jurors simply cannot unravel
the instructions they get from trial judges in libel cases.[21] Or trial
judges themselves in some cases inadequately understand the in-
tricate rules of libel.[22]

These figures may also support the admonition that we not put
speech and press freedoms to a referendum. Poll data over time
also suggest that a majority of the American people believe in
freedom of speech and press as an abstract principle. But when
asked a specific question such as: Should an extreme radical group
be permitted to use the hometown civic center for its conference?
the majority response is almost invariably, No![23] Fifty-five percent
of respondents in a 1970 CBS poll would withhold from the media
the right to report stories the government thought dangerous to

the national interest. Forty-three percent of respondents in a more recent Minnesota study thought the government should prohibit books that "portray Communists as heroes."[24]

A Gallup poll found that less than half the public knew that the First Amendment or the Bill of Rights protected freedom of speech and press.[25] Perhaps this failure of memory is unremarkable. The same poll, however, found an overwhelming majority of the public in favor of punishment of the press through libel laws for "false" criticism of public officials. "The public neither understands nor accepts the rationale of 'actual malice'," the Gallup organization noted.[26]

Another poll found that 42 percent of the public thought the president ought to be able to close down a newspaper that he felt was biased or inaccurate, while a shocking 19 percent thought the government had a right to arrest a reporter who constantly criticizes the president.[27] At the same time, two-thirds of respondents in the same Gallup poll believed that press criticism keeps political leaders from doing harm, suggesting some kind of a watchdog function perhaps.[28] And 72 percent of respondents in a 1985 ASNE survey thought that the press helps keep public officials honest.[29]

This ambivalence or fickleness on the part of the public—keeping in mind that these data are often interpreted in historical and social vacuums[30]—seems to give credence to those who subscribe to a fortress model of free speech, the idea in part that speech freedom must be continually defended against a threatening assault force of government officials and oppressive, uninformed majorities represented by legislative bodies—the majorities whose potential tyranny both de Tocqueville and John Stuart Mill observed and warned against. However contradictory this position may seem to principles of democracy that put great store in ordinary people, bureaucrats and law makers do account for most actions that violate speech and press rights, and legislators, of course, write the libel laws.[31]

An Insensitive Press

Newspaper editors themselves, from pre-Revolutionary to the post-Industrial period, have a dismal record of standing up for those who express dissenting and unconventional political or social views differing from their own. Pre-Revolutionary editors were intolerant of loyalists, as later editors would be intolerant of abolitionists, labor unionists, and social or political extremists such as the anarchists of the turn of the century and the American Communists of the period before and after World War II, and those authors or fellow publishers who, since the beginning of printing, have dealt in erotica.

Defendants in the 1886 Haymarket case, while ostensibly on trial for murder, were prosecuted for their anarchist beliefs and their newspaper writing and public speaking. Midwest newspapers cheered while four editors were led to the gallows. A fifth committed suicide just before execution. Editors then as now were inclined to rely far too much on official sources to the extent that skepticism vanished and, in criminal cases, guilt was assumed. It did not occur to Chicago, Cleveland, Kansas City, or Minneapolis editors that a great constitutional principle might be at stake. Little if any notice of the Haymarket case is taken in the standard histories of American journalism.

Victoria Smith analyzed editorials in nineteen Minnesota dailies in 1910, 1918, and 1920 in an effort to gauge editorial reaction to legislative and extralegal suppression of dissent. Editorials unanimously endorsed freedom of speech in the abstract but denied that same freedom in reality, especially in wartime, to German–Americans, radicals, and other dissenters. In fact a majority of editorials endorsed suppression of "seditionists." Only three or four editors in the state recognized any constitutional implications in Minnesota sedition laws.[32]

Angelo Herndon was indicted, in 1933, for speaking, writing, and organizing as a Communist under a Georgia sedition (insurrection) act. Four years later the U.S. Supreme Court would revive the clear and present danger test, first formulated by Oliver Wendell Holmes in *Schenck* v. *United States* in 1919,[33] to find the Georgia law unconstitutional. Only one newspaper in the state, the Macon *Telegraph*, initially supported Herndon editorially; by 1937, it had changed its mind. Atlanta's leading newspaper, the *Constitution*, endorsed the prosecution. Some leading Northern newspapers did support the Court's ruling in *Herndon* v. *Lowry*, freeing Herndon from a 20-year prison sentence, but only two Southern newspapers, the New Orleans *Item* and the Richmond *Times-Dispatch*, joined that chorus, at least from its back row.[34]

Ralph Ginzburg, publisher of relatively sophisticated erotica in a magazine called *Eros*, went to a federal prison for commercially exploiting material not obscene by the Supreme Court's own standards in 1966 but, said Justice Stewart, offensive to "a judge's esthetic sensibilities." Few fellow publishers objected.[35]

Yale law professor Owen Fiss spoke to this historical record, at least obliquely, when he wrote that no more danger to speech and press freedoms comes from the state (e.g., FCC or the courts) than from private forces (e.g., CBS or the *Washington Post*). "Terror," he observed, "comes in many forms."[36] While the historical record strongly suggests that governments have been the principal barriers to free speech, and the First Amendment has preordained that governmental "terror" is worse than other forms, Fiss's proposition does comport with some of the institutional dynamics of our time. The values of our increasingly concentrated corporate communication system will be a central and urgent issue of the twenty-first century.

Sedition Redux

It is still a punishable crime in America to criticize the government if that criticism is of its officials—sedition redux—and if hundreds of thousands of dollars in court costs and legal fees, lost time, and an ample expenditure of nervous energy are considered punishment. Libel suits are costly to defend. If plaintiffs indeed win by suing, by getting revenge on discourteous or thoughtless editors, as the Iowa study concludes, then defendants lose by winning. Substantial segments of the public seem unaware that some public plaintiffs are using libel laws to silence their critics, or to keep their own names in the public spotlight. Between the public and the courts—the appellate courts being far more constitutionally clear-sighted than the public—there appears to be a gap in constitutional comprehension.

In the middle of the 1980s, initial awards in compensatory or actual damages (damages awarded for injury to reputation) by some estimates averaged $2 million, punitive or exemplary awards $3 million—three times higher than awards in product liability and medical malpractice suits.[37] In constant dollars, libel awards for 1980–1986 had increased more than 400 percent over the decade ending in 1964 with *New York Times* v. *Sullivan*, and million-or-more-dollar awards in the same period registered a 1,000 percent increase over the previous two decades[38]; somehow the media were not benefiting from the liberating doctrine of that landmark case. Figures from the Libel Defense Resource Center for 1987–1988 indicated a substantial drop in overall average awards, but the incidence of awards between $500,000 and $1 million was the highest of any period studied, as was the average award of $250,000 for cases in which less than $1 million was paid. These figures do not reflect court costs and lawyers fees.[39]

The American Society of Newspaper Editors estimates the minimum cost of defending a libel suit at $95,000 and insurance carriers at $150,000. At least one jurist suggests a figure of $200,000, with appeals to the U. S. Supreme Court doubling that amount.[40] A summary judgment, a decision by a judge that a defendant is entitled to prevail as a matter of law, there being no facts in dispute for a jury to decide, may require $25,000 in legal fees and court costs, with some estimates doubling that sum.[41] A successful motion to dismiss may also cost $25,000.

Whatever the precise figure at any particular time and in any particular place, legal fees do constitute as much as 80 percent of the aggregate costs of a defense,[42] court costs and damage awards constituting the remainder. (The expense of lawyers and the cost of time lost were also thought to be considerably more burdensome than damage awards in the more tolerant nineteenth century.[43])

In at least half the cases brought, according to one estimate, the media are defending against public plaintiffs. One prominent libel scholar estimated that in 1985 alone, as many as 1,000 lawsuits brought by disgruntled public officials and corporate executives were pending.[44]

"Because media defendants in libel litigation ultimately win ninety percent of all cases on appeal, while often spending crippling sums to get those victories, the message is quite clear," says William & Mary law professor Rodney Smolla. "If punishment is the motive, plaintiffs do not have to win to win, and whatever the parties' motives, defendants do not have to lose to lose. . . . Case by case, common law and constitutional law development has simply failed to produce a coherent, equitable system for redressing injury to reputation that nonetheless maintains sufficient breathing

space for freedom of speech." He calls libel law a "doctrinal sham-
bles" and a "practical morass."[45]

The overall frequency of libel cases in the 1980s remained fairly
stable, while the costs of suits to defendants increased exponen-
tially since the constitutional defense was put in place in 1964.
Journalist Anthony Lewis may be right in saying that the purpose
of libel suits now is to destroy the critics' capabilities to criticize.[46]

The cases of the generals—William Westmoreland[47] and Ariel
Sharon[48]—may be the most celebrated examples of the practical
morass Smolla speaks of. Both cases were aborted far short of
final judicial resolution. Despite substantial evidence of editorial
imbalance, inaccuracy, and unfairness on the part of CBS, Westmoreland's attorneys and a conservative Washington, D. C. foundation supporting them may have decided prematurely that they
would have difficulty proving falsity with clear and convincing evidence, a threshold burden on plaintiff before the issue of fault
(actual malice) can be reached. When the General, leading his
frontal attack on CBS, looked behind, he was all alone; his legal
troops and those who had cheered him on were leaving the field.
He had no option but to accept a less than apologetic statement
from CBS that it had not intended to impugn the General's pa-
triotism or loyalty.

Israeli General Sharon's attorneys did persuade the jury that
Time magazine's report of his collaboration with Lebanese Phal-
angists, who had massacred more than 500 Palestinian women and
children in two refugee camps, was false. But the General's prospects of proving actual malice did not seem very bright. Sharon
left a New York courtroom at this juncture in the trial declaring
himself a victor.

CBS alone spent more than $10 million defending a suit that
should have never come to trial. CBS's behavior in the *Westmoreland* case, in alliance with a powerful New York law firm,
hardly engages our sympathy.[49] CBS had violated its own internal
standards.[50] But leave Westmoreland to history. By all accounts
the General, courageous though he may have been, remained
oblivious, as did his superiors, to the complex realities of Vietnam's
political culture and the machinations of its military—a more
damning accusation than any charge of miscounting or misreport-
ing the enemy, dead or alive.[51] In its own uncanny way, the public

seemed to recognize Westmoreland's failings. Nor do we weep for Time, Inc. in the *Sharon* case and its reliance on a single doubtful source,[52] a source that had failed the news magazine before. Nevertheless, alternatives to these legal confrontations should have been explored, given the political prominence of the two plaintiffs, their participation in epochal political events, and the impossibility of any judge or jury, short of Clio herself, being able to separate truth from falsehood or fact from opinion in the snarl of events involved. Indeed, General Westmoreland has since publicly recommended, in television public service spots, news councils as a substitute for courtrooms. News councils, whether local, state, or national, are voluntary citizen panels that adjudicate complaints brought by members of the public against the media and distribute their findings.

Momentous historical events were also involved when film director Constantin Costa-Gavras, Universal Studios, and its parent company MCA, Inc., faced libel suits for their 1982 film "Missing," based on Tom Hauser's 1978 book, *The Execution of Charles Horman: An American Sacrifice.* The book detailed the apparent abduction and execution of an American writer living in Santiago, Chile, and questioned the response of U.S. government representatives in the period following the military overthrow of President Salvador Allende Gossens.

Captain Ray E. Davis, commander of the U.S. Military Group and chief of the U.S. Navy Mission, charged that the film depicted him as ordering Horman's death. Undoubtedly, said a federal court, the film included inferences, implications, and insinuations concerning U.S. involvement in the coup, but to meet the actual malice test, Captain Davis would have to prove by clear and convincing evidence that Costa-Gavras knew before filming that Davis, unmentioned in the script, was innocent of any complicity in the crime.[53]

A federal court seemed prepared to allow a good deal of artistic license to this hybrid form of presentation, the docudrama. Even so, the filmmakers in this instance had taken pains to check the facts of the case, not only with Hauser but also independent of him. While not everything in the film was faithful to the actual historical record, as it might have tried to be in a straight documentary, it contained no actual malice, that is, no knowing falsehood or evidence of reckless disregard of truth. The complaint was dismissed.

Southern Air Transport sued ABC-TV for an investigative report on "World News Tonight" that linked the company, by innuendo said a federal court, to a plan between U.S. government officials and South Africa to supply arms to the Nicaraguan Contras—another issue of great political moment. Retired Air Force General Richard Secord and Lieutenant Colonel Oliver North, both later convicted of perjury, were mentioned in the broadcast. As had defendants in *Costa-Gavras*, ABC was forced to endure protracted litigation until a motion to dismiss based on the essential accuracy of its report was accepted and affirmed by a federal appeals court. Southern Air had contended that no evidence showed its deliberate participation in the illegal project even though its president would admit to being on a plane bearing South African markings during a weapons drop.[54]

When libel suits involving such consequential issues of public policy are brought to court, courts become sweatboxes for those daring enough to voice direct or indirect criticism of government and its myrmidons. Clear signals are sent to those undecided as to what level of financial loss they can risk by participating in public debate.

Many libel suits, however, are closer to home. A defeated candidate for a municipal judgeship sued a Hamilton, Ohio, daily newspaper for quoting a "mentally unstable" grand jury witness to the effect that the unsuccessful candidate had used "dirty tricks" to fashion a bribery charge against a director of court services. The purpose of the publication, said the complaint, was to discredit an acting judge running for a permanent position on the court, and enhance the newspaper's circulation. Oblivious to an unusually large number of supporting briefs from twenty-nine news and public interest organizations, the U.S. Supreme Court in mid-1989 affirmed an appeals court ruling upholding a jury award of $200,000 to the plaintiff. The appeals court had presumed superior knowledge as to general news practices and had challenged the paper's editorial endorsement preferences. At the same time, in my opinion, it inadequately analyzed all of the evidence purporting to show actual malice.[55]

A county attorney sued a newspaper for criticizing by implication his record on prosecuting battered women cases, even though the paper had quoted both critics and defenders of his official performance. A jury awarded the plaintiff $785,000 in compensatory and punitive damages. The trial judge set aside the verdict. The county attorney appealed the judge's decision to the state's intermediate court, which reinstated the jury verdict. The case, in a category of cases that ought to be disallowed, then proceeded on a long and costly journey to the state's supreme court. True statements or statements of opinion on matters of public concern cannot give rise to a cause of action for defamation by implication, said the Minnesota Supreme Court in reversing the court of appeals and finding for the newspaper.[56] The U.S. Supreme Court declined to hear the case a decade after the original stories were published.

After deliberating only two hours, a Philadelphia jury on May 3, 1990, awarded $34 million ($31.5 million in punitive damages) to a former assistant district attorney who had been criticized in *Philadelphia Inquirer* news stories and editorials for quashing a homicide investigation as a favor to a police official whose son had been involved. The articles were published in 1973 in the context of police scandals involving the administration of former Philadelphia Mayor the late Frank Rizzo. The suit, one of forty-six brought against the newspaper in recent years by public officials, will be appealed and is expected to last well into the twenty-first century.[57]

It took the *San Francisco Examiner* eight years to shake off a $4.26 million libel award to two police officers and a prosecutor criticized by the newspaper for "misconduct" in a murder investigation. The trial judge and the intermediate appellate court appeared not to understand the concept of actual malice, as articulated by the U.S. Supreme Court (knowing falsehood or reckless disregard as to truth or falsity with the burden of proof on the plaintiff), or California's rules disallowing punitive damages in the absence of a showing of actual malice.[58]

And it took a Bellville, Illinois, newspaper nine years to get that state's supreme court to void a $200,000 judge's award (reduced from an initial $950,000) to a county board chairman. The newspaper had suggested in an editorial that the chairman might have reneged on a campaign promise. During these extended proceedings, the newspaper's editor was jailed for two days for refusing to name a source.[59]

Two South Carolina legislators didn't bother with a civil suit against the publisher of a small weekly, in 1988, for criticizing their handling of state funds. They had him arrested, charged with criminal libel, and jailed. (John Peter Zenger and his *New York Weekly Journal* faced indictment in 1734 for accusing colonial governor William Cosby of "pillage.") On sober second thought, the lawmakers withdrew their complaints, and a grand jury indictment was voided—an indictment reflecting in the first instance something less than broad public support in that community for the idea of a free press. The South Carolina statute remains in place, as do criminal libel statutes in at least twenty-four other jurisdictions, waiting to be used to inflict provisional pain on editors who express disrespect for their elected officials.[60] Seditious and criminal libel laws are usually indistinguishable; their purposes often meld. Sedition redux.

A former staff aide to Vice President Spiro Agnew, who was deputy director of administration for the Committee for the Reelection of the President (CREEP), special assistant to the Assistant Administrator of the General Services Administration, an employee of the U.S Department of Commerce, and later a paid consultant to Senator Orrin Hatch of Utah in his senatorial campaign against incumbent Frank Moss, would appear to be a man who makes a difference. Yet, in a libel suit resulting from his being called by Moss at a news conference a "bagman" for the discredited former vice president, a federal appeals court, deferring to Utah law, upheld his classification as a "private" person. Such wanton definitional flexibility leaves the law in a state of perpetual uncertainty.[61]

In recent years, the multitude of public officials suing the press has included governors, mayors, senators, state supreme court judges, state appellate judges, district attorneys, county attorneys, U.S. attorneys, law enforcement officials (the largest category of public official plaintiff), and city council chairpersons. Among the most notorious in this parade of public official cases was the suit brought by former Governor Edward King of Massachusetts against the *Boston Globe*. King claimed defamation in three cartoons, one editorial, an op-ed page piece, and two political columns criticizing his administration. It took nearly a decade for the court system to decide that the governor had no case on any count.[62]

An FBI officer involved in the deadly Wounded Knee occupation and shootout in South Dakota sued author Peter Matthiessen and his publisher, Viking Press, for $25 million in 1982 for allegations made in the book *In the Spirit of Crazy Horse*. When the suit was initiated, Viking pulled the book out of bookstores; it would be seven years before a new edition would be ready for the market. The case did not survive summary judgment but it took four years to get to that point and two additional years to go through the federal appeals process. The case cost the publisher's insurance company an estimated $2 million in legal fees.[63]

South Dakota's Governor William Janklow had earlier been rebuffed in the federal courts in a suit against *Newsweek* growing out of the same heart-rending condition of race relations in that state.[64] A suit by the same but by now former governor against Matthiessen and Viking Press was resolved by the South Dakota Supreme Court's holding in July 1990 that use of a quotation in which an American Indian activist asserted that the governor "went from raping young girls to raping Mother Earth" was a protected statement of opinion. Put in its context of sympathy toward South Dakota's Indians, the statement, said the court, lacked specificity, precision, and was unverifiable.[65]

In Greenwood, Mississippi, the president of the County Board of Supervisors sued the *Commonwealth*, circulation 9,000, for $20 million. That's more than $2,200 per subscriber. Two of three recent Philadelphia mayors have brought libel actions against local newspapers, including *Welcomat*, an alternative weekly with a staff of one and a half and an antipathy for former Mayor Frank Rizzo. A Syracuse, New York, milk co-op sued a 1,300-circulation Madison, Wisconsin, monthly, *The Milkweed*, for $20 million. After a year, the case was dismissed but the editor reported having to spend four months of his own time on the case and $20,000 of the newspaper's meager assets on lawyer's fees. Its readers had to bail it out.[66]

Few libel plaintiffs prevail, but the press is without relief from prohibitive court costs and legal fees preceding a judgment.

An outlandish current example of this litigational excess was the cross-borders libel suit brought by Mararji Desai, former prime minister of India, against Seymour Hersh, author of *The Price of Power: Kissinger in the Nixon White House.*[67] Hersh reported that Desai, while in office, had sold some of his country's state secrets to the CIA. The former prime minister sought to have Indian law apply to his American critic because Indian law and its British progenitor are not governed by U.S. constitutional limitations. Much of the judicial conjecture in the case concerned the conditions under which the libel laws of India and the U.S. would apply. Indian law, like its British counterpart, presumes falsity, injury, and fault by the very fact of defamatory publication. Differences such as these can make jurisdiction shopping very attractive.

Since Desai also filed suit in India, it is implicit in the U.S. district court's opinion in the case that the purpose of the parallel suit was the prospect of a larger monetary award in the United States than is customary in common law jurisdictions such as India. No one should be disparaged for putting a high price on his or her reputation. But surely Desai's attorneys must have anticipated failure, at least in American courts, for a suit involving speech of such obvious public import and a reporter of demonstrated competence.[68] Hersh and twenty other editors and authors were sued for libel in England by the late Robert Maxwell.

Similar questions of jurisdiction, and of liability, arose in a case that may be the paragon of sedition resurrected. Hammer DeRoburt, president of Nauru, a Pacific island republic, sued the Gannett Company for a defamatory publication by its Guam subsidiary, *Pacific Daily News*. While England's more punitive libel law is also the basis of Nauru law, DeRoburt sought parallel damages in an American forum and was, therefore, forced to storm the battlements of the First Amendment. He did not make it. Six years later the question of legal fees was still in the courts, and DeRoburt was losing on that score as well.[69]

Sir Lynden Pindling, prime minister of the Bahamas, chose to sue NBC in Ontario when the network carried a report concerning allegations that Pindling had connections with drug-related corruption. Canadian law does not require the plaintiff to prove actual malice to win damages. An undisclosed settlement was agreed upon and NBC declared itself vindicated. An outraged Pindling then sought to reopen the case, then changed his mind. Canadian courts accepted the lawsuit because Canadian cable carries NBC broadcasts.[70] The costs associated with such juridical treadmills can only be imagined.

Senator Paul Laxalt's $250 million suit against the *Sacramento Bee* and other McClatchy newspapers, eventually settled out of court, was, in its initial stages, supported by a trust fund put together by Donald Trump, Joseph Coors, Ivan Boesky, and the late Roy Cohn. After settlement, an arbitration panel awarded Laxalt's lawyers more than $647,000 in fees and costs, which amounted to only 15 percent of what they had requested. This again gives some idea of the incredible costs of libel suits. Laxalt has undoubtedly received more cautious coverage since the settlement.

The typical plaintiff, according to the Iowa Libel Study, is an important and visible male professional, elected officeholder or public employee, educated and affluent, who perceives statements about his performance as false and threatening to his position.[71] Highly placed policymakers, judges, and candidates for public office appear to be suing with greater and greater frequency. Political criticism is thereby discouraged, except for the very rich and powerful publishers who can afford to indulge their civic principles.

More ominous is the possibility that media managements may be increasingly less inclined to support the costs of protracted litigation in behalf of free speech and press.

"Seditious libel is alive and well despite attempts of judges and scholars to knock it on the head once and for all."[72] Officeholder instincts for survival and the protection of governmental appearances remain priority social values, critical, even revolutionary, speech notwithstanding.

Celebrity Suits

There is another kind of libel action that falls just short of a resurrected crime of sedition. That is the suit brought by what the law calls the pervasive or all-purpose public figure, or public personality—in lay language, the celebrity, or to be cute, the "glitterati." Here, the plaintiff may or may not intend to influence political policy but, with an access to mass media outdistancing that of many public officials, celebrities influence that policy never-theless by helping to fashion our common cultural context or a style that catches the public imagination. Frequently the identification with a particular political candidate is direct and purposeful. The political and fund-raising clout of artists should be neither surprising nor unwelcome in an age when the line between entertainment and political communication has become so blurred: Jane Fonda, Lauren Bacall, Dick Gregory, Ed Asner, Warren Beatty, Charleton Heston, all politically active and identifiable, and, of course, Ronald Reagan, come to mind as having had well-defined political agendas for most of their careers. Artist entries on an East European political activist list is today even more meaningful. Throughout the world the media serve as the battlefield of public opinion and, as in ancient times, there are still those who would slay the courier who brings bad tidings.

Pat Weaver, father of actress Sigourney Weaver and founding father of NBC's "The Tonight Show," believes Johnny Carson has greater influence than Dan Rather:

> There are stories in the papers these days about how closely watched the late-night talk shows are by Washington politicians. What Johnny jokes about is an index of potential trouble.[73]

Joining Carson in major libel suits have been Carol Burnett, Shirley Jones, Woody Allen, Norman Mailer, William Buckley, Clint Eastwood, Mohammed Ali, Elizabeth Taylor, and Wayne Newton, to name only a few of the more prominent. And it might be suggested that in some cases, at least, a reputation might be so good that a media accusation can't impair it. Indeed it may be the messenger's reputation that is further damaged by the publication.

Newton's case has attracted public attention because of a $22.7 million federal court jury libel award, mercifully reduced by a judge to $5.2 million (most of it in punitive damages), accepted by Newton, and appealed by NBC. The suit began when NBC in an October 6, 1980, program questioned Newton's truthfulness—the court said by innuendo—in an appearance before Nevada's gaming authorities with regard to his relationships with organized crime figures. While there were no falsehoods in the report, the judge held that, whatever its intention, NBC had recklessly disregarded truth in failing to have "foreseen" that viewers might infer from the broadcast that organized crime figures had financed Newton's purchase of the Aladdin hotel and casino.

NBC's New York attorney Floyd Abrams voiced frustration in having to defend against *Newsweek*'s "King of Las Vegas" in the hometown that made him its "Distinguished Citizen of the Year" and celebrated a "Wayne Newton Day." Abrams, in recounting his experiences, said, "I knew we were in trouble when we drove up to the courthouse and saw that it was located on Wayne Newton Boulevard." And all of these honors came after NBC's fateful broadcast.[74]

Newton later got his Nevada gaming license and a $19 million loan to go with it. He was also declared Nevada Republican Man of the Year, awarded a Presidential Medal of Freedom, feted in the White House, and made grand marshal of a July 4th parade in Washington, D. C. It was not clear for what NBC was being punished; the network obviously hadn't damaged Newton's reputation. It may be fair, therefore, to insist upon proof of injury in such cases.[75]

Plaintiff's attorneys in the case had to admit, on analysis of their own poll data, that Newton's popularity, or lack of same, had more to do with his moustache, his dress, and his singing than with any alleged connections with organized crime.[76]

But the "tendency" of a publication to leave an unintended defamatory impression, thought somehow to be intuitable by a jury, was all the law required in the Newton case. Major media organizations, fearing the implications of such a view, rallied to the support of NBC in *amicus* briefs.

Almost ten years after the original broadcast, a three-judge panel of the U.S. Court of Appeals for the Ninth Circuit, on August 30, 1990, found insufficient evidence of actual malice on the part of NBC to support any award for damages. This is the kind of case, it will be argued, that should never have been heard in the first place. The original jury award of more than $20 million had dwindled to zero, but at what cost to the parties and to the judicial system!

So there is this hybrid category of plaintiff: public figures who, while primarily artists and community activists, have anterior purposes. Sometimes they seek to save souls or society from the forces

of darkness. Sometimes they labor for political or social movements. Among such plaintiffs are televangelists Jerry Falwell and
Pat Robertson, well known to mass audiences; Mobil Oil president
William Tavoulareas, whose political advertorials appeared regularly in a wide array of liberal magazines and newspapers, including the op-ed page of the *New York Times;* and Ralph Nader,
who over the decades has turned large segments of society into a
consumer movement. All have brought unsuccessful libel suits
against the media.

Bob Woodward's chilling book on the life and death of John
Belushi, *Wired*, led to suits by Belushi's wife, his doctor, and by
the hotel in which he died.

Armand Hammer, philanthropist and chairman of Occidental
Petroleum, until his death in 1990, a man of inexhaustible resources, sued Steve Weinberg, former director of Investigative
Reporters and Editors, a professor of journalism at the University
of Missouri, and author of a second Hammer biography, this one
unauthorized and less adulatory than an earlier biography and
three commissioned memoirs. But, wisely, Hammer brought the
suit in England, where only common law defenses such as truth
and privilege are available and the burden of proof is on the defendant publisher or author.[77] Ultimately, Hammer could not have
won his suit in the United States. Hammer's suit died with him.
Defendants Weinberg and his English publisher were no longer
liable but they had already spent nearly $2 million in pre-trial
maneuvers. An estimated $8 million more likely would have been
spent by defendants and plaintiffs had the case gone to trial. Like
Neil Sheehan, Weinberg was so busy preparing materials for his
English attorneys in the year it took to get ready for trial that he
had no income from his own writing.

For decades Synanon and the Church of Scientology filed intim-
idation suits against their critics—Synanon as many as 144 in a
ten-year period.[78] In 1979, Synanon brought a $1 billion suit against
the *Point Reyes Light*, a 3,100-circulation California weekly that
had won a Pulitzer Prize a year earlier for a series on the ominous
changing nature of the organization.[79] ABC was reported to have
spent $7 million before settling a suit with Synanon.[80] Time, Inc.
defended against a $77 million Synanon suit before the organiza-

tion withdrew to deal with its more pressing legal problems. Between 1970 and 1979, Scientology brought more than 100 civil lawsuits against journalists, publishing companies, radio and television stations, libraries, and anyone who had the temerity to criticize the church.[81]

A survey of 167 Kentucky newspapers with circulations less than 50,000 found that 70 percent of them had been threatened with libel suits at least once in the past five years. Chilling effects appeared to be correlated with these threats and with such other variables as insurance policies, attendance at libel seminars, and ownership.[82] What merely inhibits major media may terrify the weak and the small. Plaintiffs can be major or minor also. A prominent lawyer not only demonstrated that point, but changed the course of the law of libel.

Elmer Gertz, whose lawsuit against a reactionary magazine brought libel to where it is today, fits both categories of plaintiff so far discussed. Gertz was the attorney who successfully sued the John Birch Society magazine, *American Opinion*, for linking him to a worldwide Communist conspiracy because he represented a family in a civil suit. The suit was against a policeman who, in attempting to deal with a violent family altercation, had accidentally shot the son of the family. The resulting libel case, *Gertz* v. *Robert Welch, Inc.*,[83] established most of the current rules of libel law. Gertz, said the U.S. Supreme Court, was a private person in the circumstances of the case, and therefore would have only to prove negligence on the part of the magazine to win damages. And he did.

In spite of the fact that a Chicago jury had never heard of him—an information gap that defendant's attorney could have bridged—Gertz enjoyed high status politically, socially, and culturally. His place in the social structure should not have depended on the information level of the jury, a small and unrepresentative segment of the public, not if the purposes of the *New York Times* doctrine were to be honored. Public status should be defined by informed or alert publics, by those in one's own social or professional circle. Leaving such determinations to the mass public is a meaningless gesture.

Elmer Gertz had been elected to rewrite Illinois' constitution. He was one of Chicago's best known lawyers, an expert and a bar leader in the areas of libel, censorship, civil rights, free speech, the death penalty, and housing. He was the author of books, pamphlets, magazine articles, book reviews, radio plays. He was a professor of law, a civil rights leader, a founding member of the Civil War Roundtable, the Henry Miller Literary Society, and the George Bernard Shaw Society. He won a parole for Nathan Leopold, a defendant in the classic Chicago murder case involving Leopold and Loeb and their young victim Bobby Franks. He won a death sentence commutation for Jack Ruby. Hardly a private person, Gertz's suit should have been rejected. Gertz has never appreciated the damage his victory did to the right to comment freely on significant public matters.

One is reminded of the seemingly endless libel suit brought by the wise and eloquent radio humorist, John Henry Faulk, against *Red Channels*, a reactionary publication that specialized in blacklisting anyone in the entertainment industry who wouldn't march to its drummer. Faulk eventually won his suit to the same kind of public acclaim that greeted Carol Burnett when she won her suit. Faulk, his friends, and this writer reveled in the euphoria of his victory. But how could Faulk square his victory with the ideal of free speech that he so masterfully proclaimed to audiences all over America? Could there have been a better way to punish his antagonists?

Truly public people withstand the tests of time. Publicity is their lifeline. Reputations are willingly risked for the trappings of power and public acclaim. Columbia University sociologist Herbert Gans calls them the "knowns," the establishment, leading political or cultural figures who, although they constitute less than 3 percent of the population, occupy 70 to 85 percent of domestic news space.[84] They must know they will be reviled, falsely depicted, maligned. They also know that the deadliest blow of all is to be ignored by press and public. Better to let the media incur the wrath of their readers and viewers for violating fundamental canons of decent journalism than to boycott them for fear of error. (William Seward is purported to have said of the nineteenth century party press that libel suits had become unnecessary because the "licentiousness of the Press had impaired its power to defame."[85])

Public-person plaintiffs, those with higher incomes and visibility, appear to be particularly persistent in pursuing libel suits conse-

quent to published accounts about their public or political activities. And it can be profitable, even on a *pro bono* basis, for an
attorney to represent a leading politician or a celebrity. Public
people generally may account for as many as 60 percent of all libel
suits. Private-person plaintiffs, on the other hand, are less attractive to attorneys and may end up paying a larger share of their
legal bills. Economic loss to the business or profession of these
plaintiffs due to defamatory publication can often be compensated
only by monetary damages. Even so, the Iowa Study reports that
many of these litigants would have settled for a retraction, a correction, or an apology. As it turns out, no more than 25 percent
are settled, even though plaintiffs ultimately succeed in fewer than
10 percent of these suits.

Most plaintiffs spend less than $5,000 in litigating and, even
though contingency fee arrangements are less available than in the
past, two-thirds of plaintiffs are offered some kind of contingency
plan, that is, they will have no lawyer's fees to pay until a judgment
is made and then only if the judgment is in their favor. Sixteen
percent of plaintiffs in the Iowa Study had no litigation costs and
30 percent spent less than $3,000 to win overall damage awards
averaging $120,000 or settlements averaging $7,000.[86]

One observer believes that the publicity of a libel suit can be a
godsend to a candidate for public office or a celebrity, as well as
to his or her attorney, and may militate against settlement, whatever the risks of losing the suit—and they are high. "The actual
malice rule," says Ronald Cass, " . . . discourages litigation least
by the very group with which it was directly concerned"—public
officials.[87]

We have reached a point in the oscillation of societal interest in
professional ethics where unfairness, imbalance, and exploitation,
in any of their myriad forms, no longer go unnoticed and are
increasingly matters of sharp public comment and debate. Moreover, if one genuinely wishes to repair one's public image, a lawsuit
is probably the single worst way of going about it. Given the
shortness of the collective memory, an accusation soon fades. To
litigate is to assure that a defamatory falsehood remains in the
public mind for perhaps a decade or more and in law review anal-
yses and in other literary realms for millennia. This could be called
the "Oscar Wilde" syndrome. Wilde is reported to have considered
the press in his own time the modern equivalent of the rack. His

ill-advised libel suit against the Marquis of Queensberry began his precipitous decline in creativity and his perilous physical and psychological descent.

Oscar had learned little from the experience of his father Sir William Wilde, a promiscuous Irish surgeon. Sir William's sexual escapades had been exposed to the world in a libel suit brought against his wife for a defamatory publication she had designed to rescue her husband's fading honor. While Wilde's parents were defendants rather than plaintiffs, the results were predictably unpleasant.[88]

James MacNeill Whistler, the great expatriate American artist, sued the eminent British critic John Ruskin who had called his work "rubbish." Both men found libel litigation a losing game. Whistler was awarded a farthing, in itself an insult to his artistic worth. And this added to the disparagement already heaped upon him by "expert" witnesses for the other side. Furthermore, he was required to pay his own costs at a time when he could ill afford to do so. Ruskin, now called a libeler, felt himself disgraced, resigned his professorship at Oxford, and finished his life in isolated retirement.[89]

The Westmoreland and Sharon suits served to remind many why they didn't admire those military leaders in the first place.

From a social point of view, "Libel suits today often seem to revolve around issues more relevant to lawyers than litigants," says Professor Smolla, "and often seem to lose sight altogether of the truly significant social issues . . . out of which the lawsuit originally arose. While lawyers try cases in court, the litigants try the case in the newspapers, and very few clear-cut truths ever finally emerge."[90] What is the "truth" of Lincoln's or Kennedy's assassination, of the Gulf of Tonkin episode, of Chappaquiddick, or of the Iran-Contra affair? Unfortunately the law prefers the reassurance of dichotomies that at best are elusive and at worst false in themselves.

"There is no greater fallacy," said Irving Brant in 1965, "than the belief that government can or ought to separate truth from error. Error, protected by freedom of speech, may outline truth. But freedom dies when error is repressed by law, and error multiplies when freedom dies."[91] Brant, a newsman turned historian and student of the Constitution, wrote a six-volume biography of James Madison and a number of works on the Bill of Rights. John

Stuart Mill, of course, in his famous "Essay on Liberty," gave us the same advice 150 years ago. Truth and falsehood, elusive concepts at best, become dangerous to freedom of speech when made into absolutes. They are by their very nature forever entangled, difficult to separate.

Ironically, with Glasnost and increasing freedom for the Soviet press has come a rash of libel suits that Soviet journalists consider to be "one of the greatest current threats to press freedom." The chief editor of *Soviet Culture* says, "we're taken to court virtually every day. We've had to hire a special lawyer just to handle the cases."[92] Must this be the price of freedom?

Having set out the problems for public discourse created by wanton libel suits brought by the powerful and the celebrated, it is necessary next to look more closely at the interactions of plaintiff, defendant, and audience, to consider the origins of America's raucous press, and to examine how the law of libel has developed and has failed to deal adequately with the strains between the reputations of the powerful and the celebrated and the right of others to speak publicly about those reputations.

2

Plaintiff, Defendant, Audience

Two major categories of libel-proof public plaintiff have been proposed: the public official and the celebrity. Celebrities, while they
do not always influence public policy, set trends, serve as models
for style and behavior, and strive for public adulation. Both categories have, in common, access to the public through the media,
and in the case of celebrities, welcomed access often to millions
in the mass audience.

Public officials are those persons elected or appointed to public
office who, through the power and authority of those national,
state, or local offices, set and carry out the political agenda. While
they are distinguishable, both high-level policymakers and administrators would be included.

Justice Brennan in his opinion for the Court in the 1966 case
Rosenblatt v. *Baer* was among the first to expand the definition
of public official. Plaintiff, here, was the former supervisor of a
county recreation area whose policymaking responsibilities were
minor.

"There is, first," he said, "a strong interest in debate on public
issues, and second, a strong interest in debate about those persons
who are in a position significantly to influence the resolution of
those issues. Criticism of government is at the very center of the
constitutionally protected area of free discussion. Criticism of those
responsible for government operations must be free, lest criticism
of government itself be penalized. It is clear, therefore, that the
'public official' designation applies at the very least to those among
the hierarchy of government employees who have, or appear to
the public to have, substantial responsibility for or control over
the conduct of public affairs."[93]

Note how Brennan would permit the public's perception of

power to influence the definition. Nevertheless, clerks, secretaries, and janitors need not be included in any libel-proof category, nor those lower-level functionaries whose policymaking or enforcement powers are minuscule. Nor should the relatives of public officials be included unless they in some way insinuate themselves into the decision-making process or have problems so severe as to debilitate the officeholder in the performance of his or her duties.

Generals, admirals, sheriffs, police chiefs, and police officers, at least when on duty, ought to be included because they have been accorded powerful means of enforcing the law. Police officers interpret the law as they enforce it; firefighters, in contrast, are completely reactive to physical events and are, therefore, seldom policymakers. Doctors, lawyers, teachers, clergy, top corporation executives, labor leaders, and those who do business with the government, all may influence the body politic by voluntarily ministering to or exacerbating its needs.

Even more expansive in applying the actual malice rule was Justice William O. Douglas, concurring in *Rosenblatt*.[94] He would have applied the test to anyone on the public payroll, night watchman, file clerk, typist as well as government contractor, industrialist, labor leader, and those engaging in speech about science, the humanities, the professions and agriculture.

I agree with Harry Kalven, the late University of Chicago law professor, that Douglas may have had the right tilt in the case, but he went too far.[95] I would not go so far as to include minor public employees in a policymaking category.

Pervasive public figures are those plaintiffs who have reached celebrity status through their interaction or communication with mass audiences. Those who, through their talent, charm, or charisma, play a role in setting the cultural agenda, and often, whether intended or not, play an indirect but sometimes compelling role in public policymaking. Included are artists, athletes, perhaps a few restaurateurs, broadcast personalities, editors and publishers, and all those whose social positions depend on public approval and the public conferment of status.

Unless their family members bear importantly on their trend-setting efforts, they also should not be assumed to have celebrity status. Like politicians, celebrities have put themselves in the public spotlight, and that light often generates heat. Sometimes it even burns.

Assuming that criminals exercise a modicum of free will, they also fall into the all-purpose public figure category, although most would choose not to.[96]

Many public people remain fairly permanent in the social structure and are often as important out of office as in office, off the stage as on the stage. Reputation as honor, a socially ascribed status, says Berkeley law professor Robert Post, tends to remain fixed.[97] Their private lives are entwined with their public lives in such ways that attempts to untangle them lead to endless difficulty and disagreement.

As we shall discover, judging a person's social role and influence, although highly subjective, is constitutionally preferable and far less daunting than taking apart media content to measure its public importance or its truth, or investigating an editor's mindset to assess intentions. After all, it is conscious people who sue and are sued, not lines of type or sound waves or superegos, and the Constitution could not have anticipated, nor would it condone, the application of any kind of "truth serum" to editors.

Not included in the celebrity category are those private persons who, faithful to the obligations of citizenship, take up a public cause, demonstrate, petition, or otherwise seek to change or influence the passage of a law, and, for a moment in time, walk across the public stage. Such persons the courts call vortex or limited-purpose public figures, and they are not fixed in the social hierarchy. They lack reliable access to the mass media. They do not make or carry out public policy on any kind of continuing basis. Instead they try to influence or change that policy at a particular time and place, unlike the Ralph Naders of the world who become fixed in the public consciousness through their access and their influence over time. Libel law should remain available to the occasional activists, when they are "thrust into the public eye by the distorting light of defamation."[98] These people may be defendants as well as plaintiffs. Nader, for example, sued General Motors successfully for clandestine attempts to discredit his personal life, and columnist Ralph de Toledano unsuccessfully for questioning his motives. The latter suit was clearly unjustified, given Nader's influence and access to media.

SLAPPs

While my concern is primarily with media defendants, I have great sympathy and respect for those more humble political participants, many of whom emerge briefly and courageously from their private lives to influence public policy. A legal assault on these limited-purpose public figures for their speech activities illustrates dramatically another way in which libel laws are being used to destroy public debate and discourage political criticism.

Two Denver researchers have collected data from 200 libel suits that resulted when ordinary citizens sought to influence public policy. Suits were filed after these people circulated petitions, wrote letters to public officials or to editors, reported violations of law, made complaints to governmental bodies, conducted elections, testified at public hearings, demonstrated or boycotted; in other words, when they petitioned the government, directly or indirectly, for a redress of grievances.[99]

The Denver authors call these legal actions Strategic Lawsuits Against Public Participation, or SLAPPs. Clearly, some of these are preemptive strikes against public interest lawsuits. Others are designed to obscure the real issues at stake.

People unexpectedly become libel defendants because of their interest in such things as metropolitan development, the use of basic resources, civil rights, the performance of licensed professionals, and the adequacy of governmental services.[100]

For example, the NAACP and residents of the district of Bayview, California, protested police brutality and cover-ups; the Police Officers Association sued for $50 million. Critical comments regarding child-care services made before a U.S. Senate Subcommittee resulted in a $200,000 defamation suit.[101] Pat Haworth of San Lorenzo Valley, California, protested a land development scheme in a letter to the editor; the result, a $3 million libel suit. A $200,000 suit was the response to an assertion that a coal company polluted a West Virginia river.[102] Condominium developers in Beverly Hills sued the president of the League of Women Voters, the leader of an anti-development initiative, a local citizen, and 1,000 "John Does" for $63 million.[103] The town council of Braddock, Pennsylvania, a Pittsburgh suburb, sued the leader of a civil rights group for calling the council "racist" after the dismissal of a black secretary.[104]

A university professor hired by a housing coalition to document racial bias in a housing development was sued for libel by the landlords. His lawyer told him not to worry: he had such a good case it would cost only $10,000 to win.[105] Clearly the law is being used in these cases to recover through the judicial process what has been lost in the political process.[106] If you can't win at the polls or in the court of public opinion, you sue. When the government is plaintiff, the action carries the mark of sedition. Sedition redux.

"We, as a society," says Eugene Roberts, executive editor of the *Philadelphia Inquirer* until his retirement in 1990, "have now delivered into the hands of government officials the nation over—indeed, the world over—a simple but effective weapon against freedom of expression. It is the capability of using protracted litigation to harass, intimidate and punish the press and private citizen alike for views and reports that officials do not like."[107] Nongovernmental plaintiffs, obviously, have also come to appreciate the effective intimidating power of libel suits.

This is not to say that some who sue the media don't have good cause. It was gratifying to me, I must admit, when Carol Burnett won her libel suit against the *National Enquirer*, and when John Henry Faulk's suit against Aware, Inc., effectively put that Red-baiting organization out of business. But Burnett's successful libel suit had the stars of stage and screen lining up behind her to strike their own blows for accuracy. Such people have better ways to respond than through a court action. They have their microphones, their celluloid, and their stages.

Media Effects

Often absent from legal considerations of plaintiff and defendant is curiosity about the audience, the relevant community that, under the law, assigns reputational harm. Stanford University researchers have found evidence to suggest what may be a "vast gulf between the damage juries think defamatory articles cause and the damage they actually cause."[108]

Using W. Phillips Davison's "third-person effect" hypothesis, which holds that people exposed to media messages believe that they are not as strongly affected by those messages as others, the Stanford group found that jurors will reach a verdict based on that perception. They also found that emphasis given in the trial to the defendant's harmful intent heightened the jury's perception that the plaintiff's reputation was damaged, whether it was or not, and intensified animosity toward the defendant communicator. Davison himself, in an 1983 article, observed, "Exaggerated expectations about the effects of dissident communications have caused countless people to be incarcerated, tortured and killed."[109]

While we are not facing life or death issues in libel, the law still relies on an outdated "hypodermic needle effects" model of communication, the notion that the opinions of reasonable people are forever changed by a single defamatory publication and that audience members give no thought to the credibility of source or message or to countersources.[110] Or the law presumes that our minds absorb media messages the way our bodies absorb a vaccine. For too long legal reasoning has underestimated the astuteness of ordinary people and has largely ignored cumulative evidence of media effects in a wide array of settings, including voting behavior.[111]

Empirical evidence indicates that to a degree media messages socialize, inform, persuade, and set agendas for us by suggesting on front pages and in television's headline newscasts what we should think about. Nevertheless, media messages are more inclined to reinforce our existing attitudes than to convert us to new points of view. And sometimes they may have effects counter to what was intended by a communicator or what might have been reasonable assumptions about effects.[112]

In a broader social framework, media messages influence social change by bringing innovations we are ready for to our attention and by dramatizing social problems such as crime, drug abuse, and homelessness. At the same time, these messages are being mediated, filtered, or screened through the norms and values of our group memberships, the age, education, religion, and economic categories in which we fit or with which we identify.

These social relationships together with our predispositions, individual differences, and our particular needs, desires, or moods of the moment will largely determine how we use the media. Effects, of course, also depend on the skills of communicators—their power, their talent at manipulation, and their attractiveness. Audience reaction to particular communicators partly explains why some media or media offerings survive and prosper while others wither and die.

We are much less certain about the more subtle, indirect, and cumulative long-range effects of mass communication. Violence on television is only one example of a content form that may through constant repetition have deleterious effects on the behavior of some viewers. The resulting behavior may be mimetic or imitative, or it may be cathartic. The degrees of each are difficult to measure in general populations. Certainly all of us, to some extent, model what we see on television and we share symbolic meanings with other members of the audience for good or for ill; but we adjust our attitudes and thereby our opinions and actions based on those opinions ever so cautiously so as to keep them congruent or in balance with what we have learned or been taught in the past.[113]

By assuming "unbridled power of media representation," note Professors Bezanson and Ingle, writing in the *California Law Review*, "constitutional privilege analysis tends to obscure the role of readers, viewers, and listeners in the communication process, a role at least as important to the formation of reputation as what is meant or what is said.... [W]e should draw ... lines in ways that more accurately reflect the communication process than do distinctions between fact and opinion or falsity and truth.... [W]here the form of expression involves the representation in another medium of essentially aesthetic or value-based judgments, libel should not lie."[114]

Perplexity over the fact–opinion distinction, for example, one particular dimension of audience reaction, is as old as Madison.[115] The Supreme Court has so far sent mixed signals, as shall be noted. And only recently have the federal appeals courts made an attempt to, distinguish fact from opinion only to be countermanded by the U.S. Supreme Court.[116]

In a celebrated 1980s libel case that audiophiles might have appreciated the issue was the sound qualities of Bose loudspeakers. The relevant audience was assumed to be a lump of clay when in reality that audience had been alert to and sharply divided for years on the question: One either loved or hated Bose loudspeakers for the sound that "tended to wander about the room,"[117] the opinion that was initially held to constitute actionable libel. Here again five years of litigation should never have begun.

And it should be remembered that the public prints or air waves are far superior to the courts in airing these kinds of disagreements. Carson's or Burnett's monologue reaches a far wider audience and has a much greater impact than fragmented reports of a libel suit can possibly have in responding to a *National Enquirer*. For the mayor or the celebrity who has been falsely accused of child molestation by an opponent or a competitor and this has been reported, the press has a clear obligation to print or broadcast his or her denial, or better, a full and fair retraction if the defamation is false.

3

Revolutionary Origins

However oblivious courts remain to evidence concerning the nature of the communication process, it is incumbent upon them to recall from time to time the revolutionary origins of the nation's press. The grounds for punishing criticism of government and its agents today will not bear historical scrutiny. Merrill Jensen, in reviewing Leonard Levy's landmark work, *Legacy of Suppression*,[118] reminded his readers of that heritage when he wrote in 1961,

> No governmental institution, political faction, or individual was free from attacks such as few newspapers today would dare print.[119]

Presidents Washington, Adams, and Jefferson head the list of those political leaders savaged by the press of their day. Washington held criticisms of his administration to be "outrages on common decency." Adams was charged with "ridiculous pomp, foolish adulation, and selfish avarice." To the Federalist press Jefferson in office was the "infidel" bound to the prostitute "Goddess of Reason." The great interpreter of press freedom was said to be a swindler, a seducer, and the keeper of a slave mistress, Sally Hemings. He was finally driven to respond, "Our newspapers, for the most part, present only the characteristics of disaffected minds. Indeed, the abuses of the freedom of the press here have been carried to a length never before known or borne by any civilized nation."[120] Jefferson did not sue for libel. Nor did Hamilton, who, after a merry chase by the press of his day, admitted to adultery with Maria Reynolds. Neither Federalist nor anti-Federalist editors were sued by Jefferson or Hamilton, although the latter chose to respond to his tormentors in a Federalist newspaper.

The tradition of press assaults on the character and reputation of presidents and presidential candidates has never ceased, although the tone of such aspersions has become increasingly temperate and depersonalized. Following the Founders, there were Andrew Jackson and his beloved Rachel, who was ostracized by Washington society because it was rumored that her divorce had not been final when she married the future president. Martin Van Buren was depicted as effeminate, William Henry Harrison and Franklin Pierce as drunks. Abraham Lincoln, once referred to a "that monkey in the White House," was spared few epithets found in the English language. And Grover Cleveland was forever reminded that he had sired an illegitimate child.

Practice seldom tracks with theory. It didn't then and it doesn't now. The press didn't do for democracy what it was supposed to do and those who managed the democracy found it difficult to control their tempers. Indeed, Texas law professor David Anderson has demonstrated that notwithstanding a number of celebrated and spectacular wins in the Supreme Court the media throughout our history have not done as well as the general run of litigants when appealing to that body, although the success rate in prior restraint, privacy, and libel cases is higher than in other areas of media law.

Interestingly, media success in libel and privacy cases appealed from federal courts, in Anderson's study, was almost half of what it was in cases appealed from state courts.[121] Data from this study, as shall be noted, point, at least slightly, in the same direction for the comparatively brief period studied.

Levy's 1960 revisionist analysis of the principles and policies underlying adoption of the First Amendment's speech and press clauses, however controversial, began a fruitful debate that has diminished little over the decades. Did the First Amendment intend to revolutionize and mandate a new role for the press in America, putting aside the crime of seditious libel for all time, or did it merely reflect a Republican or Jeffersonian Party fear of federal authority, as Levy contends, and leave to the states the power to punish the common law crime of seditious libel, defamatory assaults on authority? To begin with, of course, the common law of England was the only law the American judiciary had, and English precedents were therefore persuasive if not conclusive.[122]

A reading of both pre- and post-Revolutionary newspapers, however, leaves little doubt that editors and pamphleteers on both sides of the Atlantic, whether or not they had developed anything resembling a theory of freedom of speech and press, were fully prepared to challenge the arbitrary authority they saw encased in common law. Indeed, by the end of the seventeenth century the Colonials had already established a tradition of fearless free speech. And when the lines of permissible speech were crossed, government-imposed penalties were generally surprisingly light, if a jury had not already acquitted.

Pre-Revolutionary newspapers, such as Edes and Gill's *Boston Gazette*, would prove to be powerful catalysts to patriot fervor. As for the common law of defamation, the Philadelphia *American Weekly Mercury* in its November 6, 1740 issue, for example, made a distinction between private and public libels. It promised not to print private or personal defamation, but offered this caveat, "The Rules there laid down, when applied to the Behaviour of those in Authority, will admit of many Exceptions."

There is evidence also that when newspapers did step over the legal line in the Colonial period grand juries often wouldn't indict nor petit juries convict.[123] Legislatures did punish breaches of parliamentary privilege, a crime closely resembling, if not synonymous with, sedition, but, technically, they relied on contempt citations that could generally be purged with a profuse and abject apology.

But old habits, especially when mixed with fear, persist, and much in the record of the eighteenth century seems to support Levy's thesis. Patriot Francis Hopkinson could write as late as 1776 that,

> . . . the liberty of the press hath been justly held up as an important privilege of the people. . . . But when this privilege is manifestly abused, and the press becomes an engine for sowing the most dangerous dissensions, for spreading false alarms, and undermining the very foundations of government, ought not that government, upon the plain principles of self-preservation, to silence by its own authority, such a daring violator of its peace, and tear from its bosom the serpent that would sting it to death.[124]

The endurance of British precept was suggested 25 years later by James (Chancellor) Kent, New York Federalist, legal scholar, and Blackstonian. He thought the common law appropriate to America because "[W]here vituperation begins, the liberty of the press ends"—particularly when that vituperation is directed at public officials.[125] The robes of authority were not to be sullied.

Once republican government was secured, however, many of its champions in turn believed that its survival would depend on limiting attacks on its basic assumptions. Thus, early in our experience there emerged the sometimes convenient but always destructive rationale that "saving" the system justified occasional violations of individual rights guaranteed within that system. These sentiments, while a minority view, would persist through the twentieth century and provide a rationale for Communist conspiracy indictments as late as the 1950s,[126] the government's side of two great *New York Times* cases of the 1960s and 1970s,[127] and further support for Levy's historical analysis of sedition.

Neither prominent reputations nor democratic structures, it was believed, would be safe from a vicious press and revolutionary speech. Free speech must not be used to destroy free speech. There is no freedom not to be free. And only rational speech is worth protecting. This would become Walter Lippmann's view and the view of many legal theorists. And George Will in the popular press would use the aborted march of Nazis in Skokie, Illinois, to make a similar argument. "But the right to compete," he wrote, "implies the right to win. So the logic of liberalism is that it is better to be ruled by Nazis than to restrict them. . . . There is no such thing as an amoral Constitution, neutral regarding all possible political outcomes." Put more abstractly by Walter Berns, to whom Will pays homage, there are political purposes for protecting free speech, and some speech is incompatible with those purposes.[128]

Between the Blackstone era and its theory of free speech limited to "no prior restraint" and the end of World War II, many legal writers held that, because of their destructive potential, defamation, sedition, and obscenity remained outside the boundaries of First Amendment protection.[129]

Radical Theorists and Practitioners

There was radical–liberal opposition to this view, of course, but it was sparse. For example, Theodore Schroeder, secretary of the

California-founded Free Speech League, forerunner of the Civil Liberties Union, argued, while seeking a system of free speech to shield minorities from majoritarian excesses, that seditious speech must be tolerated.[130] And Henry Schofield of Northwestern University Law School called the practice of holding newspaper editors in contempt for criticizing judicial conduct "intolerable."[131]

While not a matter of libel as such, the loosening of the contempt power from its English moorings meant a far wider range of freedom from governmental power for the American press. Schofield's implicit goal would be reached in 1941 when, by a close vote, the U.S. Supreme Court took from American judges the power to punish editors for contempt committed outside the courtroom in the columns of their newspapers.[132] This is not to say that "contempt by publication" no longer leads to citations by state court judges. It does.

More than 110 years before Schofield, two Jeffersonians, George Hay and John Thomson, had made even stronger arguments in favor of freedom for public speech. Hay would go so far as to contend that there could be no such thing as a verbal crime. He advocated complete freedom for falsehood and error, even if maliciously motivated and harmful.[133] These minority voices represented the body politic in the early nineteenth century no better than Schroeder and Schofield in the twentieth. But they were voices with staying power.

The most influential of nineteenth century dissenters may have been Thomas M. Cooley, an erudite Michigan judge writing in the last quarter of the period. He flatly rejected the English common law of seditious libel. Public men, said Cooley, ought to expect searching, even libelous, criticism of their character, habits, and mental and moral qualifications.[134] "[T]he evil likely to spring from the violent discussion," he wrote, "will probably be less, and its correction by public sentiment more speedy, than if the terrors of the law were brought to bear to prevent the discussion."[135]

Dissenting in an 1881 case, he urged his colleagues to think of quasi-public institutions, in this case Detroit's Board of Trade, as government agencies. He argued that a privilege ought to extend to "all schemes, projects, enterprises and organizations of a semi-public nature, which invite the public favor and depend for their success on public confidence," including the activities of banks, insurance companies, private asylums, and public fairs.[136]

The idea "that a judge who is corrupt and debauched in private life may be pure and upright in his judgments," wrote Cooley, was "false to human nature" and "contradictory to general experience."[137] James Scripps' tabloid, the Detroit *Evening News*, whose publisher was proud of "protesting everything" and whose motto was "Whatever is, is wrong,"—and this included the law—sorely tested the judge's theory and made it hard sometimes even for Cooley to sustain his tolerant view.[138]

But Cooley's was also a minority view. Unable to accept the notion that the First Amendment had abolished preexisting liability at common law, especially where the reputations of public figures were concerned, almost all courts continued to adhere to the strict liability standards of English law. But many newspaper editors did not honor those standards, nor did all of those who read and were influenced by newspapers.

A radical view of the meaning of freedom of the press seems to have existed from the very beginning of the American experience.[139] Levy himself, in modifying his earlier thesis in a subsequent book, expresses amazement that so many courageous and "irresponsible" seventeenth and eighteenth century editors daily risked imprisonment.[140] But he leaves undisturbed the core of his earlier work: the framers had no intention of abandoning the common law of seditious libel; what the Congress was forbidden to do by the First Amendment was still within the authority of the separate states. Even the incorrigibly radical Thomas Paine, Levy believes, countenanced common law prosecutions for sedition.[141]

This theory, it would seem, could never catch up with the perverse practices of printers. In 1788, a writer in *The Pennsylvania Gazette* confessed, "I am every week publishing things which in another country would bring the author to the gallows, as a seditious disturber of the public . . . and nothing comes of it."[142] One editor who probably would have been hanged in a less permissive society was Eleazer Oswald of Philadelphia's *Independent Gazetteer*. No one was too elevated in the power structure not to feel Oswald's editorial sting. Both George Washington and his political ally, Thomas McKean, chief justice of Pennsylvania, were targets of "Junius Wilkes," a pseudonym Oswald drew from John Wilkes radical *North Briton*, scourge of the British establishment. But Oswald and fellow Philadelphia editors, such as John Dunlap of the *Pennsylvania Packet* and Thomas Bradford of the *Pennsylvania Journal*, had a purpose beyond vituperation: they railed against the crime of seditious libel.[143]

On November 9, 1782, Oswald wrote in the *Gazetteer* that "the press might blemish a good reputation but the damage amounted to far less than the evil of restraining the press. The unjustly-maligned official should bear his injury rather than allow the public to suffer from a restriction on the press . . . politicians assumed the risks of office and could always answer unjust accusations in the press."[144]

One of the first to draw attention to the similarity between severe punishment after publication and prior restraint, Oswald would later be tried and convicted before the same Chief Justice McKean for a gross criminal libel against a private person.[145]

Oswald was not to be deterred. "The doctrine of libel," he said, "[is] a doctrine incompatible with law and liberty, and at once destructive of the privileges of a free country in the communication of our thoughts."[146] Of course, he was thinking of the libel of public men.

Oswald was by no means alone in his defiance of authority. As late as 1791, the year the Bill of Rights was ratified, Edmund Freeman, publisher of Boston's *Herald of Freedom*, could still be indicted for criticizing a legislator from Massachusetts. A jury acquitted him.

John Daly Burk, editor of New York's *Time Piece*, in a July 4, 1798, editorial wrote that only wicked governors of men dread what is said of them. Since all public business is transacted for the people, the deeds of magistrates should be open to public examination. It was deplorable, he concluded, that a situation should occur that made it possible for Federalist administrators to charge their opponents with Jacobinism because the latter refused to acknowledge the "heaven born genius of an Adams."[147] Sedition charges were brought against Burk and others even before passage of the infamous 1798 Alien and Sedition act on the assumption that the federal government possessed common law jurisdiction over the crime of seditious libel.

Benjamin Franklin Bache, grandson of Benjamin Franklin and editor of the Philadelphia *Aurora*, was arrested just two weeks before passage of the Sedition Act, an act intended both to discourage the formation of political parties and to break the pens of those supporting opposition to the Federalists. But it was an Act that would eventually ring in doom for John Adams and his party, if not for the crime of seditious libel itself.

Bache's trouble began when, in attempting to defend himself against a charge that he was either a pawn or an agent of Foreign Minister Talleyrand and the French, he was accused of a libel on the president. His arrest was a forerunner of the trials that would follow. Under the headline, "The Foul Charges of the Tories against the Editors of the Aurora...," Bache concluded his jeremiad in the June 19, 1798, issue of *Aurora* with this description of his tormentors:

"They are officers not even known to the Constitution, mere creatures of the Executive, subject to his will and pleasure, and independent of the People. Shall such men be permitted to place themselves above the law with impunity: to interpret private correspondence and run down private character?"[148] Note the appeal Bache makes for "private character," even though to him John Adams was not only "blind, bald, crippled, toothless (and) querulous" but also guilty of nepotism, squandering public money and warmongering.[149]

Abijah Adams was found guilty, in 1799, of publishing a libel on the Massachusetts legislature; he did 30 days, paid costs and put up a $500 good behavior bond for one year. The judge, in charging the jury, declared the common law of England the birthright of every American—"printing and publishing hath a direct and manifest tendency to stir up uneasiness, jealousy, distrust, sedition in the same Commonwealth of Massachusetts."

That idea was endemic. "The Sedition Act," said its chief enforcer, Secretary of State Timothy Pickering, "prescribed punishment only for 'pests of society, and disturbers of order and tranquility' and could not be considered as an attack on freedom of speech and press.[150]

Levy's contention that the thread of seditious libel runs through the American experience is difficult to dispute because evidence of it is ubiquitous; yet it was not the only thread in the emerging tapestry of American law and journalism. Levy's thesis somehow misses the spirit of the times, a refusal "to succumb to the legal or political consequences of the British theory that accepted seditious libel as a crime."[151]

David Frothingham of the *Argus* of New York was sued in 1799 by Alexander Hamilton for allegations of attempted political bribery. He was found guilty, fined $100 and sentenced to four months in jail.[152] James Callender, for a time a favorite editor of Thomas Jefferson, was indicted for his acerbic political opinions and had to flee Pennsylvania for Richmond, Virginia, to avoid punishment. His guilt was presumed by a Federalist judge and jury. Callender continued to attack John Adams in the Richmond *Examiner* and in pamphlets. Finally, he was tried under the Sedition Act, even though Virginia's House of Delegates had declared it unconstitutional, as had Kentucky's legislature earlier. Callender was sentenced to nine months in jail and fined $200.

In 1800, two years after passage of the Sedition Act, the accountant of the Navy was said to be $2.5 million short in his accounts. War Department records were mysteriously burned as Jefferson was making his transition to the presidency. The *Aurora* called it the "Federal Bonfire." Shortly thereafter, Treasury Department records were also destroyed by fire. The *Aurora* called the Secretary of the Treasury a man of "blazing fame."[153] This episode could have been a prelude to Watergate or Irangate, although in those cases some of the principals were of "erasing" and "shredding" rather than "blazing" fame.

Historian Frank Luther Mott counted twenty-five arrests, fifteen indictments (eight of them against newspaper editors), eleven trials and ten convictions under the 1798 Sedition Act. Five more convictions were gained under the common law of seditious libel.[154] After the 1812 case of *United States* v. *Goodwin & Hudson*,[155] the federal government was blocked from punishing common law crimes, including sedition, in the absence of a federal statute. The states would move into the breach.

In the meantime, among the "pests of society" Secretary Pickering spoke of was Matthew Lyon, a U.S. representative from Vermont, who spent four months in prison and paid a $1,000 fine for asserting that President Adams had a fondness for "ridiculous pomp, idle parade, and selfish avarice." He was reelected to Congress while in prison.

Republican or Jeffersonian editors were thought to be the "crazies" of the late eighteenth and early nineteenth centuries. Yet they should be credited as our true journalistic forefathers, given their verve, courage, and contrariness. And they published the mainstream newspapers of the day.

To Bache's *Aurora*, George Washington was an "assassinator," an inferior general, a mediocre politician, and an ordinary planter, hungry for money and glory and willing to blink corruption. Noah Webster was an "impious, disorganizing wretch." (It is difficult to think of the compiler of a dictionary as "disorganized.") Federalist editor John Fenno was "a scoundrel and a liar." On August 8, 1800, Bache's paper dedicated two lines of doggerel to Justice Samuel Chase: "Cursed of thy father, scum of all that's base, Thy sight is odious and thy name is (Chase)." The same Chase is remembered for his devotion to British precedent when in the trial of Thomas Cooper, temporary editor of the Sunbury and Northumberland (Pennsylvania) *Gazette*, who in 1799, was also charged with criticizing President Adams, he wrote:

> All governments which I have ever read or heard of punish libels against themselves. If a man attempts to destroy the confidence of the people in their officers, their supreme magistrate, and their legislature, he effectually saps the foundation of the government. A Republican government can only be destroyed in two ways: the introduction of luxury or the licentiousness of the Press. This latter is the more slow, but more sure and certain, means of bringing about the destruction of government.[156]

Boston's *Independent Chronicle* called Alexander Hamilton that arrogant, fraudulent "adulterer"—"immersed in mischief, brothels, funds and banks, lewd slave to lust."[157] Philip Freneau's *National Gazette* specialized in ridicule and irony. Sam Adams' *Boston Gazette*, the New York *Argus*, the New London *Bee*, the Baltimore *American*, the Lancaster *Intelligencer*, Callender's Richmond *Examiner*, all masters of invective, became Thomas Jefferson's flying wedge and the clattering nemesis of President Adams.

For a time such editors were pursued relentlessly by Federalist officials. Federalist editors, calling them "trumpets of the devil," often gave as good as they got, although they were outnumbered and would eventually be ground down by public pressure. But they would go down howling. Russell's *Gazette* of Boston, commenting on the premature death of Bache, said "this scoundrel cannot be too highly execrated."[158] William Cobbett's *Porcupine Gazette* was so virulent in its anti-Jeffersonian commentary that John Adams was considering having Cobbett deported to his native England under the very Alien and Sedition act that Cobbett supported editorially.[159] Against the Jeffersonian *Aurora* and *Chronicle*, Boston's Federalist *New England Palladium* made this rococo attack:

> By newspapers, prejudice finds eyes, and passions a tongue . . . Excellent in their use, intolerable in their abuse, we are forced to ponder about newspapers, whether we can do without them, or endure them. Liberty would be a goddess and really immortal, if she could be thus dieted on poisons, if she could play unhurt with the forky tongues of the Chronicle and Aurora.[160]

But the Republican tradition was not without a darker side that reflected less than a delicate appreciation for the deeper meaning of freedom of the press. A Newport, Rhode Island, Committee of Inspection, in a resolution endorsing the boycott of a Tory newspaper, had raised a cry for a free press, then choked on it by damning "infamous falsehoods, partial facts, the fomenting of jealousies, the exciting of discord and disunity, the supporting of worst men and measures and vilifying the best"[161]—the very skills the Republican press would later master.

Even the great Cato (the letters of John Trenchard and Thomas Gordon, first published in England in 1720), strongest of influences on the radical press, could lapse into ruinous qualification—"True and impartial Liberty" for "every Man to pursue the natural, reasonable, religious Dictates of his own Mind; to think what he will, and act as he Thinks, *provided he acts not to the Prejudice of another* [emphasis added]."[162] A neat trick if one could manage it.

Seventy years later Bache's successor, William Duane, had managed by his bellicosity to call down sixty libel suits upon his head in a single year, 1806.[163] James Cheetham's New York *American Citizen*, famous for its political acumen and flamboyant language, once had fourteen libel suits pending against it at one time.[164] Little is known about these lawsuits.

Jefferson as president suffered as much as anyone from press attacks. In a letter to then Govenor Thomas McKean of Pennsylvania he had suggested that a few "selected" prosecutions for criminal libel might have a "wholesome effect in restoring the integrity of the presses."[165] Did he mean it? Perhaps he did. He was called an atheist, radical, coward, libertine, and thief after his election in 1800.[166] In an August 28, 1789, letter to James Madison, Jefferson had written that he would have preferred language regarding the press clause of the federal Bill of Rights to have included, "The people shall not be deprived or abridged of their right to speak, to write or otherwise to publish anything but false facts affecting injuriously the life, liberty, property or *reputation* of others or affecting the peace of the confederacy with foreign nations [emphasis added]."[167]

By 1804, he had decided that such power to punish the press, while denied the central government, still resided in the hands of the states in their "provisions for punishing slander, which those who have time and inclination resort to for vindication of their characters."[168]

Croswell's Case and the Federalist Backlash

It was just such an attack in Alexander Hamilton's *New York Evening Post* that led to Harry Croswell's case. Croswell, editor of the Hudson, New York, *The Wasp*, a vicious pro-Federalist paper that even Federalists avoided, reprinted the editorial. It alleged Jefferson had paid James Callender, who, having fled Philadelphia, was now editor of the *Richmond Examiner*, to call George Washington a traitor, robber, and perjurer, and Adams a hoary-headed incendiary. Croswell was indicted under a New York State sedition law on a charge of libeling the president. Found guilty, he appealed to the state's highest court where Hamilton argued his case, pleading as a defense "truth with good motives and for justifiable ends." The court divided evenly, upholding Croswell's conviction. The New York Assembly, in 1805, turned Hamilton's argument into a statute, but not before a long debate over whether the English common law permitted truth as a defense in a criminal, as opposed to a civil, libel suit.[169]

"A free discussion of public measures, without descending to delineate private vices," said the prosecution in *Croswell*, "is sufficient for all beneficial purposes. To expose personal vices, defects and foibles to the public eye, corrupts the morals of the community, tends to drive useful men from office, and to render the press a vehicle to scatter firebrands, arrows and death."[170]

Similar criticisms would dog the doctrine of *New York Times* v. *Sullivan* a century and a half later.

Texas law professor Richard Robertson believes that powerful and irresponsible media interfere with legitimate government functions by unfairly and inaccurately exposing public officials and public figures to undeserved criticism.[171]

"A legal system that offers only niggardly safeguards against false assaults on the reputations of public officials," legal scholar Bruce Fein argues, "encourages an atmosphere of suspicion and cynicism surrounding government. Such an atmosphere impairs the ability of government to undertake bold and decisive measures to address many vexing problems that confront contemporary society."[172]

Experience teaches that cynicism and lack of incentive toward "bold and decisive measures" is much more profound in those societies prohibiting or cautioning against assaults of any kind on the reputations of public officials. A parallel argument found in critical reaction to the Court's holding in *New York Times*—that good people would be discouraged from seeking public office—may be "simply too conjectural to warrant restrictions of speech."[173]

Croswell's case occurred after the Sedition Act had self-destructed by means of what is now called a sunset clause. Written into the statute was a provision for its automatic repeal unless reenacted. But defamation of the state did not disappear with the coming of a Jeffersonian administration. Punitive damages in civil suits were replacing criminal indictments, to be sure, but they were no less onerous. In fact, money damages were just as effective in quelling criticism. And criminal libel remained particularly hardy in New York, a state that took time to forget its magisterial past.[174] So did civil libel.

In a study of New York libel cases between 1776 and 1860, legal historian John Finnegan found newspaper editors losing three of four civil cases in the first two decades of the nineteenth century, a difficult time for libel plaintiffs. Then as now many public plaintiffs were government officials. While criminal libel cases had all but disappeared by the period 1821–1840 due to their association with the hated Sedition Act, New York libel plaintiffs were winning more civil suits than ever. Public officials were suing less often, but, when they lost at trial and appealed, they won 89 percent of the time. Other studies suggest that civil libel suits were infrequent nationally in the Jacksonian period.[175] Any discrepancy may depend on how the Jacksonian period is measured.

In debates about criminal libel in the proposed 1821 New York constitution, New York Federalists believed that judicial independence, lifelong tenure for judges, and adherence to British legal traditions would keep the state and nation on a proper course. Republicans, on the other hand, viewed the judiciary as essentially unaccountable to voters, abusive in its exercise of power, and mindlessly fixated on technical and outmoded legal procedures belonging to a foreign culture.[176]

In the period 1840–1860, defendant editors in New York were at least breaking even in libel cases, and sometimes winning on appeal. In the last twenty years of the nineteenth century the state's newspapers, in spite of futile efforts by newspaper organizations there and in other states to rewrite the libel laws, were still breaking even and doing better against a less aggressive breed of public official.[177] This may not have been true everywhere; Norman Rosenberg found libel suits generally a problem after 1870; libel law had slipped back into what he called a Federalist mode: very little latitude for the criticism of government officials.[178] Editors of the time were convinced that jurors and the law favored plaintiffs; malice was presumed in any defamatory publication. They also railed against opportunistic lawyers and the sometimes crippling costs of beating back frivolous suits. And, then as now, a substantial 20 percent of libel suits may have been brought by public officials, another 30 percent by professional and business persons.

Some of the nineteenth century New York cases prefigured the contemporary libel scene. Editor and founder of the *Albany Evening Journal*, Thurlow Weed, was forced to defend five times against the hypersensitive and patrician novelist James Fenimore Cooper. Weed's biggest financial setback was the $17,000 in costs he had to pay in the only libel case he *won* against his tenacious adversary. Cooper, who was being challenged editorially for daring to instruct America in politics after a long self-imposed exile in France, seemed prepared to sue every editorial critic who crossed his sights between 1837 and 1845 (as many as ten suits in all, depending on how you count them).[179]

Horace Greeley who thought the state of the law of libel at the time a "perversion,"[180] was one of the hunted.

In a series of thoughtful and amusing articles on libel in his *New York Tribune*, Greeley recognized the futility of defending an opinion when truth was the only defense, and a failure to demonstrate truth was taken as evidence of actual malice. In a memorable paragraph addressed to Cooper, Greeley wrote:

> If you would simply sue those of the Press-gang who displease you, it would not be so bad; but you sue and write too, which is not the fair thing. What use in belittling the profession of Literature by appealing from its courts to those of the law? We ought to litigate upwards, not downwards.[181]

Greeley seemed to be saying that Cooper had substantial resources for reply to criticism.

Cooper's numerous suits sharpened perceptions of the "fair comment and criticism" defense, the privilege to go to the utmost lengths of denunciation, condemnation and satirization in criticizing men, measures and social institutions seeking public approval. The Cooper cases also provided prolonged protection in laws still in place to this day for the private dimensions of the lives of public people. The common law defense of fair comment, the opinion defense, would eventually be absorbed into the *New York Times* doctrine (specifically the "no false idea" rule of *Gertz* v. *Robert Welch*),[182] and it remains a precursor to the current dialogue on the troublesome distinctions between fact and opinion and private and public reputation in libel litigation—how to criticize the work without criticizing the author, or the character of a public official without infringing upon his or her private life.

Radical Rebuttal

For every assertion of orthodoxy in the Federal period and beyond came a radical rebuttal, establishing a tradition of dramatic overstatement from which we may tend to hide in today's tangled underbrush of libel litigation. Nevertheless, it can be argued that every charge carried in today's vast and complex communication system brings a countercharge, or an earnest defense made somewhere by someone. Literati and the less orthodox organs of journalism take pride in punching holes in conventional wisdom, challenging facts and pointing out exceptions to every norm claimed, followed or violated by mainstream America.

The early years of the republic clearly were accompanied by an acceptance of—and an eagerness for—political polemic, part of what some called the "politics of controversy."[183] Readers did not take libels literally. Unrestrained public debate was part of the price to be paid for liberty. And it was entertaining. Should we lose that appreciation for political wordplay because we can't afford the cost, the time, or the aggravation of a libel suit, we shall be poor in spirit as well as in polity.

The First Amendment, as well as its earlier and later conditional and unconditional manifestations in state constitutions, existed to protect a press scurrilous as well as responsible. But many state constitutions and statutes included the ominous qualifier of press freedom—"being responsible for the abuse of that liberty." Truth alone would not work as a defense against libel in nearly half the states. The English common law of libel would not be discarded easily.

Robust journalism also marked the later nineteenth century. Again practice outdistanced theory. James Gordon Bennett's *New York Herald* estimated, in 1869, that newspapers nationally at any one time faced 1,000 libel suits asking for some $50 million in damages. While threats may have been combined with formal actions in these estimates, the *Herald*'s editor counted 100,000 libel actions in New York alone in a ten-year period, attesting to the virility of the press of the period. Bennett's statistics may have been colored by the fact that he fought a single opera manager he had criticized for fourteen years in the courts.[184] Celebrities could be every bit as oppressive as public officials, then and now, when enlisting the state to their causes. The paper editorialized:

> This complaint refers especially to the system of libel suits against the publishers of newspapers, by means of which every censoriously criti-

cized public officer, or every exposed rogue, seeks to re-establish himself in public esteem by attempting to bleed the publisher or editor, and fill his own pockets at the latter's expense.[185]

A respected crusading editor of the period, Samuel Bowles of the Springfield (Massachusetts) *Republican*, speaking of the press wrote, "I know that it withholds unjustly to the public one hundred times, where it speaks wrongly once of the individual. Certainly nine out of ten of all libel-suits against the press are brought by adventurers, and speculators, and scoundrels, whose contrivances to rob the public have been exposed."[186]

Among those qualifying as "tyrants" in Bowles' editorial judgment were New York financiers Jay Gould and James ("Jim") Fisk, Jr. Fisk arranged to have Bowles arrested on a charge of criminal libel and held in jail overnight when Bowles visited New York City. Bowles continued to defend the press "against those critics who objected to the type of searchlight journalism that seeks to expose evils in society and government."[187]

Edwin Lawrence Godkin of *The Nation* and the *New York Evening Post* fought the same battle against municipal maladministration and corruption, much of it focused on Tammany Hall. It is said that he was arrested for criminal libel three times in one day in 1890 for publishing records and character profiles of hundreds of Tammany candidates for city offices. Since the accuracy of his reporting was never controverted, the suits amounted to no more than nuisances.

Alexander McClure's Philadelphia *Times* and Wilbur Storey's Chicago *Times* had experienced the same travails for their exposure of municipal corruption.[188] In 1875, the latter found itself defending against twenty-four suits at the same time, six brought by members of the Chicago City Council.[189] Then as now, the libel suit was meant to distract and threaten rather than remedy.[190]

The bumptious Theodore Roosevelt revived criminal libel in 1909 in an effort to punish the Indianapolis *News* and Pulitzer's *World* for reporting that well-placed Americans has profited from the purchase of the Panama Canal. Seemingly oblivious to the constitutional problematics of sedition, Roosevelt contended that since a libel against him and his Secretary of War was a libel against the American people, "It should not be left to the private citizen to sue Mr. Pulitzer for libel. He should be prosecuted for libel by the governmental authorities."[191] This is the same Roosevelt who, in the fullness of hindsight, could call Thomas Paine, a moderate voice by contemporary standards whose *Common Sense* catalyzed the American Revolution, "a filthy little atheist."[192] Both of Roosevelt's suits failed.

The case against the *World* did reach the U.S. Supreme Court in 1911 during the Taft administration. Indictments brought in the U.S. District Court in New York charged that six copies of the newspaper had been circulated at West Point and had found their way to a U.S. Post Office, laying the ground for a federal case. Holding that the federal courts had ignored the laws of the State of New York and, therefore, lacked jurisdiction in the case, the Court upheld a motion to quash.[193] The decision was trumpeted by the *World* as "the most sweeping victory won for freedom of speech and of the press in this country since the American people destroyed the Federalist party for enacting the infamous Sedition law," and predicted that "no other President will be tempted to follow the footsteps of Theodore Roosevelt, no matter how greedy he may be for power, no matter how resentful of opposition."[194]

In his second term, Roosevelt brought a petty civil action against the editor of the Ishpeming, Michigan, *Iron Ore* for reporting that candidate Roosevelt had been drunk during a campaign visit to the town. A long line of friends and supporters took the witness stand in Roosevelt's behalf, followed by the president himself. A chastened, beaten defendant apologized, withdrew his report, paid nominal damages of six cents and his own court costs and lawyer's fees.[195]

One of the last serious attempts to use criminal or seditious libel against a publication was Chicago's suit against the *Tribune* for libeling its credit in the bond market and impairing its functioning as a municipality. Under Mayor William Hale (Boss) Thompson, said the *Tribune*, civic corruption was bankrupting the city.

"No court of last resort in this country," the Illinois Supreme Court declared in response to the suit,

has ever held, or even suggested, that prosecutions for libel on government have any place in the American system of jurisprudence . . .

and . . . assuming that there was a temporary damage to the city and a resultant increase in taxes, it is better that an occasional individual or newspaper that is so perverted in judgment or so misguided in his or its civic duty should go free than that all of the citizens should be put in jeopardy of imprisonment or economic subjugation if they venture to criticize an inefficient or corrupt government.[196]

The Court also observed that the civil suits under which American writers were laboring had done more to inhibit freedom of the press than had the criminal prosecutions of the eighteenth century.

Criminal libel prosecutions, while few in number between 1812 and the Civil War, had increased dramatically after 1876 and would survive until the mid-1960s. Of approximately forty cases of seditious libel brought between 1916 and 1965, the majority were brought by state prosecuting attorneys defending their performances in office. Newspapers were defendants in a quarter of these.[197]

Clearly, admonitions against criminal suits have been replaced by an acquiescence to sedition redux in the form of civil suits and a perplexing panoply of variations in libel laws among states as to malice, damages, mitigation, privilege, opinion, republication, intent, and the difference between public and private people, all of which serve to mystify.[198]

It has not been easy to uphold the daring tradition of a revolutionary past. Only in 1964 would the U.S. Supreme Court finally attempt to bring down the curtain on seditious libel suits. Unfortunately, as we shall see, the curtain got stuck part way down.

4

New York Times v. *Sullivan:* Lost Opportunity

Legal historian Alfred Kelley also believes it probable that the penalties of civil libel under which writers labor today are more damaging to the practice of press freedom than the criminal prosecutions of the eighteenth century.[199] There is evidence to support his view. Economic disaster may attend today's libel suits. Substantial but smaller newspapers have been forced into bankruptcy or near bankruptcy by a single lawsuit, the most recent a daily in Alton, Illinois.[200] That also happened in the eighteenth and nineteenth centuries—it happened to William Cobbett—but it was rare.

The *Alton Telegraph* was reduced to bankruptcy because of a memo two of its investigative reporters sent to the Justice Department, a memo containing information alleging a developer's connections to organized crime that the newspaper did not publish for lack of complete documentation. Segments of the public cheered the newspaper's subsequent losses in a libel suit.[201] Cobbett, in 1799, had been sued and heavily fined for calling Dr. Benjamin Rush of Philadelphia a "quack." Unable to pay the fine, Cobbett fled the country and returned to England. As an exponent of a free press, Cobbett's practice was far superior to his theory: his thoughts about freedom of press were inconsistent, but he was an indefatigable fighter for the right.

Eighteenth and nineteenth century printers, with few exceptions, seem always to have recovered from a few months' imprisonment, imposition of a good conduct bond, or modest damage awards.

Nevertheless, twentieth century newspapers continued to labor under the threat of having to defend against criminal libel suits, however constitutionally misplaced they may have been by this time, and against constitutionally legitimate civil suits with defenses little improved over English common law.

Columbia University law professor Herbert Weschler in his powerful brief for the *New York Times*, in the 1964 landmark case, argued, "Sound would soon give place to silence if officials in 'complete control' of government agencies instead of answering their critics, could resort to friendly juries to amerce them for their words."[202] He could not have foreseen that, even with a victory for the newspaper he was defending, what he wished most to avoid would be the result.

For a long time before its formal promulgation by the U.S. Supreme Court in the *New York Times* case, however, there was a minority view in state libel cases. That view held that great latitude must be given speech concerning the character and qualifications of public officials and candidates for public office. The Charleston *South Carolina Gazette* had said it well on May 7, 1772:

> But this we faithfully promise, and are determined to perform, whenever public Characters appear deserving of general Detestation, neither Promises of Reward, or Threats of Punishment, shall prevent our exposing them to public Scorn and Contempt.

An 1808 Massachusetts case also reflected the minority view's persistent effort to break the chains of seditious libel. Judge Parsons wrote in *dicta*:

> And when any man shall consent to be a candidate for a public office conferred by the election of the people, he must be considered as putting his character in issue, so far as it may respect his fitness and qualification for the office. . . . And every man holding a public elective office may be considered as within this principle. . . . [203]

An 1845 U.S. Supreme Court ruling put the question, a question it considered "important to society," even more succinctly, if only rhetorically. The case involved a letter to the president from a citizens' group critical of a Georgetown collector of customs:

> How far, under an alleged right to examine into the fitness and qualifications of men who are either in office or are applicants for office—or how far, under the obligation of a supposed duty to arraign such men either at the bar of their immediate superior, or that of public

opinion, their reputation, their acts, their motives or feelings may be assailed with impunity—how far that law, designed for the protection of all, has placed a certain class of citizens without the pale of protection.[204]

The minority rule was just that. It did not commend itself to most courts and would not be legitimized until a landmark Kansas ruling in 1908. Protection for public criticism "must apply," said the Kansas Supreme Court, "to all officers and agents of government, municipal, state and national; to the management of all public institutions, educational, charitable, and penal; to the conduct of all corporate enterprises affected with a public interest, transportation, banking, insurance; and to innumerable other subjects involving the public welfare."[205]

There is no better example than the 1908 case of *Coleman* v. *MacLennan* in demonstrating the influence progressive state rulings could have on the federal judiciary. The Topeka *State Journal* had seriously questioned the official conduct of a candidate for reelection as attorney general. The newspaper's concerns had to do with the suspected "manipulation" of state funds and the purchase of county bonds. The candidate, C. C. Coleman, sued the publisher F. P. MacLennan.

"[A]lthough the matters contained in the article may be untrue in fact, and derogatory of the character of the candidate," said the trial judge in instructing the jury, a newspaper's editorial opinion about a public official believed to be true and published for the benefit of the electorate is privileged. The jury, persuaded by the trial judge, found for the newspaper and Coleman appealed to the Kansas Supreme Court.

In an opinion of historic consequence, Justice Rousseau Burch upheld the jury verdict and in language from which the U.S. Supreme Court would quote liberally fifty-six years later he concluded that the so-called majority rule would put the law about where Blackstone had left it, based on the pretense that criticism would drive good men out of politics.

> [A] candidate must surrender to public scrutiny . . . so much of his private character as affects his fitness for office. . . . The narrow (majority) rule leaves no greater freedom for the discussion of matters of the gravest public concern than it does for the character of a private individual. . . .

Federal courts in time would also reflect this view. Listen to Judge Learned Hand in the 1917 *Masses* case:

The "right to criticize whither by temperate reasoning or by immoderate and indecent invective [is] normally the privilege of the individual in countries dependent upon free expression of opinion as the ultimate source of authority."[206]

Coleman would provide the bedrock for *New York Times* v. *Sullivan*[207] in 1964. And that case would turn the minority rule into the law of the land.

The private right to reputation would become subordinate to the constitutional right of unfettered public discussion, the right of others to speak to a candidate's reputation before an election. The importance of such discussion to state and society was seen by the *Coleman* court as "so vast and the advantages derived so great that they more than counterbalance the inconvenience of private persons whose conduct may be involved, and occasional injury to the reputations of individuals must yield to the public welfare, although at times such injury may be great."[208] By 1945 as many as sixteen states subscribed to the minority rule that, in time, would be the only rule.

Clearly this view, which some will find callous, has deep roots in American history. It is a view that over centuries had to be torn from the grip of authority, sacred and secular, often by individual speakers at great risk to their lives and liberty. The *New York Times* doctrine, as it would come to be called, reflected this past. In the fertile mind of Justice William Brennan, who fashioned the opinion of the Court in the case, it also reflected the free speech theories of Alexander Meiklejohn, a legal philosopher who, although he came to his subject late in life, had enormous influence on generations of legal scholars and jurists, both of the Left and Right, including Brennan.

It also reflected the classic core formulation of Justice Louis Brandeis in his famous concurrence in *Whitney* v. *California* that the remedy to be applied against falsehood is "more speech, not enforced silence."[209]

Meiklejohn believed that freedom of expression must be absolute in areas of public affairs. What he called speech of "governing importance," speech that constitutes the thinking process of the community, could not be burdened beyond reasonable time, place, and manner qualifications. Its content was sacrosanct; its protection absolute. Meiklejohn also believed that, while the First Amendment gives no protection to private defamation,

> If... the same verbal attack is made in order to show unfitness of a candidate for governmental office, the act is properly regarded as a citizen's participation in government.... And the same principle holds good if a citizen attacks, by words of disapproval and condemnation, the policies of the government, or even the structures of the Constitution. These are 'public' issues concerning which, under our form of government, he has authority, and is assumed to have competence to judge. *Though private libel is subject to legislative authority, political or seditious libel is not* [emphasis added].[210]

A Crippling Compromise

As elated as Meiklejohn is reported to have been by the Court's ruling in *New York Times* v. *Sullivan*, a ruling that appeared to adopt his theory of protection for political speech (he said the ruling was cause for "dancing in the streets"), he would have to have been greatly disappointed, had he lived, in the course it would take after 1964. This is due in large part to a fatal qualification or compromise in Brennan's theory, a compromise, of course, without which he might not have been able to bring with him a majority of the Court in the *New York Times* case.

As has been noted, the compromise Brennan made against the advice of Justices Hugo Black, William O. Douglas and, in large part, Arthur Goldberg is the actual malice test requiring a reading of a publisher's intentions or motives. The Court held that a public official suing a news organization for libel would not only have to prove falsity and injury at the threshold to collect damages but also actual malice, that is, "knowing falsehood or reckless disregard as to truth or falsity." And evidence of actual malice would have to be of "convincing clarity."

Certainly the new rule was an improvement over the strict liability standards of the common law where, absent a privilege, truth or truth with good motives was the only defense. The burden of proof would now be on plaintiff rather than defendant, and it seemed that few public officials would ever be able to meet the actual malice standard. In a few years the new constitutional defense would be stretched to include public figures and eventually, but, as it would turn out, temporarily, to private persons involved in matters of public interest.[211]

Harry Kalven, Jr., in an influential article interpreting the landmark decision, predicted that this extension of the actual malice rule would take place when he wrote:

> But the invitation to follow a dialectic progression from public official to government policy to public policy to matters in the public domain, like art, seems to me to be overwhelming.[212]

Private persons not involved in public events would also carry the burden of proof in libel suits under *New York Times*, but their standard of fault would be negligence rather than actual malice, and individual states could be guided by their own libel statutes and constitutions in defining it.

Arguments against the *New York Times* doctrine were the same arguments made against criticism of public persons in New York in 1827: no honest person would run for office with such distended protection of an irresponsible press.[213]

On still another side, Justice Black, joined by Justices Douglas and Goldberg, in concurring opinions, sensed that Brennan had compromised his own standard, a standard that had been formed by Brennan's reading of Meiklejohn. Black, of course, by this time on record as declaring all libel laws unconstitutional, wrote in his concurring opinion that the defendants had an "absolute, unconditional constitutional right" to criticize state officials. "[L]ibel laws," he added, "threaten the very existence of an American press virile enough to publish unpopular views on public affairs and bold enough to criticize the conduct of public officials."

Douglas agreed. Although he wrote no opinion in the case, he was as close to being a First Amendment absolutist as any justice in the history of the Court. In fact, Douglas always led Black, sometimes dramatically, in voting for speech rights, which he defined far more broadly than Black, although libel cases were an exception for him until the ascension of Warren Burger to the position of Chief Justice of the United States. Then, both Black and Douglas, perhaps as a defensive measure, were 100 percent pro-press in libel cases.[214] Justice Goldberg, although he may have mispoke in viewing the First and Fourteenth Amendments as affording "privileges" rather than rights, mirrored Black's declaration in writing of "an absolute, unconditional privilege to criticize official conduct despite the harm which may flow from excesses and abuses."[215]

Legal scholar Thomas I. Emerson, among others, found Brennan's actual malice test "inconsistent with basic First Amendment theory"—at least with his own (Emerson's) First Amendment theory.

"[S]uperrefined attempts to separate statements of fact from opinion," said Emerson, "to winnow truth out of a mass of conflicting evidence, . . . to probe into intents, motives and purposes . . . all these do not fit into the dynamics of a system of freedom of expression. The health and vitality of the system depend more upon untrammeled freedom of discussion, in which all citizens contend vigorously, than in judicial attempts to establish the motives of participants."[216]

Emerson was prescient. In the next twenty-five years, libel law would become so convoluted as to defy understanding. Presentations on the subject by the best and brightest in the field would leave one with an impression of semantic chaos. Dean Prosser had spoken much earlier of "anomalies and absurdities" in the law of libel.[217] The contemporary voice of a New York lawyer saw the rules of libel as "hi-tech legalities to confound the confusion."[218] A leading constitutional scholar calls libel "a mysterious labyrinth for those seeking to clear their names and a costly and unpredictable burden for the speakers the first amendment is designed to protect."[219]

There seemed to be no standard definitions for the constituent elements of libel. The topic was awash in dichotomies (truth/falsehood, public/private, malice/lack of malice, deliberate/nondeliberate, fact/opinion)—alien absolutes in a world of probabilities. And the Supreme Court was fragmented as to its limits of tolerance for defamatory speech. There was a confusing interplay between common law and constitutional principles. State courts tended to go their own way, and, going back to *Herbert* v. *Lando*, the complicating 1979 Supreme Court case defining procedures for finding fault on the part of defendants, lawyers were now permitted to probe the unconscious minds of reporters and editors and to interject themselves into newsroom procedures to establish by hunch, impression or inference the existence of actual malice.[220] The *New York Times* doctrine, which had intended to liberate the press from the last vestiges of sedition, seemed more to shackle it. Courts were defining journalistic responsibility. What the *New York Times* doctrine might have intended was in tatters. The actual malice test had had a boomerang effect.

A small priesthood of libel lawyers and insurance adjusters would soon assume the role of editorial assistant, if not editor. As sociologist Susan Shapiro describes what lawyers do in evaluating stories for their tone, temper, imprecision, hyperbole, consistency, balance, fairness, and sensitivity, it becomes abundantly clear that lawyers are doing now what experienced editors and copyreaders did in the past and ought to be doing still. Why has the press abandoned this most creative part of the editorial process to lawyers? Is it due to the pressures of libel law? While media lawyers report never advising that a story be killed, it is difficult not to imagine that the accumulating dangers expostulated by lawyers don't lead editors to the same result.[221]

And one result of authoritative warnings may be an increasing dependence on official records, mainstream sources, and an avoidance of those prickly private power centers that contribute much to the character of modern society. Jack Anderson, a modern muckraker, told an interviewer that "every column is now approved by lawyers before dissemination." Fear of lawsuits cannot help but change the course of investigative reporting.[222]

More discouraging, there were as many libel suits as ever after 1964 and in some respects the press appeared to be in a worse condition than it had been before *New York Times* and the constitutionalizing of the tort.[223] Even Justice Byron White, stingy about expanding press freedoms and wary of the *New York Times* doctrine, thought protracted discovery periods would be detrimental to the press.[224]

Damage claims would become prohibitive. No longer the people's champion confronting a repressive colonial master or trumpet of a political party, the media had become in the minds of jurors corporate giants with deep pockets, and commercial giants are expected to be bad as well as rich.[225] Jurors would often find fault where, under First Amendment doctrine, none existed.

In a perverse and unexpected way, actual malice has become the banner of lost but debilitating causes. Some, including members of the U.S. Supreme Court, Chief Justice William Rehnquist and Justice White among them, would soon recommend a return to the pre-*New York Times* common law rules, thus repealing or greatly modifying the constitutional defense.[226]

A forceful argument for abandoning the *New York Times* doctrine and returning to the strict liability rules of the common law for the press, but with some control over damages, has also been made by Richard Epstein of the University of Chicago law school. He sees, correctly in my opinion, no provision for determining truth in the present system and he believes that in a world of misinformation honest people will hesitate to speak and the public dialogue will be diminished. His argument is weakened, however, by dependence on property law analogies (e.g., speech = fraud), a total neglect of audience studies where they seem to be needed (do distinguished people lose their reputations automatically when attacked in public debate?), and an inner contradiction in his thesis: *Time* magazine may have paid the highest price of all in having its reputation for accuracy forever sullied within its peer group, Epstein suggests. As a result of criticism by journalist Seymour Hersh and others—criticism much more informed and telling than that delivered by the jury in the libel trial—the level of public discourse was raised. If indeed it was, what additional public purpose can be served by libel laws in public-plaintiff cases except that of a public whipping?[227]

Others argued, as some Jeffersonians had in agreement with Federalists two centuries earlier, that vigorous enforcement of libel law was necessary to good government. Irresponsible attacks on public officials would keep the best people from running for office, they claimed. But what was an irresponsible attack? Was it irresponsible to include relevant elements of a public person's private life in criticism of his or her public performance?

5

Public and Private Reputation

The law has never successfully explained how the character of a candidate for public office or an official holding that office can be evaluated without entering the *private* realm of reputation and personality. The perplexing distinction between public and private life, however, has a long lineage in Anglo-American law, and very likely derives from the earliest canons of Western jurisprudence.

The distinction was made in a Star Chamber decision, *De Libellis Famosis,*[228] in 1605. In justifying the crime of criminal libel, the court wrote that an offense against a private person should be punished because it could lead to a breach of the peace. An offense against a public official was far more serious because it was a scandal on the government. The court was unprepared to make any distinction between officeholder and office.

In 1768, Governor Francis Bernard brought suit against publishers of the *Boston Gazette* for a letter signed "A True Patriot" written by Dr. Joseph Warren. A grand jury voted against indictment, noting the distinction that ought to be made between defaming public and private people.[229]

Even the most radical of early libertarians, George Hay, in a revision of an earlier essay, came around to the view that a line must be drawn at what he called private reputations, even to the extent of recommending criminal proceedings against those he called the notorious libelers of private character.[230]

Although he preferred civil actions, the seemingly incorrigible Eleazer Oswald would also have condoned criminal punishments for those who defamed private lives, even those of public officials.[231] In proposing to his readers what his principles of journalism would be for the *Independent Gazetteer* (or the *Chronicle of Free-dom*) of Philadelphia, he wrote with masterful equivocation:

> A considerable latitude must be allowed in the Discussion of Public Affairs, or the Liberty of the Press will be of no Benefit to Society. As the indulgence of private Malice and personal Slander should be checked and resisted by every legal Means, so a constant Examination into the Characters and Conduct of Ministers and Magistrates should be equally promoted and encouraged.[232]

Adding to the confusion, a Virginia court, in 1811, recognized truth alone as a defense if the libel dealt with the public as opposed to the private life of an official.[233]

One of the major themes in Jeffery Smith's *Printers and Press Freedom: The Ideology of Early American Journalism* is the historical distinction generally assumed between public and personal reputation from pre-Revolutionary times.[234] He concludes that the result was endless confusion in defamation law. "How could comments on conduct in public life be separated from comments on personal character?"[235]

Capable though he was of "searing personal attacks," Benjamin Franklin would have approved of legislation protecting personal reputation.[236] Thomas Jefferson may never have given up the idea that the press ought to pay for inflicting personal injuries.[237] "Printing presses shall be free," he wrote, "except so far as by commission of private injury, cause shall be given for private action."[238] Justice Holmes, in a famous dissent, would imply the same qualification nearly 150 years later in *Abrams* v. *United States*: "It is only the present danger of immediate evil or an intent to bring it about that warrants Congress in setting a limit to the expression of opinion *where private rights are not concerned* [emphasis added]."[239]

Levy writes that "No printer, writer or theorist had ever contended that the right to bring a private suit for defamation of character abridged the freedom of the press or that its freedom required junking of damages awards in civil cases."[240]

And yet earlier statements out of our long libertarian chronicle cast doubt on the generalization, although these statements themselves were sometimes contradictory. Cato (Trenchard and Gordon) had written that it was "certainly of much less Consequence

to Mankind, that an Innocent Man should be now and then as-
persed than that all Men should be enslaved."[241] The original and
influential Junius (John Wilkes) had observed that "the public evils
he and others complained of lay not in the description of government officials, but in their character and conduct."[242]

"Perhaps the enormities of private slander should be checked,"
wrote "Brutus," speaking to more conservative fellow patriots in
an 1783 issue of the *Gazette of South Carolina*, "but at the same
time, I think it would be dangerous to suffer even an excrescence
of this PALLADIUM of public liberty to be lopped off, as the
breach of innovation once made, widens every moment, and . . .
if it was once opened, there is no saying where it might end."[243]

Professor Gerald Baldasty noted similar uncertainty in a study
of five late eighteenth century Boston newspapers. While their
editors claimed to be sensitive to the right to one's personal character, they seemed not the least hesitant to enquire into that character. It was as if editors of the day were sincerely trying to separate
public from private lives but were finding it no less difficult than
we find it today.

William Parks, the first Virginia printer, was able to defeat a
charge of libel by proving from court records no longer thought
to be available that a member of the house of burgesses in Wil-
liamsburg, unfriendly to the printer and to press freedom, had
earlier been convicted of sheep stealing. So, wrote Isaiah Thomas
in his history of printing in America, the burgess "withdrew, over-
whelmed with disgrace from publick life, and never more ventured
to obtrude himself into a conspicuous situation, or to trouble printers with prosecution for libels. Thus, it is obvious that a free press
is, of all things, the best check and restraint on wicked men
and arbitrary magistrates."[244] A character evaluation? It would
seem so.

If we admit that we can differentiate public and private plaintiffs,
then logic compels us to make a microcosmic distinction between
the public and private dimensions of the lives of public people.
The common law of privacy recognizes that the disclosure of some
kinds of embarrassing private facts can outrage a community's
sense of decency or shock its conscience, although the courts have
not said how degrees of unconscionability are to be measured. In
suits of this kind, it must also be assumed that there is no genuine

public interest in the publication since the privacy claim can be defeated by the seemingly limitless defense of newsworthiness.[245]

Still, no measure beyond that of deferring to an editor's judgment has been developed by courts of last resort to assess newsworthiness, and it is doubtful that such courts would be constitutionally comfortable in doing it any differently.

Again, to indulge oneself in the public–private dichotomy in defining plaintiffs requires one to recognize a public interest in some kinds of information and not in others. In the absence of any mechanism to measure public interest, one can only ask if the private and assumedly embarrassing fact has any bearing on policymaking or social agenda-setting. Since politicians deal in power, a closer association ought to be assumed between their public and private lives than between the public and private lives of celebrities, but, there also, the private realm often impinges on the public. Where the connection between public and private can reasonably be made, no libel remedy should be available.

"Given the realities of our political life," the Supreme Court noted in *Monitor Patriot* v. *Roy*, in 1971, "it is by no means easy to see what statements about a candidate might be altogether without relevance to his fitness for the office he seeks. The clash of reputations is the staple of election campaigns, and damage to reputation is, of course, the essence of libel."[246]

Grievous ethical lapses will occur. Media too often hide behind unidentified sources. They break promises to those sources. Those sources are too frequently unchallenged "official" sources, or sources representing only a mainstream view. Reporters sometimes misrepresent themselves to get a story. Media misquote or quote people out of context. They invade personal privacy in gathering information. They ignore other constitutional rights, for example, fair trial, as the price of a good story. Reporters and editors sometimes serve private interests clandestinely. But better the news media face public and professional censure for unnecessary invasions of privacy and unjustifiable libels than win doubtful libel victories against plaintiffs who are destined to fail under the legal rules that have evolved.

Without filing suit, however, a person wronged by the media may have no other way of bringing the matter to the attention of press and public, except in Minnesota, the one state with a news council, a voluntary citizen group prepared to hear legitimate complaints against the media. One study shows an appreciable drop in media libel cases after establishment of the council,[247] although many states without councils have proportionately fewer libel cases than Minnesota.

6

Legal Band-Aids

Libel law, as has been noted, is awash in dichotomies. One of the most prevalent is the truth–falsehood dichotomy. No less ephemeral than the psychological search for editorial intentions in attempting to prove fault on the part of the communicator is the idea establishing truth as the compelling purpose of a libel suit. Pursuit of truth means litigation equally expensive and protracted as that needed for investigating motivation. It simply substitutes the search for one phantom for another.

Why in a post-scientific age the law continues to rely on the belief that truth in some pristine form will emerge from political debate can only be explained by its continuing reliance on a classic libertarian theory: the notion that a truly competitive marketplace of ideas exists and that in that marketplace truth, because of its empyreal merit, ultimately prevails.

Truth in most civil and criminal suits depends on probabilities, reflected in standards ranging from a "preponderance of evidence" to "beyond a reasonable doubt." While libel law settles for a middle level of evidence in determining actual malice—"clear and convincing"—were truth to replace fault as the ultimate goal of the libel suit, a plaintiff, would not only be required to prove a negative in demonstrating falsehood, but also would be faced with a task that has long defied philosophy. What is truth? Is it simply the correspondence of our beliefs or statements to known facts? Or, in reality, are there no facts, so that our judgments or statements can never be more than partially true? Or, pragmatically, is a belief true if we find it expedient to act upon it? Or does truth have everything to do with the structure of the particular language we are using? Or is truth no more than internal consistency within a system of related propositions?

While I am not prepared to answer these questions, their introduction suggests that the concept is anything but simple. Truth is a more baffling concept than fault. Political or social truth, as divined by a jury torn between the rhetoric of partisan lawyers, can only be a crude approximation of truth, or worse, a momentary reflection of the feelings of a jury, that sliver of the public; it may have little to do with truth, however one decides to deal with the concept. Only tyrants would pose more danger to free speech than total reliance on juror estimates of truth.

It is argued that equity demands that every wrong have a remedy. In libel law, a tangible remedy for most public plaintiffs is now so remote and unlikely that a denial of a remedy altogether for certain classes of plaintiff will change the law very little. It will, however, do away with thousands of hours of futile litigation and lost time and energy, and perhaps add more speech to public channels. The threat of libel has undoubtedly silenced some speakers, both the weak and the strong. Many more are likely inhibited unjustifiably.

A denial of remedies also raises due process objections, although the U. S. Supreme Court has held, over the strenuous objections of Justice Brennan, that reputation is not a "liberty interest" protected by the due process clauses of the Fifth and Fourteenth Amendments.[248] This raises an important and difficult question. If the notion of individual-centered rights is to be the fulcrum of an individual right to speak, then must there not also be an individual right to defend one's reputation—related to what Justice Stewart called our "basic concept of the essential dignity and worth of every human being?"[249] It seems reasonable to expect so, except that a second question must be considered: Does not a defense of reputation depend on reputation having been unreservedly harmed? No such condition attaches to the defense of a right to speak, given the constitutional status of speech. Speech is free whether or not it serves to rectify a wrong.

And, in light of *New York Times* v. *Sullivan*, the "notion of encouraging 'uninhibited, robust and wide-open' expression, and 'vehement, caustic and sometimes unpleasantly sharp attacks' . . . is scarcely in harmony with efforts to foster (individual interests in economic ventures, standing in the community, or general good feelings)."[250]

Deliberate, calculated falsehood is rare in American journalism;

ignorance, inaccuracy, simplification, and omission are not.
Courts, so it would seem, have a fixation with "true facts," cer-
tainties that simply do not emerge from social debate or its reporting in the major media. What facts there are too often combine
with values, opinions, and emotions in making reality a blur of
conflicting variables. Justice Louis Brandeis declared long ago that
the remedy to be applied to uncertainty, confusion, and error is
more speech, not enforced silence.[251] The bruising libel suit is
hardly conducive to more speech.

It is with that principle in mind that I now examine and take
issue with most of the recommendations that have been made for
libel reform. Some of these proposals do indeed tamper with the
process of libel litigation; but few of them recommend any major
structural changes in the system itself, rule changes that might
bring some degree of certainty and consistency to the law.

Much attention is given to declaratory judgment, a judge's declaration as to the rights of the parties to a suit or his or her answers
to legal questions, before any damages or other forms of relief are
awarded. It is assumed that declaratory judgment would fore-
shorten the litigation process. This and other proposals would
make truth rather than fault the central issue of the libel case.
Jurors would decide what historians can't agree upon. Editors
could be condemned for broad misinterpretation of conflicting social facts in the *Westmoreland* and *Sharon* cases of the future. Fault
would now be a matter of content rather than motivation: forget
an editor's intentions, were his reports accurate, did he tell the
truth? The judicial system would soon find itself on quaking constitutional ground.

Proposals for Reform

Charles Schumer, a New York congressman, was among the first
to recommend that libel litigation end with a declaratory judgment.
He did this in a study bill (H.R. 2846, 99th Cong. 1st Sess. 1985).
A prevailing plaintiff under his proposal would be entitled to attorney's fees unless the defendant published a retraction within
ten days of judgment or demonstrated that every effort had been

made to determine the truth of his or her report. Under no circumstances would punitive damages be awarded.

Marc Franklin, a Stanford law professor, while recognizing that some rich and powerful plaintiffs will never be deterred from suing, would provide plaintiffs on a state-by-state basis with the alternative of declaratory judgment.[252] His colleague, David Barrett, would give both plaintiff and defendant the option of declaratory judgment, but Franklin and Barrett agree on a prohibition of punitive damages, a one-year statute of limitations, and fee-shifting to the losing party.[253] Caps of any kind on damages, however, have had little appreciable effect on overall jury awards, and would not decrease the frequency of suits if damages are not to be the primary goal anyway.

Franklin believes that the media should be willing to trade the burden of damage awards for more frequent confessions of liability, even though a loss in a reputation for journalistic accuracy might follow. Why an insured defendant with any pride of profession would make that choice is difficult to discern. Franklin's proposal might increase the social interest in robust debate, but there are better ways than punishment to achieve that purpose.

Rodney Smolla, a William & Mary law professor, would approve some form of declaratory judgment in the interest of restoring a plaintiff's human dignity. While he characterizes libel law as a quagmire of archaic, arbitrary, and internally inconsistent rules, he would retain a good part of the snarl, including fault requirements (public officials would still have to prove actual malice), proof of actual injury, and the common law privileges. The jury would be left to untangle the strings. Space for reply or equal time would be acceptable, if voluntary. Losers would pay all legal fees. Caps would be placed on all nonpecuniary losses, and punitive damages eliminated. Most germane to my own proposal, Smolla would eliminate suits brought by high-ranking political policymakers.[254]

The Annenberg Proposal

The Annenberg Washington Program Proposal for the Reform of Libel Law has been the leading voice for a declaratory judgment approach. In 1988, a panel of nine lawyers, one journalist, and a public relations practitioner, directed by Professor Smolla, reached consensus after long deliberation on a three-stage model statute: (1) a complainant would seek specifically either a retraction or an opportunity to reply; failure to do so within thirty days of publication of the libel would bar future action; (2) either party having elected to try the suit as an action for declaratory judgment, a suit would conclude with a declaratory judgment as to truth or falsity; and (3) having chosen this process, the losing party would pay the winner's attorneys' fees in what is known as fee-shifting.

If the declaratory judgment option were rejected, under the Annenberg proposal, actual damages only would be considered in an ensuing libel suit. There would be no presumed or punitive damages. Panel members disagreed on whether special damages incurred before trial ought to be considered separately in a mini-trial, and, as criticism and defense of the proposal on that and other grounds continues, libel issues move right back into their definitional and procedural quagmire, the vexing truth–falsehood dichotomy being one of them. *New York Times*, of course, requires plaintiff to show some level of fault on the part of the defendant for damages. No-fault suits are the only option the proposal contemplates. Choosing the declaratory judgment option, therefore, could be tantamount to a defendant waiving a constitutional right. Private-person plaintiffs under the Annenberg proposal would have little to gain by not bringing suit and much to lose.

It must have been distressing to the Annenberg panel that on the very day that its proposal was issued Judge Pierre Leval in a luncheon address to the panel condemned the idea.

Judge Leval, who presided over the General Westmoreland trial, believes that the *New York Times* rule need not apply to a plaintiff who desires only to clear his or her name. But neither, in his opinion, should a plaintiff be forced to follow the declaratory judgment route by a defendant's decision to do so. He is also worried that inattentive plaintiffs might miss the thirty-day deadline for reply or retraction, and he is concerned about length and form limitations imposed on those who do choose to reply, especially those who have been libeled on television. I would suggest a more serious problem: private-person plaintiffs may not know how to reply effectively.

Judge Leval calls his solution a no-money, no-fault suit. All suits would qualify as such except those where the plaintiff suffered actual money loss.[255] Judge Leval, it would appear, has not decided what to do about lawyer's fees and court costs.

In a vigorous defense of the proposal Professors Smolla and Michael Gaertner pointed out that, presumably, plaintiffs have only to demonstrate "substantial truth." In the next sentence the same plaintiff is said to bear the burden of proving "falsity." Are these two burdens or one? And, if two, can they be separated? "Designing *any* libel system that does not include truth or falsity as an issue for litigation," they add, "is impossible. . . . Courts must determine who is a liar and who is not."[256] It is precisely this obligation that my proposal asks the courts to forego in the interests of the First Amendment where policymaking and agenda-setting public plaintiffs are concerned.

While the Annenberg proposal is clearly an improvement over current law, it could conflict with both *Miami Herald* v. *Tornillo* and *New York Times* v. *Sullivan*. In *Tornillo*, Professor Jerome Barron, George Washington University law professor, tried and failed before the Supreme Court to establish the constitutionality of a statutory right to reply.[257] To what extent does the Annenberg proposal mandate a right of reply? Clearly, if you don't comply with a request for reply space or a retraction, you go to court.

Zechariah Chafee, an eminent First Amendment scholar, was one of the first to propose a right of reply statute.[258]

Anthony Lewis, *New York Times* columnist, favors mandatory retraction, believing it would serve both the demands of reputation and the public interest in information.[259]

Martin Mayer imagines a custom of public apology by the author of a libel.[260] But he provides no blueprint.

Richard Winfield, a leading New York libel lawyer, believes that attorneys' fees might exceed damage awards if declaratory judgments were the only option for unwilling defendants. He would insist that defendants retain the right to choose between declaratory judgment and the constitutional or *New York Times* defense, doubting that many defendants' attorneys would opt for the former since it seems nearly impossible for plaintiffs to prove actual malice and thereby win their cases. Likewise, how many plaintiffs would settle for an admission of error while there remained any chance of winning money damages?[261] There is an air of resistance to change in Winfield's analysis, however valid his arguments, and a seeming unawareness that attorneys' fees already exceed damage awards in many cases.

"[A]llowing declaratory judgment actions for judicial findings of falsity," says Harvard law professor Laurence Tribe, "protects against large damage awards, but also stretches the competence of courts and offers scant relief to plaintiffs who suffer actual harm."[262]

A National Conference of Commissioners on Uniform State Laws committee was asked to take the Annenberg proposal under consideration in drafting a model libel law for states to consider. Their draft uniform act would also be a two-stage procedure: stage one would deal with publication, defamation, reputational harm and falsity, stage two with privilege, fault, and damages. Defendant could terminate the process at the end of stage one by paying costs, attorney's fees, and publishing a retraction. Both defendant and plaintiff would take risks in moving on to stage two, but risks to defendant would be greater because there would be no equivalent fee shifting when a plaintiff files a frivolous suit to harass, punish, or gain publicity. Immediate opposition to the proposal came from the Libel Defense Resource Center (LDRC), which felt that it was based on a desire to protect reputation or plaintiff's rights at the expense of defendant's right of free speech. Major segments of the press agreed.

In a surprising statement, given the messy condition of libel law, LDRC opted for continuation of "the salutary process of common law and constitutional evolution." But the Center was correct in noting that the National Conference proposal asked legislators to do what only the experience of judges could comprehend.

Additional Proposals

A flurry of additional recommendations for libel reform occurred in the 1980s. Well reasoned, though lacking in consensus, the proposals received little if any attention from the courts. Perhaps there is a "Rumpole" factor working here. More likely, courts are simply reluctant to engage in sudden or dramatic change. And these are perilous times in which to promote the cause of freedom of expression. The enemies of free speech exercise political power. The public is cynical about the press. The Supreme Court is dominated by conservatives whose full range of views on speech and press questions are so far only partially revealed.

Some of the proposals include mandatory retractions or rights of reply. These appear incompatible with constitutional precedent.[263] All statutory recommendations, of course, would have to comport with constitutional requirements.

There has been some agreement on the need to do away with punitive damages. The Schumer bill would have abolished them.

The American Tort Reform Association recommends that punitive damages be awarded only after a finding of liability at trial; juries would decide whether punitive damages are justified, judges would decide the amount. At least four states—Virginia, Georgia, Montana, and Kansas—have imposed limits on punitive damages. Three others—Oklahoma, Colorado, and Florida—limit punitive damages to specific multiples of compensatory or actual damages.

The American Legal Exchange Council (a group of 200 state legislators) model statute would limit punitive damages to twice the award of actual damages and put a cap of $250,000 on non-economic damages including injury to reputation, humiliation, mental anguish, and emotional distress.[264] Other suggested manipulations would lessen the blow of punitive damages, but, in a patchwork way, have opened up new vistas of legal argumentation.

Alternative Dispute Resolution or a Federal Libel Law

The Iowa Libel Project, introduced earlier, would, in cooperation with the American Arbitration Association, circumvent the judicial process altogether. As of this writing the joint project, a form of alternative dispute resolution (ADR), has only one case that it believes will follow the process to its conclusion. But the project's coordinators cannot be certain because the very availability of arbitration seems to have a "settling" effect on litigators who otherwise mark time by letting filed libel cases lie dormant. The Iowa arbitration option seems to have led to the settlement of a number of cases.

Some states have found arbitration in other areas of tort law a way for people who can afford it to short-circuit lengthy trials to get quickly to appeal levels in regular civil courts. As healing as this arbitration proposal could be, plaintiff's lawyers will still advise clients that the system offers little compensation for a damaged reputation. Defendant's attorneys, on the other hand, will advise against giving up constitutional press rights embodied in the *New York Times* doctrine.

A comprehensive statutory solution was advanced by Judge Lois Forer of Philadelphia in a 1987 book proposing a uniform federal libel statute.[265] Her proposal is not new. As far back as 1890 newspapers were trying to make sense out of libel laws by proposing legislation that would create a uniform statute across states.[266] There is no federal libel law. Since we have a national interstate communication system, Forer believes that we should have a national libel law. Such a law would deter fruitless suits and help judges who now have a welter of cases and state laws out of which to make sense. State courts now have exclusive jurisdiction over all criminal and civil cases governed by state law. Where plaintiff and defendant reside in different states—what is called a diversity suit in civil law—a case will go to federal court but the law of the state where the case is heard will be deferred to by that court.

All recommendations for increasing federal judicial power, including the central proposal of this essay, today must swim against the Supreme Court's currents of Jeffersonian federalism that seek to decentralize judicial power to the benefit of the states. Despite that hurdle and the damage Forer believes libel litigation does to the public dialogue, she would leave "public policy" suits squarely in the hands of the courts. Assuming her statute could pass constitutional muster, it would have to accommodate myriad fact situations, rules of procedure, standards of liability, and a plethora of inadequately defined concepts. Court interpretations might soon mystify her statute and return libel to its present state of confusion. Nevertheless, the idea of a single libel statute in place of fifty is appealing.

Judge Forer would extend an absolute privilege to those who criticize "the actions of government officials, employees of government (she goes too far down the ladder of authority), aspirants to public office, and recipients of public funds."[267] Her categories are crudely delineated, but no more so than my own, and she believes that public officials and public employees generally give up many rights when they win or accept public office. She nevertheless makes a powerful argument for predefined plaintiff categories since those who now sue for libel have no prior knowledge as to what category of plaintiff courts will put them in.

But Forer's standards of fault are as complex as anything now in place for those libel plaintiffs who would retain some chance of victory; and she would further complicate her statute by engrafting upon it rights of privacy and publicity (the right to benefit commercially from one's own public name and image), and the right to know, that is, the right of citizen access to political information. Negligence, her standard of fault for all plaintiffs, while less intrusive than the actual malice test, would be a major setback for the press if public officials and pervasive public figures somehow brought suit. Punitive damages would be reserved for those defendants guilty of actual malice.

And "truth" in her proposal is again assumed to be readily ascertainable. Because, in Forer's view, "facts" are easily "proved" in policy debates, there would be punishment for falsehood, where negligence is shown. How does truth apply to editorials, cartoonists, humorists, letters to the editor, fiction, satire, parody, culinary reviews, advertisements, and other categories of opinion that the Annenberg proposal would exempt from libel laws?

Judge Forer prefers retraction to declaratory judgment, but doesn't appreciate the problems created by coerced retractions. Newspapers resist having to proclaim doubts about their own veracity. The *New York Times* for this reason never settles out of court in the name of the newspaper, although the New York Times Company may do so in behalf of the newspaper, nor does the *Times* carry libel insurance, even though it appreciates the extravagant costs of libel litigation. How then would the *Times* react to an ill-founded demand for retraction?

Even less acceptable to the press would be Judge Forer's statutes preventing publication under all circumstances of the names of rape victims and juvenile offenders.

Martin Shapiro, a Berkeley political scientist, would also subscribe to a truth standard, not recognizing that this is as severe a
form of governmental intervention as any fault standard can be.
While truth may be a performance evaluation rather than a process
intervention, it requires governmental scrutiny of content. But
Shapiro approves of a declaratory judgment solution because, he
says, it permits the media industry to correct errors at relatively
low cost.[268] The cost is higher than he imagines.

Donald Meiklejohn, emeritus professor of philosophy and social
science at Syracuse University, would adopt something like the
Rosenbloom or "public interest" test giving an absolute privilege
to all comment on public affairs. What would qualify? That question is still unanswered. Is "public interest" defined by editors or
by judges? This problem has been exacerbated by recent Supreme
Court libel cases, notably *Dun & Bradstreet* and *Hepps*.[269] In *Dun
& Bradstreet*, the Court tied damages to whether or not a public
issue was involved; in *Hepps*, the Court said that speech of public
concern had to be proven false by a plaintiff before any damages
could be collected.

Judges apparently will make *ad hoc* decisions on what qualifies
as public speech, and the rest of society will have no idea as to
what principle informs their decisions. Meiklejohn, sensitive to
historical tradition, believes that "attempts to exclude the deliberately false or reckless statement from first amendment protection
harks back to the concept of seditious libel which *Times* v. *Sullivan*
has generally been understood to have rejected. . . . " He is correct.
Clearly he is in favor of more speech, but only if a mandatory right
of reply accompanies it, and a mandatory right of reply has already
been rejected by the Supreme Court.[270]

Other Remedies

The American Civil Liberties Union (ACLU), after extensive debate in 1983, promulgated a new position on libel. Defamation
suits, it said, violated the First Amendment when brought by public
officials on matters relating to their public position, by public figures on matters relating to their public status, and by private or
public figures on matters of public concern. All the foregoing plain-

tiffs would have to prove actual malice to win a verdict and there would be no payment of punitive damages under any circumstances. In many respects this is also a revival of the *Rosenbloom* or "public issue" test. That test severely fragmented the Court in 1971 and led to the *Gertz* ruling three years later, which, in effect, brought private plaintiffs back under the protection of libel law.

The ACLU in its 1983 report reiterated its opposition to criminal and group libel laws, opting instead for reply, rebuttal, and debate.

"Libel actions," said Ira Glasser, executive director of the Union at the time, "places a price on free speech, a price that the speaker or writer frequently cannot pay." Few, since William O. Douglas left the Court, had articulated a clearer preference for the First Amendment than the ACLU in its libel law report.[271]

Arlen Langvardt, Indiana University business law professor, recognizing what he calls the "the unconquerable maze of public controversies, public concerns, and public interests," prefers that fault requirements hinge on the status of the plaintiff.[272] He finds support for his position in what might have been the last fully aired sedition case in the federal courts, *Garrison* v. *Louisiana*, in which the Supreme Court said:

> [A]nything which might touch on an official's fitness for office is relevant. Few personal attributes are more germane to fitness for office than dishonesty, malfeasance, or improper motivation, even though these characteristics may also affect the official's private character.[273]

While my proposal echoes Langvardt's, his elaboration of a solution leaves the law largely where it is now.

In an approach that combines aspects of law and ethics, Michigan State media law professor Todd Simon would use professional codes of ethics to set broad standards against which journalistic malpractice could be measured. While a creative approach, it assumes uniformity in press ethics and practice where none exists and a specificity of ethical rules not to be found in general statements of moral behavior. It also raises the question of whether there ought to be or can be "expert" witnesses in a field as perverse and as diverse as American journalism. Where courts have assumed responsibility for deciding what journalistic ethics ought to be, we experience a judicial role not contemplated by the First Amendment.[274]

Paul LeBel, William & Mary law professor, proposes a "right of repair" as a voluntary alternative to payment of damages. A defendant under his plan could devote resources equivalent to those expended in defaming a plaintiff to correct errors and by doing so restore a reputation. Plaintiff could still collect damages for actual injury. This restorative procedure would compensate only for damage to reputation. Courts have not, however, developed a clear rule for distinguishing actual injury and reputational injury, nor has LeBel.[275]

Attorney Seth Goodchild speaks for those who believe the best defense is a good offense, even though the media shouldn't be perceived as promoting libel suits by filing countersuits. Where it appears that a suit has been brought either to intimidate or to garner publicity, he contends, countersuits might be justified. Such actions might argue (1) abuse of process (an ulterior purpose in bringing a suit), (2) malicious prosecution (a wrongful civil proceeding in which there is no probable cause to believe that a defendant acted maliciously), (3) a complaint alleging an intentional interference with constitutional rights, and (4) a claim of violation of Rule 11 of the Federal Rules of Civil Procedure, which imposes sanctions and attorney's fees on those who initiate frivolous suits.[276]

In 1988, thirty-three states had laws imposing penalties for frivolous suits, some of which applied to libel. An example of a frivolous suit law that includes libel is the one from New York (N.Y. Civ. Prac. Law Rules, sec. 8303(a), June 12, 1986).[277]

Los Angeles attorney David Hollander believes, upon analysis of the economics of libel litigation, that fee-shifting, the loser-pays rule, would eliminate the incentive to bring harassment suits. But Hollander concludes that any absolute protections would lead to greater media carelessness and inaccuracy.[278]

Franklyn Haiman, Northwestern University First Amendment theorist, would punish the most outrageous cases of "deliberate, knowing, calculated falsehood(s)," but only where there were no means of response. He would continue searching for a reply mechanism. And he would make no distinction between public and private plaintiffs.[279]

It is with these recommendations for reform in mind that I now proceed to rationalize the proposal that is central to this work:

Public officials at policymaking level and celebrities, those persons the courts designate as pervasive public personalities, shall have no remedy in libel law. For such persons to claim this kind of legal remedy subverts the underlying purposes of the *New York Times* doctrine by reviving sedition in the guise of a civil suit and subjecting the press, large and small, weak and strong, responsible and irresponsible, to a danger not anticipated by Justice Brennan's 1964 opinion for the Court in *New York Times* v. *Sullivan*. Only a structural change of the magnitude suggested by this proposal will serve the historical purposes of the First Amendment.

7

The Limits of Tolerance

Theories of freedom of speech and press are notable for their complexity, their currency, and their controversiality. And, of course, they are not theories in the true sense of that term; rather they are fragments of theories that don't yet exist. Speech theories don't explain much and they certainly have little predictive power. Sometimes they seem to be nothing more than biases about freedom of expression. They emerge from expansive philosophical frameworks, however, and are often the products of clashing views about very real problems.

In today's intellectual arena, traditional liberal, neo-liberal, and post-Marxist critical theorist confront one another in the philosophical ring while neo-conservatives quietly take over the levers of judicial power. The central belief, on or off the Court, of neo-conservatism—majoritarianism in constitutional terms—is that the elected representatives of the people, not judges, are best equipped, and indeed are delegated by the Constitution, to determine public policy. This view permits judges to protect against manifestly unconstitutional legislative assault only those rights that are clearly delineated in the actual text of the Constitution. An extremist wing of neo-conservatism is prepared to sacrifice even basic Constitutional rights when they are at odds with higher values such as God, family and country, values that are often impervious to debate. Free speech, though set out unmistakably in the First Amendment, does not generally survive this approach to the weighing of values. And when it does, many reject the results and clamor for amendments to the Constitution.

Meanwhile liberalism has never quite recovered from the tragedy of Vietnam. Liberal elites, it seemed, handled power badly and pursued unworthy imperialistic goals during that regrettable period. What had been an optimistic and pragmatic liberal mainstream was giving way to various radical alternatives. Liberty, a core concept of classical liberalism, was challenged by the idea of equality, an idea that never quite found a satisfactory definition, but a powerful idea in the Western tradition. Liberty, as part of a contemporary dialogue, may have been put back into play by the liberal intellectual John Rawls in his *A Theory of Justice*, a theory that nevertheless makes equality its central thesis.[280] Rawls proposed that all social primary goods—liberty and opportunity, income and wealth, and all the bases of self-respect—be distributed equally unless an unequal distribution of any or all of these would be to the advantage of the least favored. Speech in Rawls' paradigm would belong primarily to the powerless.

Various forms of collectivist thought, never completely alien to liberalism but less comfortable with it since the end of the New Deal and the rise of authoritarian regimes of Right and Left, also began to press against liberalism's academic citadels. Civic obligation and community spirit were said to be more crucial to the body politic than individual liberty. Alasdair MacIntyre's Left Communitarianism, for example, stressed duties as well as rights, as had the 1947 Hutchins Report in its delineation of a social responsibility theory for the media. Right communitarians preached tradition, authority, hierarchy as a substitute for individual freedoms. Younger liberals began to defect, disdaining identification with a traditional, old guard orthodoxy, that had been insensitive to the stakes of the Vietnam Conflict and seemed to have few solutions for the injustices and inequities of contemporary society. They also feared exclusion, perhaps, from a younger, if directionless, political avant-garde. Calls would be heard for a more cooperative, participatory society, whatever it might eventually be called. The difference for speech? One example: Liberals, while they might not like it, would defend obscenity whether in the form of eroticism or marching Nazis; communitarians would ban it.

While individual rights remain central to liberalism, there has grown within that tradition a greater willingness to doubt the moral certainty of one's position, to be reflective about the views of others, while maintaining respect for rational process and the experience of the empirical world. Liberalism still looks good when

its alternatives are closely considered. Ronald Dworkin of Oxford
and New York universities appears to be one of its current champions.[281]

Today, free speech as a core concept of liberalism is in dire need
of a champion. It is under the same kind of political, social, and
ideological pressure now that it faced in the 1920s. The government
feasts on secrecy and keeps speakers it doesn't like out of the
country. Segments of the professoriate and the American Library
Association, for example, are defining new standards of acceptable, approved, or politically correct speech, cleansed of its racist,
sexist, or homophobic elements. Interest groups of all kinds attempt to enlist government in banning whatever speech is contrary
to their views. This is how books, many of them classics of their
genres, disappear from school libraries. Our literary history would
be rewritten under such regimes. To some extent zealots cancel
one another out, but they still cast a shadow over free expression.
Even more damaging in the long run may be the ridicule and
cynicism liberalism faces from the radical left's charge that free
speech is the voice of power alone and that liberals are in fact
defending nothing more than hypocrisy when they defend free
speech.

Some critical theorists have resurrected an extreme form of legal
realism that places political power at the core of all social processes.
Little else determines human action. Power not principle, in this
view, is the fulcrum of all social relations and the law is its hand-
maiden. There is, of course, nothing "neutral" about the law.
Other critical theorists call for a nonrevolutionary but confronta-
tional restructuring of society to do away with the evil concentrations of private power that traditional and partisan law has
permitted to form, among these concentrations of the mass media.

But would they not simply exchange older forms of power for
new forms, and institutions that have evolved logically over long
periods for ill-defined and potentially dangerous ideal systems?
The goal of such proposals, at least vaguely, is an egalitarian,
interactive, and noncoercive society, a humane society of participatory rational discourse in which communicative activities would
lead to consensus about universal principles. Positive though this
goal may be, there remains a suspicion that it depends on the
Hegelian assumption that, because society creates the individual,

individual rights are secondary to the needs of the organic whole.[282] Unfortunately for the critical agenda, the contours of its utopian future never quite come into focus. To be sure, a better society must be striven for, but how much do we dare mortgage to achieve it? Theories of freedom of speech and press seem puny and irrelevant in a larger critical conceptual framework. But it may not matter since most "theories" or fragments of theories of freedom of expression in the twentieth century have come out of a diverse postliberal tradition of which critical theory may or may not be a part.

The Liberal Tradition

Early fragments of conventional liberal theory would be Holmes' and Brandeis' clear and present danger test, which brooks no interference with speech until a substantial governmental interest is imminently and irreparably about to be endangered by that speech or press. As an early proponent of the "balance-of-interests" doctrine, another approach to constitutional decision-making, Roscoe Pound distinguished between Kantian private or natural rights and the public or policy rights of the community. Often these must be balanced against one another, but private rights, he argued, ought to be balanced against private rights and public rights against public rights lest the public always win over the individual in the balancing.

Alexander Meiklejohn's more fully fashioned concept of near absolute First Amendment protection for public speech, at least that which contributes to the process of self-government, has influenced both liberal and conservative positions. While Meiklejohn, the strict utilitarian, was much more concerned with the general welfare than with the value of personal expression, Justice Brennan credited Meiklejohn with being his philosophical mentor.

Whether influenced by Meiklejohn or not, Robert Bork, George Will, and other conservative thinkers also argue that only political speech is protected by the First Amendment; other forms of speech may be protected to the degree that the majority decides they are needed for the welfare of the community; the public speaker who advances ideas designed to destroy the republic need not be protected because what he or she espouses is not rational political speech. While conservatives are more likely to cite the work of Walter Berns,[283] echoes of Meiklejohn are still to be heard in their presentations.

Counter to these is Justice Harlan Fiske Stone's broader and more encompassing suggestion of a doctrine of preferred freedoms, free speech being among them, a doctrine that has come to incorporate a clear and present danger test, to reject any kind of *ad hoc* balancing where speech is being weighed against other constitutional values, to reject prior restraints, and to place severe limitations on fiercely punitive subsequent punishment.[284]

Since a magazine article purporting to give instructions on the making of a nuclear bomb became the *Progressive* case, prior restraint may still be a constitutionally permissible government strategy where "immediate, direct, irreparable harm to the interests of the United States" can be demonstrated. This may be another version of the older clear and present danger standard. Weighing freedom of speech and press against the right to live, a federal district judge in the *Progressive* case chose the latter and accepted the government's argument that the Atomic Energy Act, prohibiting communication, transmission, and disclosure of certain categories of information, also restricted publication of information that was either "classified at birth" or of a "technical" nature not protected by the First Amendment.[285]

The Supreme Court's denial of certiorari in November 1990 to an appeal to consider the constitutionality of a temporary restraining order prohibiting CNN from broadcasting tapes containing recordings of allegedly privileged conversations between General Manuel Noriega and his attorneys may suggest that fair trial claims in the future will also support prior retraints on publication. The Court's decision, over the dissents of Justices Thurgood Marshall and Sandra Day O'Connor, had the effect of requiring the network to produce the tapes in its possession for *in camera* inspection.[286]

Thomas Emerson in a seminal work, *The System of Freedom of Expression*,[287] explored the possibility of developing a general theory of freedom of speech and press, what he called a "full protection" theory. His most original proposition, and one often applied to actual cases, is the speech/action model that gives constitutional protection to speech but not to conduct, when the two can be differentiated. Emerson has also put forth an "affirmative" theory of the First Amendment that he and others believe will promote the enhancement of speech through such legislative acts as postal subsidies, exemption from antitrust laws, public access to the media, and the privilege of journalists to keep the identity of sources confidential.

Here a paradox: freedom of expression implies an absence of government intervention; yet the conditions under which freedom of expression can successfully take place in modern society increasingly require governmental involvement.

Laurence Tribe, a critic of Emerson's model, prefers what he calls a "track one/track two" approach for protecting freedom of speech. Only in the most critical of circumstances would governmental interference with the content or communicative impact of speech be permitted (track one). But when the government does not aim at ideas or information directly but seeks to advance a significant public interest independent of communicative content or impact, such balancing may be condoned, as long as the effects on speech would be indirect and, supposedly, minimal (track two).[288] Justice Brennan, in an October 17, 1979, speech at Rutgers University used a similar construct, except that he labeled Tribe's track one, the speech model, and Tribe's track two, the structural model. Near absolute protection would be afforded publication itself, said Brennan, but access to information or the right of a journalist to protect the identity of a source, for example, could in some circumstances be restricted. There is little difference between Tribe's and Brennan's models.

In recent years, C. Edwin Baker's "liberty model" has been getting wide attention. Baker puts the individual back at the center of First Amendment theory and proposes broad protection for speech, or activities containing elements of speech, until they become violent or coercive. His theory will provide support for my proposal later in this work.

Of course, there are many more theories of freedom of expression. John Hart Ely has advanced what he calls a "specific threat" approach, not unlike Tribe's. Where harm to society is from something other than the message itself, such as, a sound truck in a residential neighborhood at bedtime, balancing would be permitted. Where the perceived harm comes from the message itself, that is, the content of the message, the Court should adopt an "unprotected messages" standard—his example, instructions on the building of nuclear weapons—the *Progressive* case. Ely's goal is a narrow, precise set of standards so that tests for protected speech don't revert to simple balancing or tests of reasonableness.[289] These few example are not meant to be exhaustive, nor do they fairly represent myriad views on the topic.

Generally speaking, justices make decisions and legal scholars, most of them writing in the influential law reviews and intricately analyzing the work of one another, make theories; scholars are pleased when it appears that their theories have influenced the courts, and often they do. Some First Amendment theories are exquisitely complicated, others simply impenetrable. And certainly no general theory of the First Amendment has emerged, nor should there be such a foreclosing theory in a free speech society. The best First Amendment theory may be that there is no First Amendment theory.

Louis Brandeis was certainly an exception to the generalization that judges are seldom theoreticians. His concurring opinion in *Whitney* v. *California,*[290] which has been referred to throughout this presentation, gave the ages a remarkable truism concerning the First Amendment that appeared to be part of a larger theory, a theory or a perspective that Professor Vincent Blasi of Columbia University law school refers to as "civic courage."[291] Hear Brandeis:

"Those who won our independence by revolution were not cowards," he wrote. "They did not fear political change. They did not exalt order at the cost of liberty. To courageous, self-reliant men, with confidence in the power of free and fearless reasoning applied through the processes of popular government, no danger flowing from speech can be deemed clear and present, unless the incidence of the evil apprehended is so imminent that it may befall before there is opportunity for full discussion."

"If there be time," Brandeis added, "to expose through discussion the falsehood and fallacies, to avert the evil by the processes of education, the remedy to be applied is *more speech, not enforced silence* [emphasis added]."[292]

That trenchant final sentence, it seems to me, in itself a theory of discourse well within our own historical experience, would support both a relevant observation concerning the First Amendment and an assumption about it that those who drafted and debated it and who experienced the revolutionary milieu out of which it came might have found valid.

1. The speech and press clause of the First Amendment is *an unqualified declaration*[293] with respect to Congress and has come, by means of a controversial twentieth-century interpretation of the due process clause of the Fourteenth Amendment, to have the same application to state and local governing bodies, and

2. Any speech theory purporting to interpret, explain, or apply the free speech and press clause to the empirical world ought to serve to *expand and enlarge* those freedoms rather than to constrict or diminish them.

If there is to be a theory of the First Amendment, it must be a priori "expansionist." An expansionist First Amendment theory for the twenty-first century will recognize and support the protection of speech in its many forms, some not yet fixed in the public consciousness. To regulate commercial speech or labor picketing—the latter an example of what theorists have come to call "speech plus"—is difficult enough. To leave them unprotected entirely so as not to dilute other kinds of speech thought to be closer to the "core" of essential communication, or to favor a competing social interest, is unthinkable.

Advertising in eighteenth- and nineteenth-century American newspapers, for example, tells us at least as much and maybe more about the Charleston, the Boston, or the Philadelphia of the period as do the mellifluous and 60-day-old news reports from London and Vienna. Today, Reuters and Dow Jones are the world's leading suppliers of computerized business information; they are also significant *news* agencies. If advertising and other forms of commercial speech do no more than advance one's economic well-being, they have done a great deal. As Eastern European politicians have learned, it is impossible to divorce economic well-being from politics; they are Siamese twins.

"Those with greater resources and power," Professor Martin Redish observes, "do not need to picket to express their view."[294] Some theorists would sacrifice or severely limit certain categories of speech such as advertising, as nothing more than the voice of the affluent. Others would limit "fighting words" and symbolic speech, often the only means available to the dispossessed and the disadvantaged, who are forced to use what have been called the media of desperation. In either case the goal of those who would limit speech is to avoid trivializing what they believe to be the heart of protected speech—calm and reasoned debate about the body politic.

Justice Hugo Black, erroneously labeled an absolutist as far as speech and press were concerned, was equally willing to sacrifice peripheral forms of speech by adopting a powerful commitment to what he defined as "pure" speech, or speech in its classic written or spoken forms; Alexander Meiklejohn, as has been noted, did the same by providing full protection only to speech that palpably had to do with politics or with what he perceived as speech within the communicative boundaries of rational self-governance.[295]

Such theories law Professors Harry Kalven, Jr. and Thomas Emerson called "two-level"—protection for all speech, except one or more discredited categories, or protection for specified categories of speech with the exclusion or the conditioning of others. Emerson feared these exclusionary theories.[296] In making one exception it will be too easy to make a second and then a third, until the foundations of a theory are so weakened that its entire structure is in danger of collapse. Agreeing with this part of Emerson's system, I will call the approaches he rejected "contractionist" theories, remembering, however, that he himself placed libel and obscenity in some circumstances on the unprotected or "action" side of his speech/action paradigm because injury was immediate and there was, in his view, no opportunity for effective reply. And he excluded labor picketing from First Amendment favor altogether.[297]

Collectivist Alternatives

Another danger to First Amendment freedoms has been the propensity of some theorists—Vincent Blasi's "checking value," for example—to define these freedoms as belonging primarily to behemoth social institutions sparring for political advantage, such as, the giant media conglomerate confronting the bulging governmental bureaucracy, the idea being, perhaps, that it takes one to know one, that only powerful media can deal with the power concentrated in modern government.[298]

While a respectable position to take, within this concept abuse by government is assumed to be more serious than abuse by private power, for example, the corporate defense contractor or for that matter the corporate media, a choice the First Amendment, of course, has already made for us, perhaps naively given the evolution of concentrated capitalist power. However alert Blasi may be to the dangers of official power, the human elements of speech are lost in such a construct and the individual citizen becomes remote, helpless, and redundant. Whatever is published, broadcast, or televised, regardless of the vehicle of communication, comes originally from individual minds, and often from a single mind. Someone is creating, someone is reporting. Someone is speaking to someone else.

A precursor to Blasi's checking value was the much earlier idea that the press as a public surrogate had a "watchdog" function beyond normal news gathering and publication responsibilities, a function that may not be well served by modern media, particular those media whose managers claim to be serving the interests of free speech but who seldom allow those they malign in the context of controversial issues of public importance to respond in kind. The watchdog notion, of course, is also powered by collective goals such as the "public good" and the "public interest."

Editors in the nineteenth century, with the gradual concurrence of the courts, writes Oregon Professor Timothy Gleason in a historical study of the concept, came to claim "a duty to observe, investigate, comment and report on official proceedings of government and on the performance and moral character of public officials and candidates in order to serve the public interest. They assumed, for the purpose of defending against libel actions, the role of institutional watchdogs in a democratic society."[299]

While the idea of a public benefit is not offensive to the democratic ideal, it does impose upon the press, and for that matter upon any speaker, a duty to live up to what is often an official, a collective, or at least a formal standard of service to the community. Theoretically, if the duty were neglected, the speaker could be punished or curtailed. Expression that did not meet the criteria of a judge or a legislator would not merit protection. Free speech is checkmated in such a strategy.

As long as the value of speech depended on the public good, defined in terms of majoritarian interests, Gleason observes, "great potential existed for the discovery of improper motives and unjustifiable ends."[300] The trick has been to develop a theory that will accommodate both the paramount private right to speak and the public interest in free speech.

The right to speak, says Ronald Dworkin, is more principle than policy, more an individual right and need than a benefit to social welfare. While press rights may seem more institutional than individual, the editorial page editor, the community editor, the pamphleteer, the leaflet writer either represent or are not far removed from the original thoughts of a particular person. Protect the speaker on principle, says Dworkin, and you are less vulnerable to the limiting demands of other interests and may attain most of your policy goals anyway, for example, the public's right to have information upon which to base its political decisions.[301] Neglect the speaker and the information needed for self-governance will not be generated in the first place.

To protect the small town editor, the street corner orator, or the wandering minstrel, the system must also protect the powerful media conglomerate, for the strong and the weak, the respectable and the unrespectable are all kin to the same First Amendment.

That "filthy little atheist" Thomas Paine, strident father to a revolution, could have been speaking of the threatened but aborted Nazi march in Skokie, Illinois, replete with swastikas, which the Illinois Supreme Court said was a form of protected symbolic speech and, in the circumstances, did not constitute "fighting words,"[302] or Larry Flynt's tasteless, vulgar attacks on imaginary political (life-style?) enemies in *Hustler Magazine* v. *Falwell*[303] when he wrote:

> He that would make his own liberty secure must guard even his enemy from suppression; for if he violates this duty he establishes a precedent that will reach to himself.[304]

Paine might even have included Robert Cohen's famous "Fuck the Draft" T-shirt in his classic admonition, a T-shirt carrying words that Los Angeles authorities must have thought were too "strong" a political message for Angelinos, words no more shocking today than Paine's must have been in an earlier time and place. Here, for all to see in a county courthouse, was what for many is the single most offensive, and in some ways the most powerful, word in the English language. But hardly a test of our limits of tolerance.

In a wise opinion for the Court, Justice John Marshall Harlan, preferring "verbal tumult, discord, and even offensive utterance" to no debate at all, saw Cohen's conviction under the California penal code for what it was: "a conviction resting solely upon 'speech'."[305] The words on the T-shirt did not stimulate erotic reactions, however unacceptable such imagined effects may be as a justification for censorship, said Harlan; they were not "fighting words" in the sense of a personal challenge to physical combat; nor was there evidence of a "hostile audience" ready to tear the T-shirt from Cohen's body. A weak "captive audience" argument might have been made for those persons who by reason of public business had to be in the courthouse on that particular day, but that possibility was smothered in an argument for privacy, inapplicable anyway in the public setting of the case. Hugo Black, it should be noted, joined Justice Harry Blackmun and Chief Justice Warren Burger in dissent. This was not the pristine kind of speech that in Black's mind deserved First Amendment protection.

Exclusionary Theories

Law Professor Robert Post, rebutting Harlan's premise in the *Cohen* opinion, argues that only a thoroughly demoralized community can tolerate everything. He contends that tolerance must come to some reasonable end if community life is to survive. Does a four-letter word in a county courthouse bring us to the boundaries of tolerance? It is difficult to think so, unless Post's community is a community of some kind of idealized past no longer recognizable. It simply cannot be Los Angeles in the 1990s, or even the 1960s Los Angeles of Robert Cohen.[306]

In his widely discussed book, *The Tolerant Society*, Lee Bollinger of the University of Michigan Law School makes an impressively comprehensive argument for public tolerance of the extremes of political speech to effect the higher social purpose of creating a society of self-restraint. But his thesis provides little tolerance for obscenity, "fighting words," and libel, even though the "extremes" of political speech often occur in the latter two categories; and, in the minds of many, the way political candidates are packaged and sold these days is in itself an "obscenity."[307]

The defamed individual, Bollinger believes, is punished not only by the defamer but also by the community that believes the defamer's message and responds in an excessively coercive manner— "the truth rarely catches up with the lie."[308] One need only take a longer view to make that aphorism suspect. People do suffer from inaccurate and/or vindictive publication, but the ultimate and deserving victim may be the careless or insensitive communicator who over time loses the respect and credibility of his audience and his peers.

At the same time, Bollinger, in advancing his encompassing self-restraint theory of free speech, believes, and I agree, that "the idea of free speech seeks to develop a mind that is comfortable with uncertainty and complexity" and that the "tolerance function of free speech focuses primarily on the reform of those who possess *social power*, on the community as a whole or on those who, because of their numbers or position, effectively hold (or have a reasonable chance of holding) the reins of authority."[309]

How can this reform be accomplished in a society in which the powerful strain to catch in libel nets those who criticize them? Criticism of public officials and celebrities, as has been noted, frequently leads to protracted and futile libel suits.

The bringing of a libel suit by a plaintiff endowed with political or cultural power is hardly an example of tolerance or, in the longer term, of self-restraint. It is instead a means of foreclosing further discussion. It is an effective political weapon. While most public plaintiffs fail in these libel suits, the litigation itself may serve to inhibit public discussion or operate as a stalling tactic to suspend discussion on an issue until the public forgets about it and goes on to new topics.

Eric Barendt observes that if congressmen enjoy absolute immunity because they would be inhibited from speaking their mind for fear of libel, think how editors, publishers, and even media managers must be deterred by the prospect of having to face public plaintiffs in court.[310]

Granted those plaintiffs not so endowed—private persons or vortex (limited) public figures—have a need to use governmental process in the form of a libel suit to compel self-restraint on those who use the power of the mass media to damage reputation. They have no alternative. Such plaintiffs exercise little influence, or sporadic influence at best, in community affairs and have only limited access to the major organs of public opinion. They cannot call press conferences, ridicule their antagonist on network television, or call out demonstrators.

Granted also that mass-media gatekeepers all too seldom retract when they are wrong. Nor do they, except on rare occasion, offer space and/or time for reply when a significant issue divides the community and a spokesperson for one side or the other has been assaulted in type or over the airwaves.

In a contest of equals, however, let us say between a governor or a mayor and a daily newspaper, the enlisting of a court process by a plaintiff tilts the playing field. The contest, no longer a putative public debate, now becomes a ritual battle between lawyers. Plaintiff and defendant become paying spectators. Jurors, either representing or misrepresenting the public, are the untrained, inexperienced, and totally perplexed referees who tend to blow their whistles predictably against the collective or corporate journalist and in favor of the defamed individual. It seems justifiable for them to do so. But the picture upon which they base their verdicts, the media giant versus the helpless public plaintiff, is seldom the whole picture, nor does it reflect the rich history of a society distinguished throughout the world for its dedication to uninhibited public speech.

Even larger areas of immunity—exceptions to the command of the First Amendment—are predicated by a University of Chicago law professor, Frederick Schauer. He includes symbolic speech, offensive speech, advocacy of illegal conduct, invasion of privacy, defamation, obscenity, and fighting words as forms of expression subject to a complex of qualifications, exceptions, and conditions. And he delineates broad contexts in which speech might also be conditioned—nonpublic forums, government employment, broadcasting, for example. Schauer is sometimes persuasive in his search for a principle governing the protection of speech, but when he speaks of excluding the "totally worthless" from coverage of the First Amendment and relies on the terribly flawed holding of the Supreme Court in the draft card burning case *United States* v. *O'Brien*[311] to do so, we wish to know more about the personal values that inform his First Amendment theory.[312] To connect the political message intended by the burning of a draft card with the ancient common law crimes of perjury and blackmail is startling. From a First Amendment perspective, the "crime" in *O'Brien* was the government's not the protestor's.

There is evidence in the legislative history of the 1965 amendment to the Military Training and Service Act of 1948[313] that a major purpose of the legislators who drafted it was to discourage anti-Vietnam war protests by "dissident persons who disapprove of national policy."[314] Far more troublesome is the Court's general rule growing out of *O'Brien* that incidental limitations on First Amendment freedoms can be condoned if governmental interests in doing so are sufficiently important and those interests are unrelated to the suppression of free expression. At the very least, the First Amendment should be interpreted to demand that the state show a *compelling* interest in enforcing laws constraining freedom of expression. Few precedents in recent history have confused the literal mandate of First and Fourteenth Amendments more than *O'Brien*. "Even speech at the core of the First Amendment," says Schauer in explicating *O'Brien*, "may be restricted if the state interest is sufficiently strong."[315] How strong is strong enough?

It is difficult to avoid oversimplifying what others have said about the First Amendment. First Amendment theory-building is a complex undertaking, one even of "enervating" complexity.[316] Some theories contain their own unassailable internal logic while others are based on assumptions that appear to be faulty. I do not favor those theories that permit or require the unjustified constriction, contraction, or diminution of freedom of expression just because that expression represents new or shocking modes, forms, and contents that have recently emerged within a changing society. A shriveled First Amendment will not serve its intended purpose.

Personal and social limits of tolerance expand at an ever accel-

erating rate. And time makes a fool of the censor. Levels of eroticism in commercial advertising, unthinkable a few decades ago,
are now commonplace. Social commentary on what used to be
intimately personal matters such as premarital sex, venereal dis-
ease, teenage pregnancy, and abortion no longer raises eyebrows.
We have become inured, regretfully, to the unrelenting sex and
violence depicted in our television news and entertainment pro-
grams. Race, ethnicity, and religion are discussed with a frankness
unknown to our grandparents. The lyrics of popular music push
against the limits of even permissive parents. We are no longer
surprised by parades, mass rallies, and demonstrations in behalf
of causes of every kind, some of them repugnant to large segments
of the population. Most of these concerns have sharp political
outlines. To reserve full First Amendment protection for an un-
definable "core" of political speech is to ignore the outer limits of
political debate where most of the verbal conflict and confrontation
occurs.

Some speech is unquestionably more valuable to society than
other speech, but who will decide? Except for lawyers and judges,
we have no one but ourselves to make these choices. One approach
has been to regulate speech according to its impact. In the *Pacifica*
case, the Court did this to a leftist broadcaster for his temerity in
allowing George Carlin to voice the "seven dirty words," although
the Court did so ever so subtly by substituting an "indecency"
standard for obscenity. Indecency has now become the general
standard for broadcasting.[317] Much that may be indecent is not
obscene by the Supreme Court's own labored definitions of obscenity. "Indecency" simply lowers the threshold for punishing
speech that some find objectionable—dirty words, for example.

In *Lehman* the Court seemed to be saying that because city bus
advertising had a captive audience, no political messages would
be accepted, but innocuous commercial advertising would.[318]
Would ads about pregnancy, abortion, AIDS be acceptable to the
city? All have political implications. Or does "innocuous" mean
product advertising only? And might not some of these also offend
the political sensibilities of some riders—environmentalists, for
example?

One could argue, in such circumstances, that speech is being penalized for its effectiveness, whatever one's answer to the captive audience question. Perhaps there should be no bus ads at all; or, alternatively, everybody's ads on a first come–first served basis.

To be sure, other compelling social interests sometimes must be weighed against speech, but not all of them have been given constitutional recognition, nor does convincing evidence always exist that those interests, whatever they are, have been harmed or will be harmed by the speech in question. Where there is evidence of harm, it is almost impossible to imagine that appellate judges will not engage in balancing of some sort, balancing that legal historian William Mayton says was never intended by the 1791 Constitution.[319]

Whatever weighing of values does take place, it should not be *ad hoc* balancing, unless judges are making choices based on the assumption that certain social interests outweigh constitutional rights, that all constitutional rights were born equal (is the right to bear arms equal to the right of free speech?), or that judges themselves function in a context of pure ahistorical eclecticism. The appeal of a different kind of balancing, *definitional* balancing, as the operating mechanism of a preferred freedoms doctrine, a doctrine that prefers the political freedoms—speech among them—to some other constitutional values, is that it takes notice of the historical primacy of speech and press in our constitutional evolution. Essentially the doctrine holds that legislation restricting political freedom, such as speech and press, must be exposed to a more searching and exacting judicial review than some other kinds of legislation. Definitional balancing, then, is balancing with a bias, a bias in favor of speech and press as constitutional rights, following from a rather clear historical mandate.[320]

Like many of his colleagues, Professor Schauer explores a number of different theoretical and empirical explanations for what he calls "a modern First Amendment." His skillful analysis, in straightforward terms, states a central theme of my position, if by "open commentary" he means libel-free commentary:

> Instead of increasingly hollow appeals to the public's right or need to know, such a theory might recognize that a system of open commentary on the qualifications and official conduct of public officials is simply the best way to run a government and the best way to guard against governmental abuse.[321]

Justice Black's pivotal opinion for the Court in *Bridges* v. *California* paid tribute to our radical speech heritage with its focus on the individual. He wrote:

> For it is a prized American privilege to speak one's mind, although not always with perfect good taste, on all public institutions. And an enforced silence, however limited, solely in the name of preserving the dignity of the bench, would probably engender resentment, suspicion, and contempt much more than it would enhance respect.[322]

Justice Black would have reserved the same privilege for those who spoke their minds about public officials as well as judges, since he later forcefully denied the constitutionality of all libel laws in an interview with a New York University law professor.[323]

But no one said it better than Thomas Jefferson:

"I deplore . . . the putrid state into which our newspapers have passed, and the malignity, the vulgarity, and mendacious spirit of those who write them. . . . These ordures are rapidly depraving the public taste. It is however an evil for which there is no remedy, our liberty depends on the freedom of the press, and that cannot be limited without being lost."[324] How, I wonder, would Jefferson measure our journalism against the journalism of his day?

Expansionists and Contractionists

Steve Shiffrin, a UCLA law professor, rejects "the extreme proposition that the Court (that is lawyers and judges) should always settle on rules in the first amendment area," a proposition of constitutionalism or judicial activism as opposed to majoritarianism or judicial restraint (positions that have come to represent, crudely perhaps, liberal and conservative judgments on what is the appropriate relationship between the Constitution and the elected representatives of the people). Shiffrin applauds the Court's atheoretic, pragmatic approach to speech and press. He rejects theories on both sides of the mainstream political dike—from Ronald Dworkin to Robert Bork—and what he calls "unproductive abstractions" about freedom of speech in favor of what is certainly itself an abstraction, John Rawls' intuitionist approach— "the complexity of the moral facts," says Rawls "defies our efforts to give a full account of our judgments and necessitates a plurality of competing principles."[325] Other approaches, in Shiffrin's view, either "reduce to triviality . . . or else lead to falsehood and oversimplification."[326]

One of these "unproductive" approaches, in Shiffrin's view, is C. Edwin Baker's "liberty" theory[327] that declares its essential principle to be the free rein of self-fulfilling individual free speech, unrestrained until it becomes coercive. Defamation, even when based on a deliberate lie, is not coercive, in Baker's view, and therefore should not be punishable. His permissive views on defamation, however, do not extend to what he calls the rights of the instrumentalist press. Using a trichotomous model consisting of "speech" rights, "defensive" rights, and "offensive" rights, Baker's views on defamation may be easily misinterpreted. Speech rights are inherently individual. Defensive rights protect the press against governmental assault, for example, grand juries, newsroom searches. Offensive rights would, for example, recognize some level of access to news. Within the model, the line becomes fuzzy between the reporter acting as an individual enjoying speech rights, free from both governmental and managerial coercion, and the reporter acting as an agent of a media organization able to claim only defensive rights and a measure of offensive rights. Baker teaches law at the University of Pennsylvania.

Shiffrin finds Baker's view "maddening" because, he says, it "sweeps away centuries of tort law" (tortured tort law, I might note) with insufficient argumentation.[328] Nevertheless, Baker's thesis deserves a closer look.

Rejecting both marketplace and market failure theories (the latter mandating equality of access to the channels of mass communication),[329] together with any form of utilitarian balancing, Baker's thesis holds that the First Amendment protects a broad range of nonviolent, noncoercive activity that either is speech or contains elements of speech.[330] Perjury, fraud, and blackmail, for example, would be excluded.

This is a fetching view. Baker draws on "expansionist" theorist Thomas Emerson to find purpose in the First Amendment: individual self-fulfillment and popular participation in change, both personal rights but with substantial social consequences. Baker plumbs the depths of the concept of free speech. Motive, content, and effects of speech are not the important considerations; what is important, he argues, is the coercive or noncoercive nature and context of an act in determining whether or not it is protected by the First Amendment.[331] In other words, does it result in harm?

Baker seems to be arguing that the assumptions underlying marketplace and market failure theories are untenable and will not result in "a timeless, ever-present objective" truth emerging from a free and open encounter, nor in a population gaining equality of access to the major organs of public opinion. The entire structure of society, he believes, would have to change before these could come about.

A great deal of speech today, to be sure, is corporate speech; speakers are not and never have been equal. To permit government to enhance some expression by burdening other expression is to risk too much. The only road open to a free speech society, in Baker's view, is to define speech broadly and let it reach, as it will, to the outer boundaries of tolerance.

Within Baker's theory, flag and draft card burning, vulgar antiwar T-shirts, a march by a dozen deranged American Nazis, and perhaps even obscenity, in most forms at least, appear trivial indeed.

Even Emerson's speech/action model, in Baker's view, threatens to be what Emerson himself rejects: a faulty two-level or exclusionary theory. Not only are many kinds of conduct expressive acts in themselves, but assembly, association and the free exercise of religion are, for Baker, threads of the same fabric.[332]

"The key ethical postulate," for Baker, "is that respect for individual integrity and autonomy requires the recognition that a person has the right to use speech to develop herself or to influence or interact with others"—even, presumably, if that person is a Kenneth Thomson or a Rupert Murdoch, or a little-known political activist victimized by a SLAPP.[333]

Baker's concern, of course, is primarily with the speaker rather than the person who may suffer from the speaker's words, although individual autonomy and one's property right in reputation could be violated by a libelous attack. Baker's may be the ultimate "expansionist" theory. He takes pains to separate the concepts of liberty and equality, both crucial elements of a just social order in Baker's mind[334]; but liberty and with it autonomy are essential to human development. Baker, in spite of his professed debt to Jurgen Habermas and Roberto Unger, doyens of the leftist critical theory movement, will be labeled libertarian (reactionary) by those who see total equality, beyond equal access to media, as the benchmark of a democratic society and who consider "liberty" a shibboleth of the socially advantaged.[335]

A chink in Baker's own theoretical armour is the exception that he makes for commercial advertising.[336] Using the same argument Thomas Emerson uses to exempt labor picketing from his "full protection" theory, Baker contends that commercial speech does not reflect anyone's voluntary or personal desire to speak. Instead it is preordained by the structure of the market and is more "property" than personal right.[337]

This again leaves human minds out of the free speech equation, as if advertising had no creative dimensions whatsoever, no human hands moulding its form and content. It reflects an incomplete understanding of how advertising is made and of an industry that is a driving force in the market economy and probably the most powerful, if most insidious, of trend-setters among social institutions. It also contradicts the protection he would proffer professional journalists against their employers, as well as against government.[338]

Political speech exerts power over people also and much of it depends for its distribution, if not its creation, on accumulations of monopoly property. One could as well exempt editors from First Amendment protection, arguing that most of them are simply the minions of faceless corporate managers in an impersonal, increasingly concentrated capitalist communications system.

Would there ever be room in Baker's construct for governmental intervention—the application of antitrust laws, for example, to create greater diversity in the structure of mass communication? Clearly there would, for he fears the limitations property and profit place on personal liberty. It is a paradox of press freedom that government intervention, as has been noted, which the First Amendment can be read to discourage, may be necessary to the full fashioning of press freedom. Examples, we have noted, include postal subsidies, statutes protecting the identity of news sources, and the antitrust exemption for once competing newspapers' joint operating agreements.[339]

Even with their qualifications, Baker and Emerson remain more "expansionist" than "contractionist" in their theoretical approaches, and serve the First Amendment admirably.

Even purer in their expansionism are New York University law professor Burt Neuborne and Northwestern's Franklyn Haiman. Neuborne advocates lifting up weak voices in an unfair marketplace rather than silencing or proscribing the powerful who tend to dominate that market. Haiman has long favored counteracting potentially harmful speech such as obscenity and incitement with opposition speech and audience resistance. Both are preferable in his view to judicial intervention.[340]

Many free speech theorists are "contractionists." One of the most sophisticated of these is Vincent Blasi of Columbia University's law school whose "checking value" construct was referred to earlier. From what he calls a "pathological perspective" Blasi argues for a *lean, trim* First Amendment, incorporating a core of relatively stable and consistently enforced central norms that are part of society's historical memory and can be conveyed, or defended, in a simple yet forceful rhetoric—what "most people would recognize as serious, time-honored forms of communication."[341]

"In pathological periods," writes Blasi, "courts need to present the forces of repression with strict, immutable legal constraints. That kind of implacable judicial posture is easier to assume when the basic reach of the first amendment is modest and compatible with widely shared intuitions regarding the natural ambit of the commitment to expressive liberty."[342] Don't make the First Amendment as complicated as the tax code, Blasi advises. The problem, however, is that libel law, as a strand of First Amendment theory, *is* already as complicated—some would say more complicated—as the tax code!

Blasi's pathological period is one in which there has been a shift in attitudes regarding toleration that threatens core values of the First Amendment. Although he provides few diagnostic tools (and his analysis is bereft of public opinion poll data or materials from the extensive public opinion literature or studies of relationships between public opinion and the Supreme Court), he does provide historical examples of periods that fit his political syndrome.

But diagnosis remains a problem. At one point he faults the

clear and present danger test for having to depend on a contemporary assessment of social conditions even though his entire thesis
hinges on a similar requirement.[343]

Another difficulty with Blasi's central construct is that the populace, finding many forms of speech unprotected, or only partially
protected at the edge, may be reinforced in believing that more
familiar forms of speech at the center need not be protected either,
and that speech itself is being devalued by the courts.[344]

Traditionally, the most serious threats to First Amendment values, it would seem from my reading of history, occur when a strong,
strategically located and vocal minority decides that the nation's
physical security is at risk, largely from powers perceived to be
external in origin and reach. Our post-Revolutionary reliance on
sedition laws came as responses to perceived threats from France
at the dawn of the nineteenth century and from Germany and the
Soviet Union in the twentieth century. Seldom have the prophets
of catastrophe become as exercised over destructive, nondemo-
cratic internal forces such as Antimasons, Know-Nothings, Ku
Klux Klan, or the White Aryan Resistance. Those movements have
been reassuringly American in origin and complexion and, therefore, have invoked little legislative hysteria.

At the one time when the United States as we know them were
clearly at risk—the Civil War—the federal government was faced
with what historian James Randall describes, quoting Lincoln, as
becoming "too strong for the liberties of its own people, or too
weak to maintain its own existence."[345] Best estimates are that
some sixty Civil War period editors and publishers were arrested
in fourteen states and the District of Columbia in an effort to hold
the North in a precarious union by constitutionally unsupportable
means.

What do we do between crises? To save the core of political
speech for a crisis that may never come at the expense of other
forms of speech that may be vital to some is to conclude construction of a free speech theory with the laying of the foundation. The
outer defenses, in my view, must be protected if the inner defenses
are to remain secure.

In anticipating "expansionist" counterarguments, Blasi appreciates the danger to unpopular speech of a theory permitting broad
exceptions, say for advertising, obscenity or symbolic conduct

(expression) and necessitating an inspection of motive and impact. "The more universal a principle," he believes, "the broader is the constituency of persons who gain from the principle."[346]

Nevertheless, "fighting words," deliberate lies (libel), hard-core pornography, and "threats" are for Blasi partially outside the limits of First Amendment protection. A "lying" press will squander the credibility needed for its checking function. He makes a principled and balanced argument for the exclusion of advertising by first noting the danger that attaches to judges speculating on the motives of the speaker or on the importance of the subject matter of the communication. He is concerned that such judgments will not be made carefully in times of stress. But, on balance, he does not believe advertising warrants the full protection of the constitution; like labor picketing it simply advances one's economic well-being:

> Were courts to grant commercial speech the same high level of protection now accorded political speech, regulatory objectives long considered important and legitimate would be frustrated, engendering in all probability a weakening of public respect for the first amendment quite a bit more severe than that now caused by the Court's middle-of-the-road approach.[347]

Blasi is a Meiklejohn disciple in that he would prescribe near absolute protection for speech that "matters" at the expense of speech that doesn't, for rational speech over nonrational speech. Although he distinguishes between viewpoint and content regulation, permitting regulation of the latter but not the former, his distinction must remain frighteningly subjective and arbitrary.

He would also grant the right of association absolute protection because the compelled disclosure of information revealing political affiliations and contributions has and will in the worst of times, he believes, lead to abuses. Surveillance by the state cuts to the core of the First Amendment, says Blasi, and deters people from getting together to exchange ideas.[348]

Likewise, he argues, students, a captive and malleable audience—as residents of Skokie, Illinois, were not—also ought to be protected against school boards who would ban or suppress ideas not to their liking in educational settings. The inculcation of censorial values in youth will be taken by students into adulthood.

Blasi wisely excludes the so-called "right to know" from his concept of protected speech, as does Baker, because, if the public has a right to know, the press may have an obligation, even a duty, to provide what the public thinks it needs. His "checking value" construct, however, seems inconsistent with this view because it could be interpreted as suggesting a press obligation to fulfill certain broad social needs that, if unmet, might lead to capricious penalties of some sort. Obligations of this kind were voiced in pre-Revolutionary America,[349] but then the conflict between press and public on the one hand and governors on the other was much more a matter of personal, political, and press survival than it is now.

I review a few of these useful theoretical constructs to suggest the categories of speech that are found to be expendable by some in drawing opaque lines between protected and unprotected speech, true and false speech, rational and irrational speech. Harm should be of high probability rather than mere reasonable expectation when establishing the outer limits of tolerance, if the constitutional protections for speech and press are to function as intended.

Harm–benefit assessments will continue to inform decisions of appellate courts; there is a reasonableness about balancing that is not found in absolutist proclamations such as the First Amendment or even in more reasonable preferred freedoms theories that appear to give advantage to one set of constitutional values or to one segment of society over others. Balancing has a common-sense appeal that looks askance at elevated or superior constitutional rights.

Yet, in balancing, harm from speech is invariably overestimated or ignored altogether. Evidence justifying exemption from First Amendment protection is seldom adequate. Threats to national security all evaporate in hindsight—except perhaps for the four years of the American Civil War—and we apologize to one another for having temporarily lost our nerve and our reason. Commercial speech, while depreciated in most First Amendment theories, in the long run is very likely to be of more benefit than harm to society, and ought to be protected to the point where the reader, viewer, or listener is helpless in the hands of the speaker and is, therefore, either captive or coerced. Moreover, the lines between what is commercial and what is not or between what is information and what is advertising or propaganda or entertainment are more and more difficult to draw. Ill-defined boundaries is a problem with all categories-based theories of freedom of expression.

Ideology has become a substitute for evidence on the question of the effects of obscenity on individual psyches or on society. And few, including Supreme Court justices themselves, can agree comfortably with one another on how obscenity ought to be defined.

Every symbolic speech case to reach the Supreme Court since the 1960s has been concerned with a triviality—flag burning,[350] affixing a peace symbol to an upside down flag,[351] burning a draft card,[352] wearing a black armband to school,[353] and promoting a candidate for a student government position by double entendres.[354] All, by any measure of common sense, attempt to communicate political ideas using what have been called the media of desperation. Only the double entendre high school case, because of its setting and the fact that no serious political speech was involved (although sexual speech was), may give one pause. Certainly it is a more difficult case.

The Supreme Court has divided in quite unpredictable ways in most symbolic speech cases and so nothing like a governing legal principle or guideline has emerged. Hugo Black, champion of classic free speech, gave its symbolic forms little or no protection in his opinions.

From its inception in *Chaplinsky* v. *New Hampshire*, in 1942,[355] the "fighting words" doctrine has been a cipher. Perhaps the triviality of that case—a religious pamphleteer calling a police officer a fascist and a racketeer—got the doctrine off to a bad start. Like *Chaplinsky*, subsequent cases have also depended on how well law enforcement officials can control their tempers.[356]

And muddle has developed over whether audiences ought to be protected against speakers or speakers against audiences.[357] A number of "fighting words" ordinances have been declared void for overbreadth, but the exact meaning of the concept itself remains difficult to fathom because few of the cases receiving appellate attention have in their facts presented anything more than speculation as to whether the words in question might have led to a riot. Face-to-face vituperation that often does lead to one-on-one violence is generally too private a matter to engage the Constitution, or even the attention of the public. But the "fighting words" doctrine has been a convenient tool for punishing or prohibiting speech that some people don't like.

It should be noted also that the state supreme court in *Chaplinsky*, with the approval of the U.S. Supreme Court, construed the New Hampshire statute to condemn as unconstitutional "other disorderly words, including profanity, obscenity and threats."[358]

Robert Bork argues that speech advocating violent overthrow of government is not political speech but a punishable rejection of the premises of our constitutional system:[359] At the other end of the political spectrum, Herbert Marcuse dismisses the First Amendment by contending that most free speech is nothing more than a ploy, a social-pressure escape valve, for preserving an entrenched political system.[360]

Certainly there are limits. On rare occasions speech alone may be damaging; Laurence Tribe's classic example of shouting "boo" to a cardiac patient may be one.[361] There are places and times where and when speech may raise serious questions of public safety—a demonstration at the city's major intersection at rush hour. In such circumstances speech may have to be moved or postponed. While it may serve as an antidote to libel, more speech will not cure a traffic jam. And speech must always give way to the protection of human life. Some forums are not public—the uninvited speaker in a church sanctuary, a college classroom, or on a private front lawn.[362]

No audience should ever be held captive, not by graffiti on a public building, by hecklers shouting down a speaker, unless the audience has somehow become captive to that speaker, nor by verbal outbursts in a courtroom or controversial advertising placards in the city bus. These are invasive and psychologically perdurable forms of speech that can't be turned off or avoided without severely modifying the patterns of one's daily life in anticipation of being part of a captive audience. One is caught in the speaker's net, unable to extricate oneself easily by averting one's eyes, leaving the scene, or responding in any meaningful way. Since listeners and viewers are a key part of the communication process, their rights ought to be reciprocal to those of the speaker. There must be freedom to hear as well as freedom not to listen.

Nor should anyone be compelled to proclaim the state's philosophy, salute its symbols, or otherwise assume the burden of be-coming its unwilling messenger.[363] These speech issues, part of a larger discourse on speech, comprise a rich and varied portion of the case law and ultimately will contribute significantly more to a meaningful consensus on the First Amendment, if that is possible or desirable, than the constricting debate over what categories of speech ought to be protected, partially protected, or sacrificed altogether to other social interests.

Speech *can* become perjury, blackmail, or a denial of one's civil rights. Advertising *can* become fraud. Symbolic speech *can* become arson and attempted murder. When these occur or are clearly about to occur it is time enough to act under criminal statutes. But to make falsity in noncriminal forms of speech punishable, as in the public–official libel case, is to demean and squeeze speech and press, rights that James Madison called the "choicest privileges of the people."[364] Social debate usually takes place with truth and falsehood on both sides.

"The 'bedrock' principle that government should not 'prohibit the expression of an idea simply because society finds the idea itself offensive or disagreeable,' " writes Geoffrey Stone, dean of the University of Chicago law school, quoting the Supreme Court in its Texas 1989 flag-burning case (*Texas* v. *Johnson*, 109 S.Ct. at 2544), "is not only a correct interpretation of the First Amend-ment, it is wise public policy in a free and self-governing society."[365]

Public libel as a category of political speech, half true or half false, whatever its imponderable motivation, ought to be protected from the endless litigation that now confronts it. Only "expan-sionist" theories of the First Amendment will advance that cause. Libel laws should be reserved for the speechless private person and the relatively speechless vortex public figure who elects to play a role in the political process or finds him-or herself unexpectedly and temporarily in the public spotlight.

Free speech is a rare commodity on our planet, a flawed or as yet undiscovered jewel in most societies. While the limits of tol-erance have expanded in our own society, counterpressures, po-litical and philosophical, for diminishing freedom of speech are found in the academies, in legislative bodies, and in the streets. Books are removed from school libraries. Universities condone the banning of speech or speakers from their campuses.[366] Faculty members argue angrily over whether certain kinds of speech can be prohibited because they are not "politically correct." Hecklers veto the speech of those who do run that gauntlet. The Supreme Court sacrifices clearly political forms of symbolic expression to trivial governmental interests without a whimper from the populace. A National Commission condemns most forms of erotic speech without making its case. The Congress bans broadcast advertising of legally sold products without considering the value of counteradvertising. And a majority of Americans condone censorship of the press by the military even when national security is not involved. But America by all comparisons is still the cradle of free speech.

Britain's increasingly centralized and unchecked political system prefers secrecy to openness in government and severely punishes those who break the code of silence; the Home Secretary, in 1989, banned the voice of Sinn Fein, a legal political party, from the airwaves. Canada's largest and one of its most sophisticated cities, Toronto, still permits a panel of volunteer citizens without any evident artistic or literary qualifications, as if that would matter, to decide what movies or parts of movies their fellow citizens shall see; and an Ottawa news service bureau chief, Douglas Small, was charged in 1989 and bound over for trial for reporting a federal government budget leak. Fortunately, a farsighted Ottawa judge, James Fontana, threw the case out of court. Ireland permits no speech on abortion. The prime minister of Singapore sued the *Far Eastern Economic Review* for libel for an article he admitted was true. He was awarded "aggravated damages" because cross-examination by the publication's attorney "exacerbates the hurt." Then the *Asian Wall Street Journal* is held in contempt of court and is alleged also to have libeled the prime minister for reporting the original court action. A new licensing system followed that effectively keeps the *Journal* out of Singapore. Under Singaporean press law, a *Journal* editor reports, the rule is: "The price of circulating freely in Singapore is that you will report nothing that poses the least threat to our political monopoly," the monopoly of the ruling People's Action Party.[367] Israel blocks publication of many major news reports not passed by military censors. The Indian press exists under Declarations of Emergency, direct governmental threat, and Defamation Bills. Nigerian journalists must register and be certified by a Media Council run by military authorities.

In most countries of the world the situation is much worse; there are no expectations of freedom and you can be shot or imprisoned for seditious libel, a crime that Professor Kalven called "the hallmark of closed societies throughout the world."[368] Death has been called the ultimate form of censorship and Freedom House reported that forty-three journalists in nineteen countries were killed in 1990, some by intention, fifty were threatened with death, sixteen were kidnapped, and 139 assaulted.[369]

In Eastern Bloc countries, where people are slowly recovering from the intellectual paralysis of Marxist–Leninism freedom of speech appears from their banners to be the first freedom demanded, whether or not many of them have any notion of what free speech really means or the trouble it can cause.

And if the mass media themselves are committed to a free speech society in which a rich and varied public dialogue takes place, they will also honor Justice Brandeis' principle that the remedy to be applied is more speech, not enforced silence, and voluntarily open their pages and their air time to those public persons who have been attacked personally or who wish to express intelligent disagreement with editorial policies or with the quality of coverage of significant public events. And in such an environment the media may be less hesitant to correct, to say they are sorry, and to admit to fallibility.

Time and space are valuable, but in the larger scheme of things what media managers would say they are worth more than freedom of speech in a society calling itself open and democratic?

Defamatory speech will always hurt. And in a free speech society there will always be defamatory speech. But what good, it may be asked, is free speech to a person whose honor and dignity have been destroyed; he may not have the heart to speak again? Perhaps not, although that seems unlikely in light of the number of libel suits that are brought, giving plaintiffs a garbled opportunity to speak through an adversarial legal system. Perhaps that is better than nothing. But surely there are better ways to rectify a defamation. Shall rectification come through a money transaction between plaintiff and defendant, with the major benefactors being the attorneys on both sides? Or shall rectification come by counterspeech and challenge to what has been said? A lawsuit or more speech? The lawsuit has failed as an answer to these questions. Seldom does any semblance of the truth emerge from a libel suit.

In 1800, Tunis Wortman, a New York lawyer and Tammany politician, made a relevant argument in one of the most seminal and influential expositions on freedom of speech and press ever published in America.[370] Focusing on the individual right of free expression and assuming that the public when given the facts could distinguish the accurate from the inaccurate, Wortman made a convincing case for counterargument and refutation against undeserved public libels. While his primary purpose was to inveigh against criminal or seditious libel, he did not overlook the private dimension.

"The Defamation of private character," he wrote, "stands upon a separate and distinct foundation. . . . We must carefully distinguish between the defamation which relates to Private Individuals and that which concerns Government. In the first case a personal injury is sustained.—Private Character being tender, and not an object of notoriety, is susceptible of suffering from Misrepresentation. The erroneous impression of a single man may be extremely pernicious to another. The prosecutions commenced for Personal Slander are founded in real damage: they aim at redress: they are entirely the objects of civil jurisdiction, and not liable to become converted into instruments of oppression."[371]

Perhaps the acceptable prosecutions Wortman envisioned for the protection of private people have become converted into instruments of oppression. Wortman does not tell us whether public officials *are* the government, although we might assume that he meant to; perhaps he would distinguish between policymakers and administrators. Nor does he suggest how we deal with the private lives of public officials.

Radical though he was for his time, Wortman would not have approved my proposal for reform; nor would most of history's commentators on the difference between public and private libel.

"The character of every man should be deemed equally sacred and of consequence entitled to equal remedy," Wortman wrote.[372] Profligate use of libel laws since the *New York Times* doctrine was promulgated in 1964, however, has undoubtedly had a deleterious effect on freedom of speech and press, however dedicated one might be to the principle Justice Stewart articulated as "the essential dignity and worth of every human being."[373] A theory of individual free speech must subscribe to the same principle but at the same time assume that freedom of speech and writing is part of that dignity and worth.

My proposal would deny the libel remedy to public officials and pervasive public personalities. Denying the remedy to public officials is where Justices Black, Douglas, and Goldberg would have taken the *New York Times* doctrine in 1964 had their concurring opinions carried the day, and they would have had the blessing of Professor Thomas Emerson.

Three years later in *dicta* in *Curtis Publishing* v. *Butts*,[374] Chief Justice Earl Warren, although still comfortable with the actual malice qualification in the *New York Times* doctrine, recommended treating public figures and public officials as one.

"To me," he argued, "differentiation between 'public figures' and 'public officials' and adopting separate standards of proof for each have no basis in law, logic, or First Amendment policy. Increasingly in this country, the distinctions between governmental and private sectors are blurred. . . . [A]lthough they are not subject to the restraints of the political process, 'public figures,' like 'public officials,' often play an influential role in ordering society. And surely as a class these 'public figures' have as ready access as 'public officials' to mass media of communication, both to influence policy and to counter criticism of their views and activities."

Combine the main thrust of the concurrences in *New York Times* with Chief Justice Warren's *Butts* observations concerning the similarities between governmental and private sectors, put them in the framework of expansionist theories of freedom of expression and the essentials of my proposal come into focus. There is no longer a place for the kind of wise compromise Wortman recommended in 1800 to rid the land of the crime of seditious libel. Civil libel run riot has taken its place.

"It is precisely the kind of retributive and punitive use of the common law remedy of defamation that so resembles the crime of seditious libel."[375] Sedition redux.

8

Evidence

"By pursuing falsehood," wrote Dostoevsky in *Crime and Punishment*, "you will arrive at the truth! The fact that I am in error shows that I am human. You will not attain to one single truth until you have produced at least fourteen false theories, and perhaps a hundred and fourteen."[376]

Perhaps all 114 theories of the First Amendment are false or perhaps in some respects they are all true. We often proceed more by feelings than logic, or by best estimates of what we can get away with.

Recall the *Rosenbloom* test.[377] Justice Brennan, writing the opinion of the Court, stretched the actual malice test from public officials and public figures all the way to public issues: that is, anyone, public or private, involved in a matter of public interest would have to show actual malice to prevail in a libel suit. The stretch was too painful for the intellectual muscle of a fragmented Court, leaving as it did the question of whether a libel was actionable pretty well up to editors' judgments as to what was or was not a public issue. Realistically, under the rule, anything an editor decided to publish was by definition a public issue.

Widely hailed though it was in press and in some legal circles, the *Rosenbloom* formula was doomed to fall. It seemed to put too much judgmental power in the hands of editors; it was too elastic a test.

Stabilizing the law three years later, *Gertz*[378] would bring private plaintiffs back under the protective umbrella of the libel laws by requiring them to prove the lesser fault of negligence rather than actual malice in suits against the media, unless they sought punitive damages.

Writing in the *Texas Law Review*, David Anderson observed

that "Rejection of the *Rosenbloom* plurality's conclusion that the constitution protects equally all discussion of matters of public concern reverses a decade of steady movement toward the more *expansive* first amendment rationale [emphasis added]."[379] He feared that private sectors of American life would be less fully explored as a result and that less conventional, more innovative media, primarily magazines and books, would be disadvantaged.[380] Of course, he was correct.

My proposal uses a different tack to achieve the same "expansive" result. For the courts to define public officials and pervasive public personalities of decision-making and agenda-setting status leaves the major responsibilities of the law, where it has always been and where it should be, in their hands. If it proves difficult to decide who belongs in the policymaking public official/celebrity categories, it should not be surprising. Courts have had little success with the public figure/private person distinction they are required to make under the present law. A contextual assessment of power, influence, and access to media would, ideally, have to be made in each case with much greater attention to common sense.

The next step is the difficult one: denying policymakers and agenda setters, once identified, the libel remedy. A review of two studies, one by the author and his research assistant, may provide empirical support for that proposal and reinforce the idea that the libel laws are indeed out of control.

Two Studies

The Lynch Study

In 1988, Attorney Judy Lynch reported in the *Oregon Law Review* the results of an ambitious study of libel suits brought by public officials between 1964 and 1986.[381] Courts appeared to confer public official status most reliably on law enforcement officers, state and federal legislators, governors, judges, and former officials. Among her findings:

1. Lower-level state and local officials sue for libel more than high-level state or federal officials. High-level federal officials

were conspicuously underrepresented in the tally, one reason being, perhaps, that they enjoy ready access to the national news media to rebut charges made against them. Lynch found only four members of Congress in her twelve-year population of plaintiffs and no federal judges or high-level members of the federal government.

2. Police officers accounted for a startling 37 percent of the 312 cases she examined. Another 6 percent was accounted for by "other" law enforcement officials such as federal, state, county, and local government attorneys. Together they constituted nearly half of all public official plaintiffs.

3. Local, state, and county executive officials accounted for another 20 percent of cases.

4. Mayors and city managers were involved in 6 percent of Lynch's cases; teachers, professors, deans, principals, and superintendents (assumedly of public schools) constituted 8 percent of plaintiffs.

5. City council members accounted for another 3.5 percent.

6. Five percent of her cases were brought by state, county, and local candidates for political office. Only three cases involved candidates for federal office, and one of these was presidential candidate Barry Goldwater (his successful libel case against publisher Ralph Ginsburg and his *Fact* magazine in 1969).[382]

7. Media defendants figured in 70 percent of cases; other public officials in 25 percent; and nonmedia or private defendants in 16 percent.

8. Defendants of all kinds prevailed in 73 percent of cases.

9. Defenses used were the constitutional or actual malice (*New York Times*) defense in 42 percent of cases; the opinion defense in less than 7 percent (a relatively new defense at the time of the study); in 9 percent of cases no defamation was found; and in 8 percent of cases the defense was conditional or qualified privilege.

10. Charges leading to libel suits were typically misconduct or corruption (tax evasion, fraud, conflicts of interest), incompetence, racism, sexual misconduct, or police brutality.

Lynch's interpretation of her data cuts to the quick of my proposal when she concludes that "for this seditious libel analogy to hold up in the context of modern civil libel suits brought by high-level public officials, it is essential that the alleged commentary be fairly characterized as a criticism of government policies and actions, and not solely a criticism of one government official's integrity or honesty."[383]

The old conundrum! How does an editor investigate and report on city hall corruption, bureaucratic incompetence, or police brutality without intruding upon personal character? Lynch acknowledges Justice Brennan's view in *New York Times* that an official's reputation would suffer from an attack on the agency of which he or she is in charge.[384] Lynch proceeds from there, however, to deny that any but a few public official libel actions in the past twenty years rise to the level of sedition. This may be due to her casting the proposition primarily in terms of "high-ranking public officials," few of whom, she finds, bring suit.

Lower-level officials have as much power and influence in their own realms as the Westmorelands and Sharons do in theirs, and it is in these more modest settings that most people live. A majority of plaintiffs in her study are from local communities. Another reason why punishment for sedition may seem irrelevant to these cases may be due to Lynch's unwillingness to combine the private and public dimensions of libel suits brought by officials—"the alleged libelous attacks," she writes, "have generally focused on the integrity and competence of the official rather than on the integrity of the governmental action."[385] Such a separation simply cannot be made. Lynch may be looking for the counterpoise between Big Government and Big Media,[386] that Vincent Blasi posits in his "checking value" construct.

Instead of relying on a wavering line between public and private plaintiffs, dependent on content or context, I am recommending that the relatively fixed status of the plaintiff in the decision-making or agenda-setting hierarchy be the determining factor of libel protection and that context be considered only in assessing policy-making or cultural power in a particular social or political community. It is not the same distinction made in *New York Times* v. *Sullivan* because there "public official" came to be defined as any government employee, and a public figure in subsequent cases, as anyone turning up in the news. My interest is in movers and shakers.

Lynch may be naive in assuming that a senator's junkets or his or her private business affairs are not related to that person's policymaking function.[387] And it is easier to measure General Westmoreland's access to media than his pain, as her solution implies one would have to do. When editors hide or bury responses to defamatory charges, they ought to risk and sometimes do risk professional condemnation, a result they may come to fear more than adverse audience reaction; their constitutional defenses remain available in either case, of course, since the First Amendment protects both unethical and ethical practices.

Anthony Lewis says that Ulysses S. Grant and other Civil War generals underwent criticism far more savage than anything dreamed of by Westmoreland.[388] Furthermore, one must ask whether Westmoreland "preserve[d] his good name," to use Lynch's words, or further damaged it by suing CBS?[389]

Of public officials Lynch writes:

> Arguably, because they are at the heart of public policy-making, their need for an avenue to maintain their reputations is even more critical. Loss of reputation can destroy an official's capacity to contribute in any meaningful way to the course of public affairs.[390]

Every despot in history would agree with that statement. Moreover, the media cannot ultimately thrive by imposing on their publics a regime of continual misrepresentation. Lynch, in what seems like a repudiation of the Meiklejohn approach, would pull back on the *New York Times* doctrine by drawing a sharp line between truth and falsehood, as the courts have unsuccessfully tried to do, so as to punish the socially useless intentional lie— although she does seem to leave the door of press immunity open just a bit where officials of sufficient stature are involved.

And Lynch has the Supreme Court on her side. In a 1985 case, the Court affirmed the notion that First Amendment rights cannot be absolute and, therefore, that absolute immunity is not available. A candidate for U.S. attorney had been libeled in a letter to President Reagan. The candidate sued and the defendant argued that he had an absolute right to petition the government for a redress of grievances. The Court, relying on the 1845 case, *White* v. *Nicholls* (see p. 65), said that no clauses of the First Amendment provide absolute immunity for libelous statements.[391] In a concurring opinion Justice Brennan, citing language from *Garrison* v. *Louisiana*, reminded his readers that there could be exceptions to the freedom of political speech:

"For the use of the known lie as a tool is at once at odds with the premises of democratic government and with the orderly manner in which economic, social, or political change is to be effected."[392] And he concluded that it wouldn't matter "whether the expression consists of speaking to neighbors across the backyard fence, publishing an editorial in the local newspaper, or sending a letter to the President of the United States."[393] As Mark Twain is supposed to have said, "A lie can go half way around the world before the truth even gets its boots on."

Walter Lippmann may have had a more acute and accurate perception of the political world:

"With exceptions so rare that they are regarded as miracles and freaks of nature," he wrote, "successful democratic politicians are insecure and intimidated men. They advance politically only as they placate, appease, bribe, seduce, bamboozle or otherwise manage to manipulate the demanding and threatening elements in their constituencies. The decisive consideration is not whether a proposition is good but whether it is popular."[394]

The Gillmor–Grant Study

In the fall of 1989, the author and research assistant Melanie Grant, then a second-year Columbia University law school student and now a practising attorney, proceeded to examine what turned out to be 614 reported libel cases involving media defendants in the period 1982 to 1988. According to Cynthia Bolbach, managing editor of the *Media Law Reporter* at the Bureau of National Affairs, few ongoing libel cases escape the attention of that publication. Bolbach's best estimate was that at least 95 percent of cases that get even to the earliest stages of a court proceeding are picked up by the *Reporter*'s far-flung cadre of correspondents, and appear in the publication, if not in official and other unofficial case reports. No equivalent record of settled media cases is available.

Settlement

Of course, only the roughest estimates of cases settled out of court
can be ventured. But an attempt was made to do this by contacting
media insurers and major law firms known to have substantial
practices in libel law. While law firms were reluctant to discuss
these matters, one insurance firm estimated that 80 percent of cases
filed are settled out of court. A second insurer put the same figure
at more than 90 percent but complained that settlement may come
after as much as $50,000 has been spent on initial legal jockeying
and the plaintiff has reaped the huge benefits of publicity. In mid-
1990, this particular company, NBC's insurer, had already spent
$9 million on the Wayne Newton case and was still waiting for an
appeals court ruling. Not even the favorable outcome for the network that did occur in the case would redeem anything but a
minuscule portion of these costs.

When a settlement comes at this stage it carries with it little
satisfaction for defendant or insurance company. Newton's case is
illustrative of those cases in which a defendant chooses to fight on
firm constitutional ground. Settlement, early or late, is unlikely,
to the chagrin of insurance companies. The accrued interest on a
$58 million jury award during the period of appeal could be enor-
mous. In such circumstances, it is not surprising that insurance
companies press for settlement One company's chief claims agent,
who suggested that the libel insurance business is "not for the
weak at heart," decried the lack of interest generally in alternative
dispute resolution options, given the huge awards made by juries
and the waste of valuable resources involved in and the predict-
ability of the appeals process.

Cases resolved in the judicial process prior to summary judgment
may still cost $25,000; cases that go to summary judgment twice
that much. Cases that go to trial may cost in excess of $100,000.
One of the companies contacted, an insurer of small- and mid-
sized publications, reported that 85 percent of its funds are spent
defending libel suits and only 15 percent on settlements.[395] Another
reported that for every $1 paid in damage claims $2 goes to lawyers'
fees.

One of largest insurers in the land, specializing in libel, privacy

and copyright, rather than incorporating libel into its general liability policies, figured that at least 80 percent of its expenditures
goes to legal fees. Millions may be spent in cases where no claim
is ever paid. In twenty-seven years the company has spent approximately $100 million in defending, and only $10 million for
settlements. A company spokesman pointed out that a major case
in Little Rock, Arkansas, might cost $200,000, whereas the same
case in Boston or Los Angeles would cost $1 million.

He also noted that until five years ago fewer than 10 percent of
cases were settled because 80 percent of publishers were wedded
to a "we-never-settle" philosophy. Journalistic arrogance has been
a costly indulgence, he suggested. Of course, in some cases there
may be good principled reasons for not settling. Contemporary
publishers are more prone to admit that "we made a mistake." As
a result, the number of cases settled has doubled. At the same
time, the company spokesman added that 50 percent of cases
should never have been brought in the first place and of those that
are legitimate one-third are settled, but usually after the expensive
judicial process has begun.

Four major companies dominate the field, one insuring approximately 75 percent of the nation's dailies. All seem to have a well-
developed sense of the importance of the First Amendment. Pre-
mium and deductible costs have held fairly steady, although the
trends for both are upward.

Settlement, consistent with earlier figures, is much less expensive
than litigation, but it does cost money. Sometimes it may take the
form of a quiet retraction, especially where the complainant is a
private person. A communication channel corrects and/or apolo-
gizes for an error publicly or privately and perhaps offers a nominal
sum in compensation; that is the end of the matter. But it may
also require the intervention of lawyers, and that can be expensive.

The Iowa study estimated that 10 to 15 percent of cases involve
money settlements, some within an insurance policy's deductible,
some outside of it, and some, presumably, without insurance coverage. Professor Franklin's insurance company sources estimated
that only 25 percent of cases are settled out of court.[396] These
discrepant figures, of course, depend on how "settlement" is defined: for example, with or without money changing hands; with

or without the involvement of an insurance company or lawyers; at an early or later stage in the lawsuit. Settlement may also be a way of avoiding crushing legal expenses, even though the law would have been on the side of the published story. Unfortunately, settlement, if it is arranged too often, may brand a prospective media defendant a soft touch and create a risk of attracting more libel suits. Moreover, our data indicate that publishers who retract lose more cases than those who don't retract. This may mean that their cases are weaker to begin with. Under some state statutes, retractions will mitigate damages substantially but they will not end the suit.

It is not known how many plaintiffs who lose at trial either appeal or drop the case at that point, or, as has been suggested, settle before trial. Many libel actions are threatened but never initiated, and cases that are brought get lost in the judicial system and become dormant.

Design

The present survey was designed to measure the level of support for the underlying assumptions of this proposal: that highly influential and visible public people constitute a substantial and fearsome segment of libel plaintiffs in media cases and that the general public would gain from an alternative system of resolution, namely, voluntary opportunities for reply through offending media.

Who are the plaintiffs? What level of influence do they have in their own social settings? What kind of access do they have to media in these same settings? Answers to the latter two questions, of course, had to be inferred from a reading of the cases.

Using categories of plaintiff developed by the courts (public official, voluntary limited-purpose public figure, involuntary public figure, all-purpose public personality, private person) and an additional category of our own making, public employee, the authors recorded the plaintiff category designated by the court in each case, and the category the authors thought most appropriate given the facts and circumstances of the case. There was often disagreement between the court and the authors as to the more appropriate designation for a libel plaintiff. The courts did not seem to have a principled method for making such decisions, and there were glaring inconsistencies from jurisdiction to jurisdiction.

The Gillmor–Grant study was concerned only with media defendants (70 percent of defendants were media in the Lynch study and 76 percent in the Franklin study, of which 60 percent were newspapers and 16 percent television). Each libel case was recorded as to media type—book, journal, magazine, newspaper, radio, television, wire service, pamphlet—and according to size of audience.

The court's determination as to whether or not there was injury to plaintiff and, if there was, whether the injury was to reputation, status, business, or some combination of these, was recorded. Also recorded was the court's determination as to whether the defendant showed actual malice or negligence in published statements about the plaintiff.

Other questions asked about each case were: Was the libelous statement about the plaintiff's public life, private life, or both? Was it true or was it false in the opinion of the court? Was it a factual statement or was it opinion? Did the defendant publish a retraction when requested or were plaintiffs given an opportunity for reply?

Finally, what outcomes followed from motions to dismiss, motions for summary judgment, trial court verdicts, and appellate court judgments? What was the final award, if any? What were the grounds for a final decision? How long did the case take and can its costs be estimated?

The initial coder, Melanie Grant, and the senior author reexamined all of the code sheets so as to reach 100 percent agreement on the coding. In addition, two second-year Columbia University law students were recruited to code a random sample of cases as a test of intercoder reliability. Their level of agreement or intercoder reliability on 1,920 items was 94.6 percent. Disagreements came most often on "author designation of plaintiff category" (public official, public figure, all-purpose public personality, etc.), and on the level of access to media available to plaintiff.

Because the judicial process is fluid, only a snapshot of cases in progress can be presented at any particular time. Although most of the 614 cases studied had reached final disposition, a few were pending at the trial level or at various stages of appeal. For this reason, we are sometimes dealing with slightly fewer than 614 cases. We report these cases, then, as we find them, trusting that our overall patterns are representative of what has happened in the courts. But, first, the major steps in the judicial process should be described:

SUMMARY JUDGMENT. If the case was dismissed on a "paper" review by a judge, then it was dismissed on a grant of summary judgment. The judge has decided that the plaintiff has no case in terms of the prevailing legal rules. If the judge felt a summary judgment was not in order, then the initial disposition would be "summary judgment denied." The case would then proceed to trial, or it would be settled, or otherwise neglected or lost in the court docket.

MOTION TO DISMISS. If the case is not dismissed summarily, the parties appear in court and present arguments. Depending on whether the judge thinks the evidence compelling or deficient, he either grants or denies the motion to dismiss. If the motion to dismiss is denied, the case moves on to the jury for further determination.

DIRECTED VERDICT. In the case of a directed verdict, a complete trial on the merits is held. After the evidence has been presented, but prior to submission of the case to the jury, the judge, considering all available evidence in the case, takes the case out of the jury's hands and reaches a final decision. But the evidence must be so compelling as to leave no doubt in the judge's mind about which party should prevail.

TRIAL BY JURY. Plaintiffs able to sustain the burden of proof may be given a jury verdict in their favor and an award of money damages. If not, the case is dismissed. No judgment is given to the defendant, but the defendant essentially "wins" the case.

APPEALS. Two types of appeals were coded: (1) appeals of summary judgments and motions to dismiss and (2) appeals of trial court decisions. Summary judgments and motions to dismiss could be affirmed, reversed, or reversed and remanded to the lower court for reconsideration. A money judgment, resulting from the trial by jury, could be affirmed, reduced (remittitur—a procedure by which an excessive jury award is reduced), completely reversed, or reversed and remanded.

Results

OUTCOMES. The number of libel cases per year remained fairly constant throughout the period studied, with no evidence of a dramatic increase in libel suits brought against the media. There was an unexplained twenty-case decline between 1982 and 1983 followed by a quick recovery in numbers in 1984, which was sustained throughout the remainder of the period studied. Remember, these are only libel cases involving media defendants, as reported in the *Media Law Reporter*. The figures follow:

1982	98 cases	16% of total
1983	78	12.7
1984	85	13.8
1985	86	14.0
1986	87	14.2
1987	83	13.5
1988	97	15.8
Total	614	100%

Media win more than four of five libel cases brought against them (see Fig. 1 for details). Aggregating motions to dismiss, summary judgments and jury trials, and looking at cumulative trends of defendant "wins," defendants won at those points in the judicial process 77.9 percent of the time, plaintiffs 22.1 percent. First appeals were decided in favor of defendants in 79.2 percent of cases, 20.8 percent of cases in favor of plaintiffs. Second appeals went 81.5 percent in favor of defendants, 18.5 percent in favor of plaintiffs. Third appeals were 81 percent in defendants' favor, 18.7 percent in plaintiffs' favor.

In more than 30 percent of the cases courts held alleged defamatory publications privileged either as opinion or fair reports. More than 20 percent were found to show no evidence of actual malice.

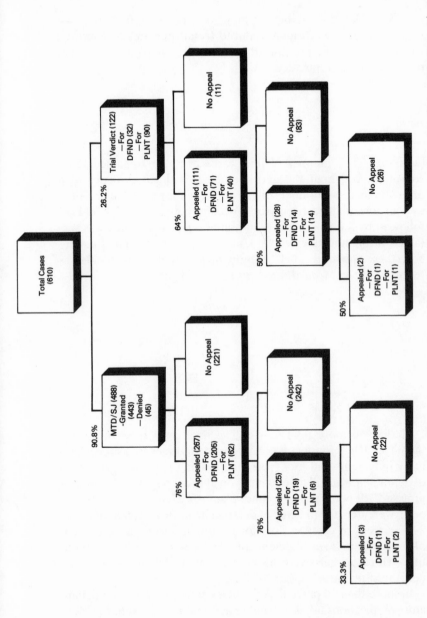

FIGURE 1. Outcome of media-related libel cases, 1982–1988. Total excludes four cases that were pending. MTD/SJ = Motion to dismiss/summary judgment. DFND = defendant. PLNT = plaintiff. Percentages on top of boxes indicate percentage

Another 10 percent were held nondefamatory. (For additional reasons for court action, see Appendix 1.)

Clearly, there is a certain degree of futility in a libel plaintiff suing for money damages. In only 33 of 614 cases were money damages eventually awarded. Of thirty-one cases for which there are dollar figures (no figures were reported for two) final awards ranged from $2,500 to $5,000,000 with a mean average payment of $504,000.

Media won 90.8 percent of the cases decided by summary judgment or motions to dismiss. When these were appealed, as they were in 267 of 488 cases, the next level of court upheld the defendant in 76.8 percent of cases. When twenty-five of those were appealed to a still higher court level, 76 percent of outcomes were in favor of defendant. Final appeals made in three cases resulted in two rulings in favor of plaintiffs, one in favor of defendant. So far, then, it is pretty much of a defendant's game. The two rulings in favor of plaintiffs at the highest court level could suggest that under current legal rules their cases were strong ones to begin with. Few cases decided by summary judgment or motions to dismiss go beyond the first level of appeal—only 25 of 267 in this study.

While media win most of the cases decided by summary judgment or motions to dismiss, they are much less likely to win if the case goes to trial.

Of the 122 libel cases that went to trial, media defendants were successful only 26.2 percent of the time. But when judge or jury verdicts were appealed the picture for defendants brightened considerably. Of 111 cases that went to the first level of appeal, 64 percent were decided in favor of the defendant. When twenty-eight of these were appealed to a higher level, 50 percent were still decided in favor of the defendant. And, in the two cases that went to the final court of appeal, one was decided in the plaintiff's favor, one in the defendant's favor, for another 50 percent split.

Of the ninety cases in this study where plaintiff won at trial, eighty-six were appealed. Only thirty-five were upheld on appeal, sixteen with remittiturs. When fifteen of these thirty-five were appealed to the next judicial level by defendants, seven more were overturned. A third appeal led to one reversal in favor of the plaintiff. Few cases get this far. Weak cases get weeded out in pretrial stages.

It might be assumed from these figures that jurors are more hostile to the media than judges. Some public opinion data would suggest that this is true. Or conversely, it could be argued that jurors are able to empathize more easily with individuals who feel wronged by institutions such as news organizations, some of which are powerful and influential. Those cases that go beyond the first level of appeal following jury verdicts were probably, under the rules of libel, strong cases to begin with, and to some extent follow the same patterns as those cases in which summary judgments and motions to dismiss are appealed.

LIBEL DIMENSIONS. *Injury* to plaintiff was identified in 324 or 52.8 percent of cases. Injury to reputation was claimed in nearly 65 percent of these cases, with injury claims to business, status, or some combination of reputation, business, and status making up most of the remainder. As for wins or losses depending on types of injury, no discernible pattern emerged (Appendix 2).

Public elements of a plaintiff's life were involved in the overwhelming majority of libel cases, 520 of 604 in this study. In only seventy-seven cases did the publication affect the purely *private* aspects of the plaintiff's life. Defendants won 82.3 percent of the time when public dimensions were at issue, 76.6 percent of the time when purely private dimensions were at issue (Appendix 3), suggesting perhaps that courts and juries are not applying the courts' own bright-line distinction between public and private lives.

Actual malice was addressed in 339 of the 614 cases studied as a motivation for injury to plaintiff. It was found in only thirty-one or 9 percent of cases. However, plaintiffs were much more likely to win in cases where actual malice was found in contrast to those in which no actual malice was found (81 percent versus 6 percent; see Appendix 4). Still, only 19 of 381 court-designated "public" plaintiffs (all categories) were able to prove actual malice sufficient for awards of money damages.

Fifteen of 166 "private" plaintiffs won money damages. Eight of these, following the rule of *Gertz* v. *Robert Welch* with respect to private persons, had only to prove negligence or some variation of that standard to make their cases. But seven of the fifteen, because they were involved in a public issue, also had to prove actual malice, the same standard of proof imposed by the Court upon public–person plaintiffs. The public nature of the case requires a higher level of fault. That rule was set down by the Supreme Court in *Dun & Bradstreet* v. *Greenmoss Builders*, a case decided a decade after *Gertz*. See p. 88.

Negligence was considered in only 79 of the 614 cases, but in the sixteen cases where it was found plaintiffs won in twelve cases or 75 percent of the time as compared with their winning in only 5 percent of cases where no negligence was found (Appendix 5).

Actual malice and negligence are often mutually exclusive factors in libel litigation. If actual malice is at issue, negligence generally will not be considered. Conversely, if negligence is at issue, actual malice will generally not be considered. Under current rules private plaintiffs will have to prove actual malice if they are seeking punitive damages or the defamatory publication grows out of a controversial issue of public importance.

In cases where neither issue of fault was considered, other factors took the spotlight. Suits could be dismissed on a number of grounds before the question of fault (negligence or actual malice) was reached. Such grounds might include lack of defamation, no identification of the persons suing, obvious truth of the publication, a privileged publication, neutral reportage, or a nonactionable opinion. It ought to be remembered that a skillful defendant's attorney will call upon every relevant defense in a libel suit. There will be complex interactions among these defenses that our tables do not reference but which future research might examine.

Opinion turned out to be a sterling defense in this study. In the 133 cases in which the claimed defamation took the form of an opinion, defendants won 97 percent of the time. Where the defamation was stated in factual terms, defendants won only 77.2 percent of the time. It could be argued that these figures suggest the traditional common law defense of "fair comment and criticism" still governs this area of the law or that the more newly defined "opinion" defense was beginning to take effect in the period of the study (Appendix 6). The opinion defense, as shall be noted, has since become clouded.

Truth or falsehood turned out to be an issue in 423 of the cases. When defamatory statements were adjudged true, defendants won their cases 90.1 percent of the time. On the other hand, when defamatory statements were believed to be false, defendants won only 76.2 percent of the time. Nearly 80 percent of these cases dealt with falsities presented as fact (Appendix 7).

In the few cases where the courts attempted to distinguish between true and false opinions—a distinction that the *Gertz* Court sought to do away with in 1974—only confusion resulted. *Gertz* held that there could be no such thing as a false opinion. An opinion as such could never be true or false.

In a 1990 case, the Supreme Court elected to go back to the earlier rule: an opinion would *not* be protected if it were based on a false fact.[397] At the same time, the Court did away with the idea of a separate constitutional privilege for "opinion." The First Amendment, it said, already protected statements of pure opinion. So confusion persists as to the distinction between "pure" and "adulterated" opinion. Perhaps now only the wildest and most hyperbolic statements will qualify as "pure" opinion. If a statement implies or asserts a verifiable or partially verifiable fact, it may not qualify as opinion.

Influence in one's social setting and *access* to the major organs of public opinion appear to be interconnected. Most public officials and all-purpose public personalities (celebrities) have high or medium access to the media and the same levels of influence in their communities be they local, regional, or national. Influence and access, at whatever level, go together. Influence—one's fixed place in the social hierarchy—would seem to be the dominant variable.

Surprisingly, perhaps, media defendants win a significantly greater number of cases against plaintiffs low in both influence and access than against those ranking high or medium on both counts. One would expect that as plaintiffs approached the private person classification and had only negligence to prove in their libel suits their ratio of wins over losses would improve. Just the opposite occurred in this study. Twenty-two percent of high influence/access plaintiffs won their cases; only 15 percent of low influence/access plaintiffs won their cases (Appendix 8).*

---

*Although influence and media access are highly interrelated, they reflect different concepts. Therefore, we are presenting separate tables that show the relationship between winners and influence and winners and media access.

Two explanations are possible. High influence/access plaintiffs may bring suits better grounded in the law and generating more sympathy on the part of the public. And they have greater access to resources, including better legal counsel.

Retractions, on the surface, seem to do considerably more harm than good to defendants. While there were only seventeen retractions recorded in all the cases studied, defendants when they did retract won 58.8 percent of their cases. When they didn't retract they won 81.9 percent of their cases. One explanation for this may be that retractions were made when the publisher already felt himself or herself in dire jeopardy because of an obviously gross and defamatory inaccuracy that might herald a losing case. In those states that limit or deny punitive and/or general damages when a retraction is made, retraction is still a good policy. And often it is the right thing to do (Appendix 9).

Reply opportunities in this study occurred only twice so that no conclusions can be drawn about their effects. This study proposes, however, that such opportunities be regularly made available by editors and publishers to policymakers and celebrities who have been attacked in print or on the air and who request an opportunity to respond.

DEFENDANTS. *Media* were classified large, medium, or small according to specific audience criteria (Appendix 10). Although two-thirds of libel suits are brought against media with large audiences (large newspapers, television stations, and magazines), audience size appeared unrelated to libel case outcomes (Appendix 11). What was apparent from the study is that newspapers bear the major burden of libel litigation, accounting for 60 percent of all cases (Appendix 12). Television and magazines followed with 15 percent and 13.7 percent of cases, respectively. Books, wire services, radio, pamphlets, and journals constituted the remaining 11 percent. (Suits brought against more than one medium are counted more than once.) These figures are remarkably similar to figures from earlier studies.[398]

A closer analysis of media defendants shows that book publishers, followed by wire services and newspapers, are more likely to win libel cases brought against them than are broadcasters. Magazines are somewhere in between. The perceived impact and dramatic, even fixating, qualities of television may account for this as against the traditional and more measured authority of print. Yet, radio fares less well than television, and the spoken word predates even print as a traditional means of communication. One might also have believed that the permanence of print would make that form of defamation more serious in the public mind. Along with the perceived power of the broadcast media, their less serious and primary entertainment function may account for the lesser protection they receive in the court system.

Overall, the press (all print media) win 83.4 percent of their cases compared with 71.8 percent for the broadcast media (Appendix 12).

PLAINTIFF DESIGNATION (AUTHOR–COURT DISAGREEMENT). In only two-thirds of cases did the authors agree with the courts' designation of libel plaintiffs (Appendix 13). No principles guiding the courts in making judgments on whether plaintiffs were public officials, public figures, or private persons could be discerned. For examples of this disagreement, the courts designated 166 plaintiffs as private persons, the authors only 117. The authors designated 164 plaintiffs "public officials," the courts only 139. The courts designated only one plaintiff an "all-purpose public personality"— their own classification—while the authors felt that forty-four, six of them winning plaintiffs, fit the category.

Among people and organizations denied celebrity or pervasive public figure status by the courts were Liberty Lobby, the Populist and Socialist Workers parties, the Irish National Caucus, Howard Hunt of Watergate fame, Roy Innis of the Congress of Racial Equality, Jerry Falwell, feminist author Andrea Dworkin, Wayne Newton, Martha Raye, Donald Trump, Dr. Amar Bose, inventor of a line of loudspeaker, Lillian Hellman, Willi Pep, a championship boxer of yesteryear, the New York Yankees, a talk show host, a television commentator, a newspaper publisher, *Billboard* magazine, and a major tobacco company. They may be either voluntary or involuntary public figures in the court's judgment, but they are something more than that given their fame, their access to communication channels, their pursuit of public approval, and their likely influence.

This difference in judgment on classification is central to this study. As long as courts make public people private and very public people only moderately public in libel litigation, the purposes of the *New York Times* doctrine will never be realized, especially when those public people are policymakers and celebrity trendsetters. Candidates for public office and former officeholders must be included in the public category in light of any doctrine of political participation. Former elected officials retain and exercise political power, and they are not without access to the media. Judges generally deny public official status to candidates for office and former officeholders. Public officials and public employees accounted for approximately one third of all plaintiffs in this study, and in earlier studies. Not all public employees in our study functioned at policymaking levels, however, and would therefore not be denied a libel remedy.

A number of plaintiffs labeled "professional," "business owners or managers," and "media related" in the Franklin and Iowa studies were part of the 7.2 percent of plaintiffs the Gillmor–Grant study called "all-purpose public personality" or "celebrity."

TIME. The table in Appendix 14 illustrates the time taken to reach final judgments in the cases studied. These cases are "final" in the sense that the last filed opinion (as of March 1990) was read. If appeals were pending and later took place, the table does not include them. Time to resolve disputes could be determined in only 427 of the 614 total cases.

A majority of cases (59.2 percent) take three or fewer years to complete; 38.7 percent take four to nine years to complete; 2.2 percent take more than nine years to complete. Cases that took only a year to resolve were generally not appealed. But many of the cases, provided the statute of limitations has not run, reappear in the courts on appeal.

STATE AND FEDERAL COURTS. Plaintiffs do somewhat better in federal courts than they do in state courts, winning 21.5 percent and 17.6 percent of cases, respectively (Appendix 15). This may be a function of state laws, no two of which are alike. It could also mean that federal courts, as they must, hew more closely to the constitutional rules laid down for libel by the Supreme Court when applying state law. Increasingly, those rules may tend to favor plaintiffs, although that is a difficult judgment to make and is certainly not supported by the data in this study.

LIBEL AND THE STATES. There are two ways of looking at states in terms of libel litigation. In a structural analysis one would expect that with increased population, especially when that population is concentrated in big cities, comes greater pluralism, social sophistication, and formal interaction. Social complexity means increased use of legal-rational methods in resolving disputes. Thus, the libel suit takes the place of such informal methods as the fist fight or the handshake in the corner coffee shop, which are more typical of traditional communities.

A second approach would be to report the number of libel cases the way crime statistics are reported, rate per million population, for example. This controls for population size and is more sensitive to the specific laws and judicial practices of a state.

Using the first approach, a correlation analysis shows that state population is strongly related to the number of libel cases in that state.[399] In other words, the number of libel cases in a state is in almost direct proportion to the population of the state.

In an attempt to identify states that have more or fewer libel cases than one would expect given the population, a least-squares regression line was plotted between population and number of libel cases. Those states lying farthest from the regression line represent those that have either fewer or more libel cases than expected given population size. It is interesting to speculate about those states that don't quite fit the model.

States that have *more* libel cases than one would expect given their population and using this analysis are New York, Florida, Illinois, Michigan, and the District of Columbia, all of which are extremely diverse and structurally pluralistic. Of course, many other factors besides population would predict the number of libel suits in those states. For example, New York, with 102 of the 614 cases in the period studied and an estimated 1987 population of nearly 18 million, is one of the publishing capitals, if not the publishing capital, of the world. New York City, with nearly half the State's population and most of its publishing houses, also has at least four aggressive daily newspapers. Chicago may account for Illinois being on the high side of the ledger with thirty-six cases. Do Miami and Detroit account for Florida and Michigan with thirty-seven and thirty cases respectively? It is not clear. Washington, D. C. is also a publishing center and one that affects a number of surrounding states that function as suburbs of the Cap-

ital. The District's population itself is only 622,000; yet a dispro-
portionate nineteen libel cases were counted in the period studied.
Washington, D. C. also experiences probing journalism.

States that had *fewer* libel cases than one would expect from
their populations were California with nearly 28 million people
and only forty-three libel cases, and Texas, Pennsylvania, Virginia,
North Carolina, Indiana, Tennessee, and Wisconsin. All have concentrated urban areas. In terms of volume and diversity of publication these states may lack the "sophistication" of a New York,
Washington, D. C., or Chicago, although it would be difficult to
defend that proposition against a Los Angeles, San Francisco, or
Philadelphia. California's ranking is particularly interesting. The
relatively low number of libel cases in the period studied (forty-
three) may be a function of the state's large and lately formed
minority population, not yet fully attuned to the American legal
tradition. It may also have to do with the entertainment industry
and its long tradition of open, original, and sometimes perverse
communication.

Pennsylvania's relatively "good" ranking, using this mode of
analysis, is also surprising given the "bad press" the state has had
recently in media law circles because of huge jury awards in libel
cases.

It may be noted that states, such as Massachusetts, Washington,
and Oregon, which prohibit the awarding of punitive damages,
gain no particular advantages for media defendants. Nor does
Michigan, a state that has generally been unsympathetic to punitive
damages.

Using the second method of analysis—rate per million population—the overall picture changes very little. The high and low
states for the most part maintain their relative positions. What is
surprising is the even more dramatic ranking of Alaska and Hawaii
(Fig. 2). A large proportion of the population of both states does
reside in the cities of Anchorage and Honolulu. Formal methods
of resolving disputes would therefore be appropriate.

These data lend themselves to various interpretations. Clearly
some state laws either make it easier to bring libel suits against
the media with some promise of success or encourage litigation in
other ways. The quality or alertness of the media bar in a state
may be another factor in either an overabundance of or an infre-
quency in libel suits.

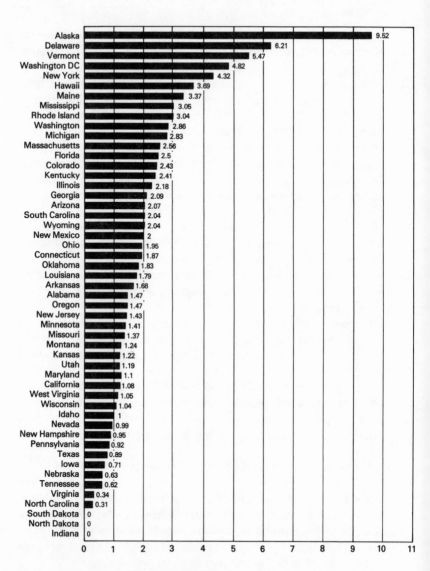

FIGURE 2. Number of libel suits filed against media in state courts from 1982–1988 (per one million residents).

Insert figure 2

The social structure of a state, as has been suggested, may also bear an important relationship to the number of libel suits recorded. It would be interesting to examine further the high ranking of both Alaska and Hawaii in libel litigation. Alaska, America's last frontier, may not fit the mold of the complex urban society. Are Alaskans more litigious than other Americans? Could this be part of an "isolation" syndrome?

And what accounts for Delaware, Vermont, Maine, and Mississippi ranking so high in libel litigation while Texas, Tennessee, Virginia, and North Carolina occupy the bottom of the scale? The New England and Northeast corridor states generally have long and mature judicial traditions that would encourage use of the courts in resolving disputes. But what about Mississippi? Obviously, urban sophistication doesn't explain all of these differences.

It is possible that the journalistic aggressiveness and enterprise of a state's newspapers and broadcast stations may account in part for that state's ranking in libel litigation. Since most lawsuits of this kind are brought against newspapers, it would be worthwhile to investigate the journalistic performance of newspapers in those states with both high and low rates of libel litigation.

Do newspapers unresponsive to political shenanigans characterize those states with little libel litigation? Certainly Texas and Pennsylvania, both low in ranking, don't support that proposition. Or do the low ranking states enjoy relatively clean state governance that simply does not elicit vigorous newspaper probes? Iowa, Nebraska, and North and South Dakota may indeed fit that model. But all of these explanations are partial explanations at best. All that has been demonstrated here is that population and the number of libel suits in a state are related.

The findings of this study are consistent with those of earlier studies, where the data are comparable. And they tend to support the central proposal of this study: An immunity for media from libel suits brought by policy-level public officials and celebrities in exchange for an opportunity to reply when the matter at issue warrants and the editor agrees. Public officials, especially, are suing newspapers with very little promise of success, or, perhaps, no expectation of success. Of the 33 of 614 cases in which plaintiff won money damages, nineteen losing defendants were newspapers,

nine large in size, four medium in size, and six small in size.
Similarly, of the five magazines that lost libel suits, one was small.
It is the smaller publications we ought to be most concerned about.

Of nine plaintiffs designated by the author as "public officials"
and awarded money damages two were gubernatorial candidates,
two deputy sheriffs, one a police officer, one a sitting judge, one
a judicial candidate, one a former U.S. attorney, one a borough
council president, and one a member of a state optometry board
(a second gubernatorial candidate was added to the original list of
nine, upon a rereading of the cases, making a "public officials"
list of ten). Four of the nine "public official" plaintiffs had high
influence and access to media in their spheres of activity. The "all-
purpose public personality" plaintiffs awarded money damages
were entertainers Wayne Newton and Carol Burnett, a major tobacco company, the National Broadcasting Company, Elmer Gertz
(a prominent lawyer and social and political activist), and a Baltimore television commentator. All six "public personality" plaintiffs had high influence and extraordinarily high access to mass
media in their particular domains.

The turnabout NBC case resulted from a counterclaim against
political personality Lyndon H. LaRouche, Jr., after he had sued
the network for libel and conspiracy. NBC convinced a jury that
LaRouche had interfered with the network's attempt to gather
news. An award of $200,000 was affirmed by the 4th Circuit Court
of Appeals.[400] Dennis Holly, a television news commentator, sued
a local radio show host and his employer for broadcasting a "joke"
about Holly that could have been interpreted by listeners as suggesting that Holly was among looters following a Baltimore bliz-
zard. A $65,000 award in compensatory and punitive damages was
upheld against the offending disc jockey and the radio station.[401]

Under my proposal none of the above plaintiffs would find a
remedy in libel law given their political and social status, their
levels of influence, and their opportunities for "more speech" to
correct inaccuracies and false impressions.

Of the 339 cases in which actual malice was considered it was
found in only thirty-one or 9.1 percent of cases, approximately the
number of cases in which monetary judgments were awarded. A
minuscule number of public officials, therefore, win libel suits, yet
they constitute a substantial percentage of all libel plaintiffs. It is

this revival of punishment for sedition in the guise of civil libel that *New York Times* v. *Sullivan* meant to suppress and failed to do so in 1964, and that this proposal attempts to remedy. Furthermore, most cases involving public officials and the press have to do with the plaintiff's public life, plaintiffs who in more than half the cases have high access to media and high influence in their social settings.

While many of these suits end in summary judgment, defendants nevertheless must spend large sums of money and expend valuable time in getting that far and beyond in defending against suits of very little legal merit, time that could be better used informing the public. Of those cases involving public officials that did go to trial, and from there to appeal, only 10 of 164 plaintiffs were ultimately victorious. The comparable figure for author-designated celebrities was six of forty-four. Ordinary public figures and, of course, private persons would be unaffected by my proposal. There would be approximately one-third fewer libel cases, many of them by far the most expensive and time-consuming examples of the genre.

Perhaps it could be argued that for an outraged plaintiff these odds still make it tempting to sue, and there is evidence in the Iowa Study that many plaintiffs do sue out of anger. But where the chances of public plaintiff victory are so slim, it would seem reasonable to focus attention on another dimension or the other end of the problem and that is the discretionary opportunity for reply, a resolution that would benefit through "more speech" a much larger segment of the American public than the litigation bar that at present seems the only beneficiary of frequent and protracted libel cases.

David Anderson has suggested that anything less than an absolute privilege would fail speech requiring constitutional protection. *New York Times* and its *Gertz* modifications tempt self-censorship because they give no protection "until both parties have incurred the full expense of trial, and often of appeal as well."[402] There may be insurmountable barriers to *successful* libel suits brought by public officials or candidates for public office, but there are no barriers to suits being initiated.

"[I]n the past few years," wrote Judge Robert Bork, concurring in *Ollman* v. *Evans*, "a remarkable upsurge in libel actions, accompanied by a startling inflation of damage awards, has threatened to impose self-censorship on the press which can as effectively inhibit debate and criticism as would overt governmental regulation that the first amendment most certainly would not permit."[403] Bork saw damage awards as "quite capable of silencing political commentators forever."

In his *Brief for the Petitioner* in *New York Times* v. *Sullivan*, Herbert Wechsler may also have had self-censorship in mind when he wrote,

> [W]e contend that an expression which is critical of governmental conduct is within the "core of constitutional freedom" and may not be prohibited directly to protect the reputation of the government or its officials. A threat to such reputation is intrinsic to the function of such criticism. It is not, therefore, a "substantive evil" that a State has power to prevent by the suppression of the critical expression; nor does the protection of such reputation provide one of those "conflicting governmental interests" with which the protected freedom must "be reconciled" or to which it may validly be made to yield.[404]

While rejecting the concept of a libel-proof plaintiff, one presumably ranking high in the governmental hierarchy, Marc Franklin, perhaps ruefully, asks the question:

> In the face of determined and successful legal resistance from defendants, might a state conclude that the efforts expended in this area were nonproductive—and *abolish* or stringently restrict the (libel) action [emphasis added]?[405]

Problems of federalism may be one reason why the Court was not prepared to adopt the theory of Black, Douglas, and Goldberg in *New York Times*. An absolute privilege or a category of libel-proof plaintiff would have deranged the common law of most states. Unfortunately for my proposal, the Court is much more states-oriented now than it was in 1964.

From a journalistic perspective "the question these days is not so much will we win or will we lose, but rather, will we go to trial? That becomes an issue because of the time that it takes to deal with depositions and with preparing for testimony," says Norman Pearlstine, executive editor of the *Wall Street Journal*. Understandably concerned about costs, he defines "public official" by assessing power and the responsibility for its exercise. Corporate executives are therefore "public officials" in his view.[406] By analogy so are newspaper publishers and their editors. I have used the word "celebrity" to represent the courts' category of pervasive public personality, those persons whose power and place in their own and often national circles are never in doubt.

And this brings me back to the proposal itself: a structural change in the law of libel that would immunize media from libel actions brought by those prospective plaintiffs who occupy the political and cultural power centers of modern society.

The proposal recalls Chief Justice Warren's observation, concurring in *Curtis Publishing* v. *Butts*, that distinctions between governmental and private sectors are increasingly blurred and "many who do not hold public power at the moment are nevertheless intimately involved in the resolution of important public questions, or by reason of their fame, shape events of concern to society at large."[407] This could mean that unknown letter carriers and misidentified shoplifters[408] will always have a cause of action while generals, prominent attorneys and television and film stars will not. One dares not predict under the Court's present pragmatic approach who will or will not be designated a public person.

It will sometimes require a painstaking effort to identify those who occupy those impregnable positions, especially those at the margins of power, but it will be less difficult and less intrusive on First Amendment interests than the courts' dependence on unprincipled judgments as to what publications are or are not socially valuable or true or false, or judgments requiring the pursuit of evidence of fault by intuitive investigations into the motivations, intentions or professional standards of those who collect, edit, and present public information.

Pearlstine takes an additional step, however, that I cannot take with him, but it does lead to the concluding concern of this work. He calls for a "compelled or mandated letter to the editor . . . or a bulletin board function in publications where a person who feels aggrieved could get equal space to write his or her own side." Since there is concern about damage to reputation, Pearlstine asks, why not a forum for reply outside of the legal system?[409] The Minnesota News Council provides such a forum—as did the National News Council before its unfortunate demise in 1984—but wouldn't the public be more involved if the media themselves performed this function? Yes, but it must be voluntary.

The media appear egregiously unprepared to provide opportunities for reply to damaging attacks in their columns. The counterpoint proposal of this paper—and perhaps it is naive—is that this be done voluntarily and in the interest of a broader social dialogue. This would diminish the threat of libel suits being used as an excuse for less than aggressive coverage of corruption and moral nihilism in government, a creeping paralysis in American journalism that does no honor to the heroic journalism of a revolutionary past.

9

Accountability

The Reply Mechanism

In the April 13, 1782, issue of his Philadelphia newspaper, the *Independent Gazetteer*, Eleazer Oswald, terror of the Federalists, wrote:

> When a Charge or other Matter, affecting the Character of any private person, is exhibited thro' the Press, there is an implied Obligation upon the Printer, to admit the Person to an equal Liberty in his Vindication.

Oswald seemed to be suggesting that editors provide an opportunity for reply to those who feel wronged—a central tenet of this book: that, where possible, public persons use the media for response and rebuttal—the press conference, the op-ed page, the television studio, for example—and, where this is not possible, media demonstrate their commitment to a public dialogue by making their facilities available to those they have hurt when the facts, the harm done, and the issue of disagreement warrant.

Whether Oswald meant to extend the same courtesy to public persons remains unknown; his editorial thunder elsewhere suggests otherwise. If we take him and Justice William Brennan, whose views on the question follow, at their word, they did not intend to indulge public people. My proposal would accommodate what public people have to say when, in a responsible editor's judgment, what they have to say is important and will contribute to reasoned or even unreasonable public discourse.

While these are pleas for voluntary extensions of a right of reply, many would join Pearlstine in making them mandatory. George Washington University law professor Jerome Barron, advocate of Florida's right of reply statute before the U.S. Supreme Court in

Miami Herald v. *Tornillo*,[410] insists on compulsory publication of what he calls "declarations of truth," controlled by complainants.[411]

Barron's demand is based on a number of questionable assumptions. One is that people who make the news—public officials and celebrities—sue because they don't have access to the mass media. While they may not always be able to compose their own copy, what they say to or about the media generally gets published or broadcast. A second is that a legally mandated right of reply would enhance the public dialogue. At one point Barron writes,

> While a right of reply to defamation may restrict the information flow, the ultimate result for the opinion process may still be beneficial. The result would be to have somewhat fewer original communications by the press, with this loss offset by the fact that those stories that were published could be tested by their subjects and would therefore be of much higher informational value.[412]

Journalists, members of a semiprofession by choice, are no more likely to turn over the controls of their institutions to lawyers and legislators than lawyers and legislators are to relinquish supervision of their courtrooms and assembly halls to reporters, anchorwomen, and cameramen. Although a mandatory postpublication right of reply might accrue to the benefit of individual members of the public, those taking advantage of it would probably be closely coached by lawyers since a libel suit would often be an alternative.

Like many suggestions for reform, Barron's seems based on a misunderstanding of what have become the primary functions of the news media—information gathering and distribution. The opinion function, that is social discourse and public debate, and the concept of watchdog over the political process, functions that may not be well served by modern media, flow from this a priori information-providing role. Legislative or court imposed replies, limiting editorial discretion, would further clutter and confuse the public dialogue, providing much less time and space for news and public information. It would be like running a government by daily referenda, without opportunity for legislative or, in this case, editorial deliberation and coherence in the presentation of information. The newspaper might become forty-eight pages of letters-to-the-editor.

Barron's reliance on Justice William Brennan for support of a mandatory right of reply may also be misplaced, and, of course, it is now academic since Brennan has left the Court. While it is true that Brennan did imply in his opinion for the Court in *Rosenbloom*[413] that right of reply statutes might provide a solution, he did not put the proposition on a very firm constitutional foundation.

"If the States fear that private citizens will not be able to respond adequately to publicity involving them," Brennan wrote, "the solution lies in the direction of ensuring their ability to respond, rather than in stifling public discussion of matters of public concern."[414] In a footnote he observed that some states have adopted retraction or right-of-reply statutes, but he did not elaborate.[415]

Clearly Brennan's record does not suggest a similar "solution" for public officials or highly visible citizens. He did not heed Barron's call for constitutional validation of Florida's right-of-reply statute in *Tornillo* (the plaintiff was a labor leader) and, in a one-paragraph concurrence, seemed to be rejecting such statutes; but he left his mind open on the constitutionality of "mandatory" retraction laws.[416] Retraction laws in the thirty or so states that have enacted them, however, are arguably voluntary; Florida's right-of-reply law was not and this is the essential difference between reply and retraction.

Dissenting in *Gertz* v. *Robert Welch*, decided on the same day as *Tornillo*, Brennan threw no further light on his retraction proposition beyond footnote reiteration of his *Rosenbloom* reference to state statutes, private plaintiffs, and a 1967 *Harvard Law Review* "Note" that proposed either by federal law or judicial rule a mandatory "order of publication," or forced retraction or reply, for public officials wishing to answer press defamation.[417] A dissenting opinion by Brennan in *Dun & Bradstreet*,[418] to which Barron refers, added nothing more to Brennan's line of thought on the question.

Many will argue, with justification, that a right of reply dependent on editorial discretion is no right of reply at all. But it is all the Constitution will allow. A legal ultimatum—provide space or pay damages—will immediately interpose the Constitution and result inevitably in legal confrontation. A self-imposed ethical approach to redressing publication injury is the only practicable form of accountability. Other models falter because they come not from the heart but from the whip, when they pass constitutional muster at all.

Categories of Accountability

There are a number of ways of looking at the concept of accountability.

The *marketplace* model of accountability has a venerable history in providing a theoretical basis for freedom of expression, but it is based on assumptions about people and society that are no longer relevant or tenable. The big soap boxes in the marketplace are now occupied by powerful entrepreneurs. In modern dress, the model posits that a publisher's self-interest will inexorably coincide with the public interest. While still the dominant paradigm, it is a mistake to assume, as this model does, that the support of local readers, listeners, and viewers implies the support of the whole society or any large part of it for the media system as it has evolved. When the marketplace fails, it is assumed, as in Barron's proposal, that government will intervene to right the wrongs or correct imbalances. But it is a paradox of freedom of press that the very government the First Amendment would keep at a distance sometimes has been called in to assure that this freedom will flourish. Consider the antitrust laws, or reverse antitrust laws, such as the Newspaper Preservation Act, the Federal Communication Act, the Freedom of Information Act and its state counterparts, postal subsidies, and state statutes that permit cameras in courtrooms or allow reporters to keep confidential the identity of their sources.

The *litigational* model, as this study suggests, has failed in the area of libel because the law is so complex and confounding that lawyers, judges, and juries unwittingly assume the role of Chief High Editor of the American press. Accountability is thus imposed on the press in a process that is slow, expensive, and punitive, the rules confusing and sometimes contradictory, and the effects often chilling to free expression. And the public may be deprived of information because the media fail to retract, clarify, or apologize for fear of how those actions may be interpreted by juries and the courts in later litigation.

The *fiduciary* model makes government agencies direct arbiters of protected speech and media responsibility, and although not as ominous or draconian as libertarians would have one believe, practitioners will continue to resist it; and it is difficult to rationalize with most First Amendment theories. Did the Fairness Doctrine, for example, serve the cause of free speech or did it persuade broadcasters to avoid controversial issues of public importance for fear of becoming caught in a regulatory spider's web?

The *voluntary* model requires sustained citizen involvement and the citizenry doesn't always choose to be involved; and some practitioners reject evaluation and judgment by outsiders. An example is the resistance to the National News Council by major elements of the American press and broadcast media, including the *New York Times* and *The Washington Post*. The Minnesota News Council, predating its national counterpart by three years, remains the only even slightly viable experiment of its kind in the land. Minnesota's Council was fashioned after the British Press Council, which, in 1991, was to be replaced by a Press Complaints Commission; some see this as a threatening first step toward a governmental regulatory system. Citizen groups, such as AIM (Accuracy in Media) and FAIR (Fairness and Accuracy in Reporting), representing political Right and Left, respectively, monitor and berate the media for bias. More detached organizations, such as ACT (Action for Children's Television), follow particular themes of media improvement to their seemingly futile conclusions. All are needed. All are important.

That leaves the *self-regulatory* model, a model that can be based on the proposition that, just as all rights are ultimately the rights of individual persons, ethics in the final analysis is a matter of the self, of personal choice.[419] Can the language of ethics become part of the language of the newsroom? Will ethical boundaries for that newsroom emerge from an ethical discourse that may or may not reflect a tenuous consensus on what is right or wrong in news gathering and presentation?

At least four additional questions arise. Can self-regulatory systems be imposed on individuals who comprise media organizations without vaporizing personal choice? Whose standards should prevail in the final analysis: those of the collective or those of the unconvinced individual? And will the newsroom ever be allowed ethical autonomy by the top managements of these hierarchical organizations? If these ethical systems can somehow function organizationally, will that serve to open the channels of mass communication to those who deserve to be heard?

Self-regulation may also include internal codes, correction mechanisms, ombudsmen, and external criticism by peers through journalism reviews because the functions of all are generally carried out by people in the field. The more fundamental question underlying all of those above is: to what extent can the journalist, who is part of complex news organization with its own rules, routines and rituals, still retain ethical independence inside and outside of that organization and influence the organization toward higher ethical standards?

University of Illinois professor Clifford Christians, in his clarion call for enforceable codes of ethics, assumes that the press' guaranteed right to disseminate information carries with it an obligation to be competent and responsible. Neither the Constitution nor the American tradition of a raucous and irresponsible press support such an assumption, although more consensual and higher standards of reponsibility are emerging and may be pushing the media toward higher levels of professional performance. Nevertheless, it is not difficult to agree with Christians that codes, whether written or unwritten, "aid in stimulating the moral imagination."[420]

We dare not shuffle along in an ethical darkness. There must be standards for there to be civilization; first, standards based on respect and compassion for individual persons and on accuracy and fairness to whatever extent they are possible; and, second, a concern for the public interest, however that interest may be defined in the complex of situations one might anticipate. For example, when do the benefits to the public outweigh damage to a person's reputation? When media wound in pursuit of a public interest, they should be willing, at least in some circumstances, to dress the wound, provide the bandages, and pay for the treatment. Treatment could take the form of an opportunity to reply at the discretion of an editor, but in the words of the defamed, unless editing with the consent of the writer would improve the message. A reply, something more than a letter-to-the-editor, ought to be given the prominence of the original allegation, whatever form it has taken. This is especially important when a reputation has been savaged.

It does not seem possible that media codes, whether stipulating opportunities for reply or not, can be written or enforced beyond the level of individual newsrooms, and even at that level there can be problems. Professional association, industry-wide, or even corporate codes (some of which are merely management directives) too easily find their way into desk drawers and do not get the attention they deserve toward improving media ethics. There are a hundred of them and they simply get lost in the daily rush of a newsroom. And their proponents, both in journalism and in the academy, provide no mechanisms for their observance. Associational codes, for example, the revised American Society of Newspaper Editors Code of 1975 and the revised Society of Professional Journalists Code of 1987, are too general to be of much use in unraveling day-to-day ethical tangles, although the latter does call for a right of reply to attacks on "reputation or moral character." In addition, it was decided shortly after the ASNE Code was first ratified in 1923 that it would not be enforceable. Ethical codes are rare in broadcast newsrooms; perhaps broadcasters see FCC policy statements as their guide to appropriate behavior. The Newspaper Guild prefers "work rules." Some media organizations demonstrate ethical sensitivity without written codes.

Newsroom codes, written or unwritten, developed out of dialogue and subject to continual reaffirmation within the newsroom, might be enforced. Editors could fire staff members who repeatedly refuse to honor ethical rules once taken seriously and agreed upon individually and collectively.

Christians dismisses the possibility that courts will use written standards of professional performance to measure liability in lawsuits. Yet that is precisely what happens, in a sense, every time a professional code is cited in a libel or privacy suit as evidence of malpractice.[421]

Attempts to enforce unwritten codes may conflict with fairness; different versions of a code may exist in the minds of those who have agreed to be governed by it. When journalists testify for or against colleagues in lawsuits involving the media they are generally expressing professional judgments as to what they would do or have done in similar circumstances with no particular written code in mind. These judgments emerge from personal values, principles, and professional experiences that may overlook unique features of a particular case. It might be asked whether it is ethical for reporters and editors to testify at all in these adversarial situations involving their peers, given the fact that they are generally paid for doing so.

While Christians seems anxious to avoid the deadening hand of "group think," he leaves us perplexed as to what he would do with renegades—he calls them "bandits"[422]—those perverse "lost souls" who constitute the minorities of one standing against the moral prescripts of the group. Perhaps he has the gossip and rumor tabloids in mind as examples of organizational bandits. What of individual bandits?

What if, after sustained, coherent, and unemotional discussion about media responsibilities to the community, I cannot agree that staging a photograph to convey graphically the complexity of a social event to the public is to be condemned as a deception? Could I be right in an ethical sense and everyone else wrong? This is the stuff of what Vincent Blasi, with reference to Louis Brandeis, calls "civic courage," only here in microcosm.

The Ethics of Hierarchy

When the chief editors of the two Twin Cities dailies, influenced by one another, decided to break a promise of confidentiality made to a news source by a senior reporter from each newspaper and identify the source in subsequent news stories, the two reporters were appalled. Their personal ethical canons had been violated. A jury subsequently awarded $700,000 in compensatory and punitive damages to the news source for breach of contract and loss of employment. And a divided court of appeals affirmed the compensatory damages part of the award.

The source, a former public official and consultant to a losing gubernatorial campaign, had sought to reverse what appeared to be a negative voting trend by the dramatic disclosure of a twelve-year-old shoplifting charge against a woman who would become the winning candidate for lieutenant governor, a charge that long since had been expunged from the record. The Minnesota Supreme Court eventually agreed with the newspapers that contract obligations did not apply where sources are promised confidentiality and that the First Amendment outweighed such promises anyway.[423] Debate over the case continues and many journalists and media attorneys are quite convinced that the editors, in the absence of any well-understood and agreed-upon newsroom policy, made the wrong decision both ethically and legally. As the state supreme court noted, "Both sides proclaim their own purity of intentions while condemning the other side for 'dirty tricks.' " The U.S. Supreme Court later reversed and remanded the case to the state supreme court on the grounds that the First Amendment does not protect the press from liability for damages under Minnesota's doctrine of promissory estoppel.[424] Reversing itself, the Minnesota court agreed.

Two other news organizations, The Associated Press and a major television station, made different ethical choices: the AP used the story without naming the source, and WCCO-TV, the Twin Cities CBS Station, elected not to use the story at all. In the case of the newspapers, principled newsroom "ethics" to cover this situation had not been developed, and the ethics of "hierarchy" prevailed.[425] Management's decision was the only decision that mattered.

We come back to the question. Can the ethics of the peer group, the workers, the individual reporter ever prevail? Newsrooms are examples of line organizations; power resides at the top. Even with newsroom personnel acting as devil's advocates, significant final decisions will remain at the top, as was the case with the Twin Cities newspapers. But group members, dialogically engaged individuals, can and must play a major role in discussing and developing ethical values and principles, in considering their consequences, and in disapproving of their breaches. Newspeople must develop sufficient ethical autonomy to be able to challenge their managements in specific cases, and have their way. There is a simplistic naivete about these declarations. Newsroom veterans will wonder how anyone could wander so far from reality. How do we get the tough guys who command and direct reporters and photographers to play the game of ethics by any rules but their own?

It is time for all teachers of journalism to put media managers on notice that the journalists they train—perhaps 60 percent of neophyte newsroom employees—will be ethically sensitive and ethically imaginative, will look for ethical dialogue in the newsroom, and will expect some freedom and autonomy in making ethical decisions critical to their own values and principles. One

162   *Power, Publicity, and the Abuse of Libel Law*

of these values could be a commitment to the accommodation of dialogue on significant issues of political and cultural policy, especially where public officials and celebrities have been attacked for their views by the media. It is time for journalism educators to present a united front to the media industry in calling for ethical discourse, debate and, yes, agonizing in the newsrooms of America.

Scoops, prizes (of which there are far too many in American journalism), or vengeful cynicism will no longer be sufficient reasons for ignoring humaneness and fairness in gathering and presenting the news. New media employees will be equipped to confront traditional norms and practices critically and with clear-cut arguments for when and where to draw the line. Our students would come equipped with the newest in ethical weaponry and they would be prepared to fight for what they believe is right. Journalism educators have it in their hands to develop new generations of ethically alert and alive practitioners.

Stanford University media ethicist Theodore Glasser would go a step farther: he would involve the "strangers" media serve, presumably members of the mass audience or the community, in ethical decision making. Following Robert Veatch's medical ethics paradigm, a "triple contract,"[426] Glasser would expect the larger community to join journalists and their subscribers in defining the limits of ethical tolerance in individual cases. To some small degree a news council could fulfill that function. But Glasser has something more formal and authoritative in mind.

It would of course be a challenge to decide who from the community, or the readership for that matter, would be representative, best informed, best qualified demographically or in terms of values, and interested in helping evolve the ethics of the organization. But it may be possible. Those professions certified by the state, law, medicine and accountancy, for example, presumably do involve the citizenry, indirectly at least, in setting down ethical boundaries; the state acts in the name of its citizens. Journalism would have to devise a non-governmental system of community input.

While there can be no doubt that the status of any calling depends in part on what the community confers and that a code of ethics cannot safely be formulated by a profession isolated from its community, collectivist solutions based on Rousseauian notions of an organic General Will, such as Glasser's,[427] create a persistent suspicion, perhaps unjustified, that an "ethics authority" waits in the shadows to ensure compliance with what, however well-intentioned, could be either a majority, a powerful interest group, or the viewpoint of someone already in power. That authority can be and frequently has been in all too many cases the authority of the maximalist state.

Compelled ethics is not self-regulation. And in the unique case of journalism the Constitution has already taken some of the choice out of our hands by greatly limiting the role of the state in supervising or raising the ethical standards of speech and press. Systems of journalistic ethics could more safely be based on the Lockean ideal of a voluntary and revocable Social Contract.[428] Glasser's proposal could just as well proceed from that premise. Nevertheless, external controls on American journalism will always be a problem, no matter how sensible community involvement may be in aiding the press to find its ethical way.

"The ambiguities of journalism are too endemic and ineradicable, its domain too wide and infinitely varied," says James C. Thomson, Jr., former Nieman Curator at Harvard University. "Indeed, that domain is life itself—the endless contours of reality. What code can be written for such a special craft other than those of the philosophers and saints who have tried to teach men how to coexist."[429]

James Madison said much the same thing when in 1799 he wrote:

That this *liberty* is often carried to excess; that it has sometimes degenerated into licentiousness, is seen and lamented, but the remedy has not yet been discovered. Perhaps it is an evil inseparable from the good with which it is allied; perhaps it is a shoot which cannot be stripped from the stalk without wounding vitally the plant from which it is torn. However desirable those measures might be which might correct without enslaving the press, they have never yet been devised in America.[430]

This does not mean that individual journalists cannot be fair, accurate, and compassionate in their search for ethical principles and practices or that they cannot discuss the consequences of their newsroom decisions with others, but, more importantly, with their colleagues. Self-regulation must be centered in individual newsrooms and editorial offices. If communicators ignore these matters, the protections of the First Amendment may gradually be worn away like old mountains by the rain, and society, speaking through the state, will set down new rules for a game in which both press and society may be losers. Editors and news directors often proclaim that they are accountable only to their readers, viewers, and listeners. If this be so, then surely affording members of those groups an opportunity to talk back when they have been verbally attacked, justifiably or not, is the least that a self-regulatory system of accountability would require. Justice, humaneness, and the nuturing of the moral imagination, it seems, would require nothing less.

10

Conclusion

I have argued for First Amendment theories that enlarge and expand rather than diminish and contract the constitutional values of speech and press. Such theories follow logically from the unconditioned constitutional protection given speech and press and the Brandeisian principle of "more speech, not enforced silence."

Theories of freedom of expression must, in my view, focus on individual persons, the individual right to free expression, the individual value of reputation, and the individual sense of what is right or wrong. It is for this reason that no meaningful proposal for reform can work outside a system in which the right to speak, in protecting the value of reputation, can be accommodated not only for those who own print media and manage broadcast frequencies but for all those persons at decision-making and agenda-setting levels who choose to participate in a public dialogue, a dialogue that can sometimes become harsh, critical, and error ridden.

Libel laws have become complicated almost beyond human comprehension. The result has been a plethora of lawsuits in which the only clear winners generally are lawyers, many of whom in my experience have only vague notions as to how libel law works. Judges have developed no principled way that can be detected for deciding who is or is not an influential public plaintiff. The categories of public official, public figure, and private person in the hands of the courts have been elastic and imprecise.

My categories of public official and what courts have called pervasive public personalities (celebrities) are limited to people of influence who generally have access to the media of mass communication. Common sense criteria should be applied to designate those who set and carry out our political and social agendas. Marginal plaintiffs should be given every benefit of the doubt so as to retain access to libel laws as limited purpose public figures or private persons. Into which category, for example, should a high school wrestling coach be placed?

A libel case involving high school wrestling coach Michael Milkovich and the Willoughby, Ohio, *News-Herald* began in 1975 and was not resolved until 1990. The newspaper had alleged that Milkovich and the school's superintendent had lied under oath about a fight at a wrestling match. While the superintendent was clearly an influential public official, the status of the coach was less obvious. A public employee? Yes. A public figure? Yes—a ruling of the Ohio Supreme Court on both questions notwithstanding.[431] Highly visible in his community? Yes. Access to media? Yes.

But to what extent a policymaker, an agenda-setter? Perhaps I underestimate the influence of a wrestling coach in a small Ohio community. Would a prominent basketball or football coach in the same community qualify as a public personality? Probably. But where there is as much doubt and disagreement about the legal status of a libel plaintiff as is possible in the Milkovich case, all doubts ought to be resolved in the plaintiff's favor so that the remedial process may continue. A summary judgment for the newspaper against the school superintendent, however, properly withstood appeal.[432]

The coach's case proceeded to the U. S. Supreme Court largely on the question of how far "protected opinion" could be pushed as a constitutional defense. And could there be libel by negative inferences being drawn by readers from accurate facts? Yes, said the Court, in reversing a trial court's grant of summary judgment to the newspaper on grounds that the charge against the coach *was* susceptible of being proved true or false. This leaves the "no false opinion" standard in limbo, as it has evolved from *Gertz*.[433] But there should be little doubt about the coach's right to bring a libel suit in the first place.

The data from this study indicate no diminution in the number of libel cases brought largely against the major and most serious purveyor of news and public information among the mass media—the daily newspaper—generally on a complaint of injury to a person's "public" reputation resulting from false allegations of fact. While few newspapers ultimately fail in defending against such lawsuits, rapidly escalating and sometimes unbelievably high costs are associated with defense strategies that can stretch on for years and, in some cases, decades.

One third of all the cases examined in this study involved what the authors called "public officials"—officeholders, candidates for public office, and former public officials, or celebrities. These are not "private persons" as courts so often hold. They are persons highly visible and influential in their own settings, and, in most cases, they have access to media and to audiences. Although, in libel suits, they are required to prove actual malice to win damages, in only 9 percent of 339 cases in which the question of actual malice was addressed, thirty-one cases in all, was actual malice found.

To permit this litigational warfare to continue not only violates the spirit of the First Amendment and denigrates and depresses a tradition of robust, courageous, and even revolutionary journalism, but revives in contemporary guise and with the sting of economic punishment what the Supreme Court took 200 years to lay to rest—the crime of sedition.

Courts in this study, as has been noted, were less willing than the author to lay the mantle of "public official" on candidates for public office and former officials, while they practically never used their own invention of the "all-purpose public personality" to designate celebrity status.

More than half of both court and author-designated public officials examined in this study had high influence in their orbits of power and an equally high access to mass audiences. Another 40 percent had at least medium influence and access to the communication system.

While summary judgments and motions to dismiss are granted in defendants' favor in two-thirds of libel suits brought by public officials, and in 90 percent of cases overall, there are still considerable costs in time and money in these early stages of the legal process—some estimates going as high as $25,000. To what extent these trying early phases of the process alone have a chilling effect on enterprise journalism is not known, but it could be considerable.

American journalism, on the other hand, too often seems unaware of the major disorganizing and destructive forces at work within society, unaware of their insidious effects, until the damage is too great to be hidden. A rush of examples come to mind, some of which have been referred to in earlier portions of the study, among them AIDS, Iran-Contra, the HUD scandals, and the S & L catastrophe. Many more problems endemic to the society go unreported and eat away at the foundations of the social structure—race, religion, and reaction among them. Could libel litigation be a factor in this journalistic malaise? Perhaps. Stephen Renas, Charles Hartmann, and James Walker in their "An Empirical Analysis of the Chilling Effect" conclude that the greater the prospects of public persons prevailing in libel suits the less the likelihood that the press will publish articles and opinion pieces of a highly controversial and potentially litigious nature.[434]

Summary judgments and motions to dismiss, when granted to the media, can be appealed, as can jury verdicts. In this study nearly 55 percent of cases involving summary judgments and motions to dismiss and more than 90 percent of cases involving jury trials reached the first appellate level; most cases ended there with defendants winning more than two-thirds of the time. Therefore, vast amounts of time and money are expended in suits that will eventually be won by more than 70 percent of defendants in this study, and in other studies, with no apparent benefit to public discourse.

In addition, proof of actual malice, the central concept of the constitutional defense against libel, was found in only 9 percent of the cases in which the matter was addressed. And, in some of these, the offending statements were said to be privileged as opinion, or true (although it is not obvious how something "knowingly false" can be true), or the court changed its mind, or it remanded.

We began this study with 164 author-designated public officials and 44 author-designated all-purpose public personalities, a total of 208 highly visible policy-level or agenda-setting public plaintiffs. People of power. Famous people. Only ten public officials and six public personalities were eventually victorious, a batting average of approximately 7 percent. Using these figures, one could argue that 93 percent of the judicial resources involved in these categories of the libel process are squandered in cases where the odds are overwhelmingly in favor of defendants who seldom apologize for errors and even less frequently invite a public person they have maligned or challenged to reply in kind. The all-around losers are members of the attentive public who would listen to and read what powerful and glorified people have to say through the major media, if given the option.

Deciding on who fits what category of plaintiff will, of course, continue to be a problem and may be the Achilles' heel of this proposal, but it is a measurable improvement over courts and juries "winnowing truth out of a mass of conflicting evidence," a truth that is seldom apparent or discoverable in the heat and passion of political and social debate, or probing into "intents, motives and purposes"—to borrow the language of Thomas Emerson—to find "fault" in editorial judgment.

I am suggesting that courts choose the least of three evils. I make my proposal with full realization that chances of the present Supreme Court adopting any rule creating a libel-proof category of public person are dim. It is important, nevertheless, for all proposals to be on the table in a period when libel reform of some kind seems particularly urgent and inevitable.

A century before *New York Times* v. *Sullivan*, George W. Childs purchased the Philadelphia *Public Ledger*, and issued twenty-four rules of conduct calling for "a fair, frank and open acknowledgement and apology" when the paper made mistakes.[435] In contrast, our study of the late twentieth century has found that practically no one got to reply to a published attack, and precious few complainants received the courtesy of a full and fair retraction where mistakes were made.

The issues touched on in this proposal are not new. One hundred years ago editors were making similar appeals for changes in libels laws, and for the same reasons: too many foredoomed suits were being brought by public officials and the rich and famous; malice was a problem because then it was presumed in all defamatory publications and supported then astronomical awards in punitive damages; the costs of defending were too high; juries, for whatever reasons, were dedicated to punishing the press; and lawyers were the only real winners in the game of libel.[436]

Access to media, like defining a public issue or separating the public dimension of one's persona from the private, is another issue that remains unresolved, an appeal for a voice on occasion in the major organs of public opinion that remains unanswered. Discretionary opportunities for reply ought to be available to those who find themselves in the vortex of controversial issues of public importance, and are attacked in the media. A "fairness doctrine" propelled by the individual consciences of newsroom personnel rather than the threatening authority of a government agency or the arbitrary decisions of corporate managers is what is intended.

This is not to suggest that our newspapers and magazines become display cases for letters to the editor or that our broadcast stations turn into "open mikes." It is rather to suggest that there are times, and a sensitive editor and his or her newsroom should be able to recognize them within the context of that newsroom's ethical rules, when persons outside of media organizations need vehicles for messages that the public ought to hear.

While editors and publishers are being persuaded, increasingly by the teachers of journalists and the journalists they train, of the rightness of making available access opportunities for decision makers and agenda setters as part of a larger system of ethical decision-making and of a necessary public dialogue, libelous charges against influential public officials and celebrities, and libel reported in the course of frenzied debate on controversial issues of public importance do not seem to press against the limits of tolerance of a confident, open society with a revolutionary heritage.

One thing heartening about the legal profession in this country, however much I have "defamed" it in this study, is that just about every imaginable point of view will eventually find its advocate. Not all legal theorists are contractionist. And, even those who are make deeply sincere and persuasive arguments for freedom of expression in most circumstances. If the legal profession is not the guardian of our rights to speak and publish, then no one is.

And no one has more appreciation for the centrality of freedom of speech and press in our supposed system of self-governance than the mass communication bar. As a group they are fully committed to protecting freedom of expression. They have an uncanny skill in finding the right argument for the particular case and in making it sound reasonable. There are few if any absolutists among them, and they are untiring in developing propositions to support their bias in favor of a free and open dialogue, even a raucous and irreverent one.

I will not soon forget the day I heard one of the country's leading libel attorneys, addressing an annual meeting of the media bar in New York City, refer to Larry Flynt, editor of *Hustler* magazine, as "killing us." He was still prepared to defend him. And the same must be said, however grudgingly, for the rumor and gossip tabloids, the so-called supermarket papers. They must be suffered for the sake of legitimate journalism. And here again the conversation seems largely between plaintiff and defendant attorneys. Lawyers for such publications as the *National Enquirer*, *The Star*, and *The Globe* discourage libel suits by warning prospective plaintiffs about what the discovery process might further expose about their private lives and by pointing to the difficulty of meeting the actual malice test. Encouraged by the Carol Burnett case, celebrity lawyers nevertheless answer the calls of their clients, while bemoaning the advantages the law gives to defendants. Most often plaintiffs have to be satisfied with nominal out-of-court settlements or retractions. And a debate continues between these two banks of attorneys over stalling tactics, an example of which may be the barrages of motions defendants' attorneys fire at plaintiffs.

As a nonlawyer, I am concerned about the intellectual and adversarial enjoyment some expert lawyers seem to get from the mind-numbing twists and turns of libel law and the lack of enthusiasm I perceive among most media lawyers for alternative dispute resolution mechanisms, whether they be news councils, self-regulatory systems, or other forms of accountability. The insurance companies that protect the clients of these attorneys are certainly ready for changes of these kinds, although they recognize regretfully the reluctance of the media bar to experiment with alternatives to lawsuits.

More attention to social data on the part of legal theorists and working attorneys would be beneficial to legal scholarship and practice. I will not soon forget the reaction I got from two of the country's most prominent libel lawyers, one a judge, when I first brought to their attention the general findings of the Iowa Libel Study. They simply wouldn't believe them. No, they responded, plaintiffs sue only for money; they could not possibly have any other purpose. Seldom had a segment of the canon of the social sciences been so easily dismissed. The researchers, of course, had talked with plaintiffs.

I am suggesting reform in remedies rather than reform in liabilities—a denial of remedies to those classes of plaintiff who have high visibility and the resources to communicate with broad sec-

tions of the public rather than readjustments to the already dizzying complexity of libel law. Limitations on punitive damages or
the substitution of declaratory judgments for jury verdicts is not
enough.

The evidence would seem to support my proposal. So few prominent plaintiffs win damages that libel suits by high public officials
and celebrities, whether television stars or corporation presidents,
appear to be a waste of public resources. The consequences of
these incredibly expensive and protracted libel suits are a depressed
environment for free speech and press and perhaps a quite unconscious shrinkage in urgent and significant public discourse,
whether out of fear or an inability or unwillingness to risk bearing
the burden of court costs and lawyers fees.

There may be serious specific consequences as well. The major
media continue to depend on mainstream and official sources.
Significant private sector sources are too often given a wide berth.
Or information is reported from unidentified sources, a practice
that the public may come to appreciate less and less. Libel suits
are having a constricting effect on the whole pattern of social
communication. Words, whether those of the irate political activist
at a council meeting, those in the daily newspaper's investigative
report on a shady bureaucrat, or those in the gossip column's
commentary on the celebrity's fifth marriage, are being punished
with greater and greater frequency.

The apparent benefits to lawyers of the present system is troublesome. The litigiousness of the American society in the late
twentieth century has been a matter of much discussion. It is good
that we seek to resolve our differences in courts of law rather than
with baseball bats on street corners. Yet good things can be abused.
And in libel we are dealing with words and sentences rather than
faulty kitchen appliances or inept medical procedures. The Constitution singles out words for special protection. There are too
many frivolous lawsuits involving words, lawsuits in which everyone loses in one sense or another except the attorneys involved.

A system in which important people fully engaged in public
debate or celebrities seeking to win a public following would be
denied a remedy in libel law would suggest to the public at large
that freedom of speech is still an important constitutional value.
And it is that public that must concern us, both those within it

who wish to speak and those who wish to hear. Also, more and more people, it appears, are in need of being reminded that the First Amendment is still a central governing precept of our constitutional system.

However, the "more speech" mechanism that I am proposing depends for its success, not only on lawyers agreeing to forego the challenge and the monetary rewards of the libel suit, but on editors, publishers, and news directors being willing to devote some of their limited time and space to speakers they deplore and have attacked on either public or personal grounds. Societal, professorial, and professional pressures are increasingly suggesting that they do so. Without this sharing of the major means of mass communication, the profits of which are as far above the norm of reasonable compensation as those of elite lawyers, future prospects for freedom of speech and press are clouded at best.

The public will continue to doubt the fairness of the mass media and will show their disdain by increasing political pressures on the press that only a Supreme Court fully alive to the fundamental necessity of freedom of speech and press can relieve. Americans seem distrustful of great concentrations of power. The American media are or are fast becoming one of those concentrations. Unless they are willing to share some of that power with those they wrong, unintentionally or with purpose, there is a danger that press freedom as we know it today will be diminished. The greater the power of an institution, the greater its responsibilities to the public. The media are powerful.

The First Amendment notwithstanding, all of us, and the institutions of which we are a part, are ultimately accountable to someone for what we do. There is no perfect freedom in an interdependent society, although many commentators underestimate the degree of free speech the community can safely tolerate. We seem to have a choice. The media can delegate to the courts the task of establishing the balance of freedom and responsibility or they can begin to perform part of that task themselves. Self-regulation must precede both alternative dispute resolution and legal process. News organizations must consider in far more deliberate ways than heretofore charges of inaccuracy, arrogance, unfairness, insensitivity to race, religion and gender, and sensationalism (making trivia seem essential to the day's intelligence).

As the Hutchins Commission envisioned in 1947 in its influential and much maligned report, *A Free and Responsible Press*, the press could serve better than it does as a forum for the "exchange of comment and criticism" so that ideas that "differ from their own" will reach the ears of America.[437]

Yet, it is important to remind ourselves from time to time that those historical editors we sometimes idealize were, in their own day, among the most irritating and uncouth, the most savage and irreverent, and the most courageous of men. Cowardly men, as Louis Brandeis reminded us in 1927, do not make a revolution.

Notes

Introduction

1. *The Pennsylvania Gazette*, June 10, 1731, reprinted as part of *An Apology for Printers*. New York: Craftsman Associates, Inc., 1955, p. 7.

2. Susan Sheehan, "When Will the Book Be Done?" *The New York Times Magazine*, April 15, 1990, p. 38.

3. Gillmor, Donald M., Jerome A. Barron, Todd F. Simon, and Herbert A. Terry, *Mass Communication Law: Cases and Comment*, 5th ed. St. Paul: West Publishing Company, 1990.

Chapter 1

4. John Mortimer, "Rumpole and the Bubble Reputation," *Rumpole and the Age of Miracles*. New York: Penguin Books, 1988, p. 10.

5. Randall P. Bezanson, Gilbert Cranberg, and John Soloski, *Libel Law and the Press*. New York: The Free Press, 1987, p. 78.

6. Randall P. Bezanson, *The Libel Suit in Retrospect; What Plaintiffs Want and What Plaintiffs Get*, 74 Calif. L. Rev. 789, 791, 808 (May 1986).

7. *Ibid.*, p. 791.

8. *Barr* v. *Matteo*, 360 U.S. 564 (1959). Chief Justice Earl Warren and William O. Douglas were among four dissenters in *Barr* who feared that such an absolute privilege would "sanctify the powerful and silence debate."

9. John Thomson, *An Enquiry, Concerning the Liberty, and Licentiousness of the Press, and the Uncontrollable Nature of the Human Mind*. New York: Johnson and Stryker, 1801. Reprinted in part in Leonard W. Levy (ed.), *Freedom of the Press from Zenger to Jefferson*. New York: The Bobbs-Merrill Company, Inc., 1966, p. 284.

10. Frederic Hudson, *Journalism in the United States*. New York: Harper & Brothers, 1873, pp. 750–751.

11. *New York Times Co.* v. *Sullivan*, 376 U.S. 254 (1964).

12. See especially *Garrison* v. *State of Louisiana*, 379 U.S. 64 (1964); *Curtis Publishing Co.* v. *Butts and Associated Press* v. *Walker*, 388 U.S. 130 (1967); *Rosenbloom* v. *Metromedia*, 403 U.S. 29 (1971); *Gertz* v. *Robert Welch, Inc.* 418 U.S. 323 (1974).

13. *St. Amant* v. *Thompson*, 390 U.S. 727 (1968).

14. 441 U.S. 153 (1979). See Stewart dissent in this case for evidence of confusion between constitutional and common law malice. While substantial majorities of newspapers of all sizes disagreed with the ruling of the Court, one study found little evidence that editors were chilled or would admit to being chilled by the case. See James Bow and Ben Silver, *Effects of Herbert* v. *Lando on Small Newspapers and TV Stations*, 61 Journ. Q. 414 (Summer 1984). A study by Stephen M. Renas, Charles J. Hartmann, and James L. Walker, "An Empirical Analysis of the Chilling Effect," in Everette E. Dennis and Eli M. Noam (eds.), *The Cost of Libel*. New York: Columbia University Press, 1989, pp. 43–68, attempts to identify the conditions under which chilling effects do occur. They conclude that the greater the prospects of public persons prevailing in libel suits, the less the likelihood that the press will publish articles and opinion pieces of a highly controversial and potentially litigious nature.

15. Lois Forer, *A Chilling Effect*. New York: W. W. Norton & Company, 1987, p. 19. The classic statement of the demise of sedition is Harry Kalven, Jr., *The New York Times Case: A Note on "The Central Meaning of the First Amendment,"* 1964 Supreme Court Review 191.

16. David Shaw, *Los Angeles Times*, Jan. 19, 1990. This is the first of four critical articles running on consecutive days on media coverage of the McMartin child molestation case. See also Larry J. Sabato, *Feeding Frenzy*. New York: The Free Press, 1991.

17. D. Charles Whitney, *The Media and the People*. New York: Gannett Center for Media Studies, Working Paper, 1985, p. 3.

18. American Society of Newspaper Editors, *Newspaper Credibility: Building Reader Trust*. Washington, D.C.: 1985, p. 13.

19. Renata Adler in *Reckless Disregard*. New York: Alfred A. Knopf, 1986, p. 242, a detailed account of the General Westmoreland libel suit against CBS, represents this point of view in suggesting that *New York Times* v. *Sullivan*, for all its liberating effects "could not . . . have foreseen that in modern life it is the press itself that has, to a degree, become unitary, powerful, and monolithic, suppressing the very diversity that it was the purpose of the First Amendment (and even of *Sullivan*) to protect."

20. Marc Franklin, "Winners and Losers and Why," *A Study of Defamation Litigation*, 1980 Am. Bar Found. J 455, and *Suing the Media for*

Libel: A Litigational Study, 1981 Am. Bar Found. J 795, "The Financial Impact of Libel Reform on Repeat Players," in Dennis and Noam (eds.), *The Cost of Libel*. New York: Columbia University Press, 1989; the Libel Defense Resource Center data point in the same direction: in 1987–1988 the Center reported that 62 percent of cases appealed were either reversed or modified in defendants' favor. See Gannett Executive News Summary, Aug. 24, 1989.

21. Linda Lawson, "Trial By Jury: Problems with Jury Instructions in Libel Cases" (unpublished conference paper, Indiana University, 1985).

22. For example see Justice Powell's critical commentary on Vermont judges' lack of understanding of the *New York Times* doctrine in his opinion for the Court in *Dun & Bradstreet* v. *Greenmoss Builders*, 472 U.S. 749 (1985).

23. John Immerwahr and John Doble, *Public Attitudes Toward Freedom of the Press*, 46 P.O.Q. 177, 181 (Summer 1982), with comments by Leo Bogart and Jamie Kalven.

24. Theodore R. Anderson and Hazel H. Reinhardt, *The Current Status of Freedom of Expression in Minnesota*. Minneapolis: Minnesota Newspaper Foundation, 1987, pp. 1, 17. See also Victoria Smith, *infra*.

25. The Gallup Organization, *The People and the Press*. Los Angeles: Times Mirror, 1986, p.18.

26. *Ibid.*, p. 36.

27. John Immerwahr, Gene Johnson, and John Doble, *The Speaker and Listener: A Public Perspective on Freedom of Expression*. New York: Public Agenda Foundation, 1980.

28. *The People and the Press*, p. 41.

29. Reported in Whitney, *The Media and the People*, *op. cit.*, p. 17.

30. See Bogart, *op. cit.*, fn. 15, pp. 187–190.

31. Lee C. Bollinger, *The Tolerant Society: Freedom of Speech and Extremist Speech in America*, Chapts. 2 and 3. New York: Oxford University Press, 1986. For a critique of Bollinger's rejection of the fortress model, see David A. Strauss, *Why Be Tolerant* (a review), 53 U. of Chicago L. Rev. 1485, 1497ff. (1986).

32. Nathaniel Hong, *They Hang Editors Don't They*? Minneapolis: University of Minnesota (unpublished M.A. paper), 1988; and Victoria M. Smith, *Newspapers and Freedom of Expression: Minnesota Press Reaction to Suppression During the World War I Era, 1912–1920*, Minneapolis: University of Minnesota (unpublished M.A. thesis), 1985.

For examples of how radicalism was dealt with in the 1930s, 1940s, and 1950s, see Paul L. Murphy, *Constitution in Crisis Times*. New York:

Harper & Row, 1972, and *World War I and the Origins of Civil Liberties in the United States*. New York: W. W. Norton, 1979. See generally John Lofton, *The Press as Guardian of the First Amendment*. Columbia: University of South Carolina Press, 1980.

D. M. Gillmor in *The Fragile First*, 8 Hamline L. Rev. 277 (May 1985) demonstrates the insensitivity of government officials and many editors to basic constitutional principles in a recent First Amendment case involving a major college daily newspaper. See *Stanley* v. *Magrath*, 719 F.2d 279 (8th Cir. 1983). The federal appeals court did appreciate the constitutional issue.

Additional evidence of failures of the press to protect the very rights that guarantee its freedom can be found in John Lofton, *The Press as Guardian of the First Amendment. op. cit.*, and John D. Stevens, *Shaping the First Amendment: The Development of Free Expression*. Beverly Hills: Sage Publications, 1982.

33. 249 U.S. 47, 52 (1919).

34. Charles H. Martin, *The Angelo Herndon Case and Southern Justice*. Baton Rouge: Louisiana State University Press, 1976. See also *Herndon* v. *Lowry*, 301 U.S. 242 (1937).

35. Stewart dissenting in *Ginzburg* v. *United States*, 383 U.S. 463 (1966). See also Ralph Ginzburg, *Castrated: My Eight Months in Prison*. The New York Times Magazine, Dec. 3, 1972.

36. Owen Fiss, *Why the State?* 100 Harv. L. Rev. 781. 787 (1987).

37. James Goodale, *Survey of Recent Media Verdicts, Their Disposition on Appeal and Media Defense Costs*, in Media Insurance and Risk Management 69 (J. Lankenau, ed., Practising Law Institute, 1985).

38. Henry R. Kaufman, Harry M. Johnston, III, and Arthur D. Sackler, *Tort Reform and Libel*. Communications and the Law, December 1988, pp. 22–23.

39. Gannett Executive News Summary, Aug. 24, 1989. See also Michael Massing, *Libel Insurance: Scrambling for Coverage*, Col. J. Rev. (Jan.–Feb. 1986), p. 36 (payments of defense costs may constitute 80 percent of total paid to clients). For a detailed account of changing damages figures see Henry R. Kaufman, "Trends in Damage Awards, Insurance Premiums and the Cost of Media Libel Litigation," in Dennis and Noam (eds.), *The Costs of Libel*. New York: Columbia University Press, 1989.

40. Lois G. Forer, *A Chilling Effect. op. cit.*, p. 164.

41. M. Garbus, "The Many Costs of Libel." *Publishers Weekly*, 230: 72 (1986), pp. 13–16.

42. Rodney A. Smolla, *Suing the Press*. New York: Oxford University Press, 1986, pp. 74–75.

43. Norman Rosenberg, *The Law of Political Libel and Freedom of the Press in Nineteenth Century America; An Interpretation*. 17 Am. J. Legal Hist. 336, 340 (1973).

44. Forer, *op. cit.*, p. 275.

45. Rodney A. Smolla in, Symposium, *Taking Libel Reform Seriously*. 38 Mercer L. R. 793, 794, 803 (1987).

46. Anthony Lewis, *Annals of Law: The Sullivan Case*. The New Yorker, Nov. 5, 1984, 52.

47. *Westmoreland* v. *CBS, Inc*. 596 F.Supp. 1170 (S.D.N.Y. 1984). CBS's "60 Minutes" is no stranger to libel suits; by 1984 it was estimated that it had been sued 150 times.

48. *Sharon* v. *Time, Inc*. 609 F.Supp. 1291 (S.D.N.Y. 1984).

49. See Renata Adler, *Reckless Disregard*. New York: Alfred A. Knopf, 1986.

50. Burton Benjamin, *Fair Play*. New York: Harper & Row, 1988.

51. Neil Sheehan, *A Bright Shining Lie: John Paul Vann & America in Vietnam*. New York: Random House, 1988.

52. Seymour Hersh, "The Price of Power," an address to the annual convention of the Minnesota Newspaper Association, Minneapolis, Feb. 16, 1985.

53. *Davis* v. *Costa-Gavras*, 654 F.Supp. 653 (S.D.N.Y. 1987).

54. *Southern Air Transport* v. *ABC*, 678 F.Supp. 8 (D.D.C. 1988), 877 F.2d 1010 (D.C.Cir. 1989).

55. *Connaughton* v. *Harte-Hanks Communication, Inc.*, 842 F.2d 825 (6th Cir. 1988); *Harte-Hanks Communication, Inc.* v. *Connaughton*, 109 S.Ct.2678 (1989). In a similar case, a political candidate who had managed to gather only 2 percent of the vote in a prior election, blamed a newspaper for what was his second defeat. *Milskovsky* v. *Tulsa Tribune Co.*, 678 P.2d 242 (Okla. 1983), *cert. den.*, 465 U.S. 1006 (1984).

56. *Diesen* v. *Duluth News Tribune*, 437 N.W.2d 705 (Minn. 1989); *Diesen* v. *Hessburg*, 455 N.W.2d 446 (Minn. 1990).

57. *New York Times*, May 4, 1990, p. A16.

58. *McCoy* v. *Hearst*, 42 Cal.3d 835, 727 P.2d 711 (1986), *cert. den.*, 481 U.S. 1041 (1987).

59. *Costello* v. *Capital Cities Communication*, 532 N.E.2d 790 (Ill. 1988).

60. "Column Puts Publisher in Jail" (*South Carolina* v. *Fitts*), *The News Media & the Law*, 12:3 (August 1988), pp. 3–4.

61. *Lawrence* v. *Moss*, 693 F.2d 634 (10th Cir. 1981), *cert. den.*, 451 U.S. 1031 (1981).

62. *King* v. *Globe Newspaper Co.*, 512 N.E.2d 241 (Mass. 1987).

63. *Price* v. *Viking Penguin*, 881 F.2d 1426 (8th Cir. 1989). See Martin

Garbus, "Afterword," pp. 589–596, in Matthiessen, *In the Spirit of Crazy Horse*. New York: Viking Press, 1991.

64. *Janklow* v. *Newsweek, Inc.*, 759 F.2d 644 (8th Cir. 1985), *cert. den.* 479 U.S. 883 (1986).

65. *Janklow* v. *The Viking Press*, 459 N.W.2d 415 (S.D. 1990).

66. Anthony Lewis, *Annals of Law: The Sullivan Case*. The New Yorker, Nov. 5, 1984, p. 52.

67. Seymour Hersh, *The Price of Power: Kissinger in the Nixon White House*. New York: Summit Books, 1983.

68. *Desai* v. *Hersh*, 719 F. Supp. 670 (N.D. Ill. 1989).

69. *DeRoburt* v. *Gannett Co.*, 733 F2d 701 (9th Cir. 1984), *cert. den.*, 105 S.Ct. 904 (1985).

70. *Toronto Star*, January 29, 1990, p. A17.

71. Bezanson, et. al, *op. cit.*, pp. 17–18.

72. Judith Schenck Koffler and Bennett L. Gershman, *The New Seditious Libel*, 69 Cornell L. Rev. 816 (April 1984).

73. Marvin Kitman, *Newsday*, Oct. 26, 1989. See also Ronald Brownstein, "Hollywood's Hot Love: Politics," *New York Times*, sec. 2, p. 13, Jan. 6, 1991, and his book, *The Power and the Glitter*. New York: Pantheon Books, 1991, for an historical account of the Hollywood–Washington axis.

74. *NBC Appeals Newton Verdict*, Broadcasting, July 24, 1989, p. 78.

75. See David Anderson, *Presumed Harm; An Item for the Unfinished Agenda of Times* v. *Sullivan*, 62 Journ. Q. 24, 30 (1985).

76. Jeremy Cohen and Timothy Gleason, *Social Research in Communication and Law*. Beverly Hills, CA: Sage, 1990, p. 93; *Newton* v. *National Broadcasting Co.*, 930 F.2d 662 (9th Cir. 1990).

77. Steve Weinberg, *Armand Hammer: The Untold Story*. Boston: Little, Brown, 1989.

78. Norman Isaacs, *Untended Gates, The Mismanaged Press*. New York: Columbia University Press, 1986, p. 127.

79. For a summary of some the Scientology and Synanon suits, see Legal Defense Resource Center *Bulletin*, No. 2, Nov. 15, 1981, p. 28, and No. 3, March 15, 1982, p. 27.

80. *Los Angeles Times*, July 3, 1982, p. 1.

81. *Libel Defense Resource Bulletin*, No. 2, Nov. 15, 1981, p. 28.

82. Elizabeth K. Hansen and Roy L. Moore, "Chilling the Messenger: The Impact of Libel on Community Newspapers," *Newspaper Research J.* 11:2 (Spring 1990), pp. 86–99.

83. 418 U.S. 323 (1974).

84. Herbert J. Gans, *Deciding What's News*. New York: Vintage Books, 1980, pp. 8–9.

85. Quoted in Norman Rosenberg, *The Law of Political Libel and Freedom of the Press in Nineteenth Century America: An Interpretation*, 17 Am. J. Legal Hist. 336, 341 (1973).

86. Randall P. Bezanson, Gilbert Cranberg, and John Soloski, "The Economics of Libel," in Dennis and Noam (eds.), *The Cost of Libel*. New York: Columbia University Press, 1989, pp. 23–34.

87. Ronald A. Cass, "Principle and Interest in Libel Law after *New York Times: An Incentive Analysis*," in Dennis and Noam (eds.), *Ibid.*, pp. 89–102.

88. Clark Gavin, *Famous Libel and Slander Cases of History*, Chapt. 4. New York: Collier Books, 1962.

89. *Ibid*. Chapt. 5.

90. Smolla, *Suing the Press. op. cit,*, fn. 32, p. 25.

91. Irving Brant, *The Bill of Rights, Its Origin and Meaning*. New York: The New American Library, 1965, p. 496.

92. Michael Massing, "How Free Is the Soviet Press?" *The New York Review of Books*, Sept. 28, 1989, pp. 55, 58.

Chapter 2

93. *Rosenblatt* v. *Baer*, 383 U.S. 75, 85 (1966).

94. *Ibid.*, 89ff.

95. Harry Kalven, Jr., *A Worthy Tradition*. New York: Harper & Row Publishers, 1988, p. 95.

96. *Cardillo* ("My Life in the Mafia") v. *Doubleday*, 518 F.2d 638 (2d Cir. 1975). See also Stephen Weaver, *Analyzing the Limits of the Libel-Proof Plaintiff Doctrine*, 62 Temple L. Rev. 405 (Spring 1989).

97. Robert C. Post, *The Social Foundations of Defamation Law: Reputation and the Constitution*, 74 Calif. L. Rev. 691, 700 (May 1986).

98. Justice Thurgood Marshall in *Rosenbloom* v. *Metromedia*, 403 U.S. 29 (1971).

99. Penelope Canan and George W. Pring, *Strategic Lawsuits Against Public Participation*, 35 Social Problems 506 (Dec. 1988).

100. *Ibid.*, p. 508.

101. *Ibid.*, pp. 506, 508.

102. Eva Pell, "The Libel Suit as a Political Weapon," *The Los Angeles Daily Journal*, July 1, 1981, p. 4.

103. *Ibid.*

104. *New York Times*, Feb. 14, 1985, p. B2. See also Ted Gest, "A Chilling Flurry of Lawsuits; Companies and Public Officials Have a New Way to Answer Criticism: Sue," *U.S. News & World Report*, May 23, 1988, p. 64.

105. *New York Times*, April 24, 1990, p. B 1.

106. Judge Stanley Mosk in *Okun* v. *Superior Court*, 629 P. 2d 1369 (Calif. 1981), reported in Pell, *op. cit.*, p. 4.

107. Eugene L. Roberts, Jr., *The Quill* (cover story), April 1985, p. 14; "A Supreme Court Decision Fosters Litigation," *Nieman Reports*, Spring 1990, p. 4.

108. Jeremy Cohen, Diana Mutz, Vincent Price, and Albert Gunther, *Perceived Impact of Defamation: An Experiment on Third Person Effects*, 52 P.O.Q. 161 (1988). Cohen and Gleason, *op. cit.*, p. 97.

109. W. Phillips Davison, *The Third-Person Effect in Communication*, 47 P.O.Q. 1–15 (Spring 1983), and quoted in Jeremy Cohen and Albert Gunther, *Libel as Communication Phenomena*, 9 Communications and the Law, 9, 17 (Oct. 1987).

110. Cohen and Gunther, pp. 27, 29.

111. Robert D. Anderson, *The Law of Defamation in American Political Campaigns; The Emerging Protection of Political Commentary, 1800–1964* (unpublished doctoral dissertation, University of Minnesota, 1989); see also Doris Graber, *Processing the News: How People Tame the Information Tide*. New York: Longman, 1984, and *Media Power in Politics*. Washington, D.C.: CQ Press, 1984.

112. W. Phillips Davison, James Boylan, and Frederick T. C. Yu, *Mass Media Systems and Effects*. New York: Holt, Rinehart and Winston, 2d ed., Part II, 1982, pp. 117–223.

113. Melvin L. De Fleur and Everette E. Dennis, *Understanding Mass Communication*, 2d ed. Boston: Houghton Mifflin Company, 1985, Part III, pp. 289–435. See also Denis McQuail, *Mass Communication Theory*, 2d ed., Chapt. 9. Beverly Hills: Sage Publications, 1987.

114. Randall P. Bezanson and Kathryn L. Ingle, *Plato's Cave Revisted: The Epistemology of Perception in Contemporary Defamation Law*, 90 Dickinson L.R. 585, 587 (1985–1986).

115. *The Writings of James Madison*. ed., Gaillard Hunt, 9 Vols., New York: G. P. Putnam Sons, 1900–1910, Vol. 6: 337, *Report on the Resolutions*, Vol. 6: 396, cited in Jeffery A. Smith, *Printers and Press Freedom*. New York: Oxford University Press, 1988, p. 85.

116. *Ollman* v. *Evans*, 750 F.2d 970 (D.C. Cir. 1984), cert. den., 471 U.S. 1127 (1985). See also Frederick F. Schauer, *Language, Truth, and the First Amendment: An Essay in Memory of Harry Cantor*, 64 Va. L. Rev. 263, 279 (1978). Schauer discusses the impossibility of distinguishing fact from opinion in most political communication. The Supreme Court, in an effort to address the question in *Milkovich* v. *Lorain Journal Co.*, 110 S. Ct. 2695, 17 Med.L.Rptr. 2009 (1990), reinstated the distinction between fact and opinion by refusing to protect opinion based on false fact. See p. 166.

117. *Bose Corporation* v. *Consumers Union*, 466 U.S. 485 (1984).

Chapter 3

118. Leonard W. Levy *Legacy of Suppression*. Cambridge: Belknap Press of Harvard University, 1960.

119. 75 Harv. L.R. 457 (1961).

120. Dumas Malone, *Jefferson, The First Term, 1801–1805*. Boston: Little, Brown, 1962, p. 224.

121. David A. Anderson, "Media Success in the Supreme Court," Gannett Center for Media Studies Working Paper, 1987,

122. An example is *Root* v. *King*, 7 Cow, 614 (New York 1827), an influential state libel holding.

123. Anderson, *op. cit.*, fn. 88, p. 510.

124. *Pennsylvania Evening Post*, Nov. 16, 1776, quoted in Arthur M. Schlesinger, *Prelude to Independence: The Newspaper War on Britain, 1764–1776*. 1957, reprinted by Greenwood Press, 1979, p. 298.

125. James Kent, *Commentaries on American Law*, Vol.II, 12th ed., edited by O.W. Holmes, Jr., Boston: Little Brown, 1896, p. 31.

126. *Dennis* v. *United States*, 341 U.S. 494 (1951).

127. *New York Times Co.* v. *Sullivan*, 376 U.S. 254 (1964); *New York Times* v. *United States* (The Pentagon Papers case), 403 U.S. 713 (1971).

128. Walter Lippmann, *The Public Philosophy*. New York: New American Library, 1956, pp. 96–103. See also Carl Auerbach, *The Communist Control Act of 1954: A Proposed Legal–Political Theory of Free Speech*, 23 U. of Chicago L.Rev. 173 (1956), George F. Will, "Nazis: The Right to Exist Implies the Right to Win," a column reprinted in the *Minnesota Daily,* Feb. 9, 1978, and Walter F. Berns, *Freedom, Virtue and the First Amendment*. Chicago: Henry Regenery Co., 1957.

129. Zechariah Chafee, Jr., *Free Speech in the United States*. Cambridge: Harvard University Press, 1948.

130. Theodore Schroeder, *Free Speech for Radicals*. New York: Free Speech League, 1916, reprinted 1969.

131. Henry Schofield, *Freedom of the Press in the United States*, 9 Am. Sociology Soc.: Papers & Proceedings 67 (1914), referred to in David M. Rabban, *The First Amendment in its Forgotten Years*, 90 Yale L. J. 516, 557 (January 1981).

132. *Bridges* v. *California*, 314 U.S. 252 (1941).

133. George Hay, *An Essay on Liberty of the Press*. Philadelphia: Samuel Pleasants, 1799; John Thomson, *An Enquiry; Concerning the Liberty, and Licentiousness of the Press, and the Uncontrollable Nature of the*

Human Mind. New York: Johnson & Stryker, 1801, reprinted by Da Capo Press (1970), gen. ed., Leonard W. Levy.

134. Thomas M. Cooley, *Treatise on the Law of Torts* (Chicago 1879), p. 218.

135. Cooley, *A Treatise on the Constitutional Limitations* (Da Capo ed., 1972), p. 429.

136. *Atkinson* v. *Detroit Free Press*, 9 N.W. 501, 523 (Mich. 1881). Cooley, *Constitutional Limitations* (1886), p. 562.

137. *Constitutional Limitations*, p. 440, cited in Norman Rosenberg, *Thomas M. Cooley, Liberal Jurisprudence, and the Law of Libel, 1864–1884*, 4 U. of Puget Sound L.Rev. 49 (1980).

138. *Ibid*. Rosenberg, p. 91.

139. See, for example, David Anderson, *The Origins of the Press Clause*, 30 UCLA L. Rev. 455 (1982).

140. Leonard W. Levy, *Emergence of a Free Press*. New York: Oxford University Press, 1985, p. xvi. Playing on the title of his earlier work, *Legacy of Suppression*, Levy learns from a reading of the press of the period that there was also what he calls a "legacy of expression" (at xi).

141. *Ibid*., pp. 347–348.

142. Jan. 23, 1788, quoted in William Mayton, *From a Legacy of Suppression to "Metaphor of the Fourth Estate."* 39 Stan. L. Rev. 139, 142, fn. 17 (1985).

143. Dwight L. Teeter, *The Printer and the Chief Justice; Seditious Libel in 1782–83*, 45 Journ. Q. 235 (1968); *A Legacy of Expression: Philadelphia Newspapers and Congress During the War for Independence, 1775–1783*, 45 Journ. Q. 445 (1968).

144. Levy, *Emergency of a Free Press*, *op. cit*., 208.

145. *Respublica* v. *Oswald*, 1 Dallas (Penn. Reports) 319 (1788).

146. *Ibid*., p. 320.

147. James Morton Smith, *Freedom's Fetters*. Ithaca: Cornell University Press, 1956, p. 210.

148. Benjamin Franklin Bache, *Truth Will Out!* Philadelphia, 1798. For a study of Franklin's influence upon his grandson, see Jeffery A. Smith, *Franklin and Bache*. New York: Oxford University Press, 1990.

149. John C. Miller, *Crisis in Freedom*. Boston: Little Brown, 1951, p. 29.

150. James Morton Smith, *op. cit*., p. 182.

151. Charles A. Miller, *The Supreme Court and the Uses of History*. Cambridge: The Belknap Press of Harvard University Press, 1969, p. 83, fn. 41.

152. Frederic Hudson, *op. cit*., p. 181.

153. Donald H. Stewart, *The Press and Political Corruption During the Federalist Administration*, 67 Pol. Sc. Q. 426, 444–5 (Sept. 1952).

154. Frank Luther Mott, *Jefferson and the Press*. Baton Rouge: Louisiana State University Press, 1943, pp. 30, 31.

155. 11 U.S. 32, 7 Cranch (U.S.) 32 (1812).

156. *United States* v. *Cooper*, 25 *Fed. Cas.* 634, 639 (April 30, 1800). See Clark Gavin, *Famous Libel and Slander Cases of History*. New York: Collier Books, 1962, p. 79.

157. Donald H. Stewart, *The Opposition Press of the Federalist Period*. Albany: State University of New York Press, 1969, pp. 531, 541, 543.

158. Frank Luther Mott, *American Journalism*. New York: Macmillan Company, 1941, p. 146.

159. George Henry Payne, *History of Journalism in the United States*. New York: D. Appleton & Company, 1930, reprint Greenwood Press, Publishers, 1970, p. 169.

160. Stewart, *op cit.*, fn. 127, p. 693. Stewart is quoting from the Feb. 7, 1801 issue of the *Dartmouth Gazette* (Hanover, N.H.).

161. Richard Buel, Jr., "Freedom of the Press in Revolutionary America: The Evolution of Libertarianism, 1760–1820," in Bernard Bailyn and John B. Hench (eds.), *The Press and the American Revolution*. Boston: Northeastern University Press, 1980, p. 61.

162. Cato's Letters, 3d ed. (London 1733) 2:248. See Leonard W. Levy, *Judgments: Essays in American Constitutional History*. Chicago: Quadrangle Books, 1972. Freedom of expression has risks, Cato realized. Men will talk seditiously, wrongly or irreligiously. Restrain their opinions and the results are worse—injustice, tyranny, and ignorance.

163. Frank Luther Mott, *American Journalism*, *op. cit.*, p. 187, and Mott, *Jefferson and the Press*, *op. cit.*, p. 30. Based on Allan C. Clark, "William Duane," in *Records of the Columbia Historical Society*, Vol. IX (1906), p. 25.

164. *Ibid.*, Mott, *American Journalism*, p. 183.

165. Ford, *Writings of Jefferson*, vol. VIII, p. 218.

166. Charles O. Lerche, Jr., *Jefferson and the Election of 1800: A Case Study in the Political Smear*, William & Mary Q., 3rd Ser., 5: 467–9 (Oct. 1948).

167. Philip Foner (ed.), *Basic Writings of Thomas Jefferson*. New York: Wiley Book Company, 1944, p. 586.

168. Sept. 11, 1804 letter to Abigail Adams in Lester Cappon, (ed.), *The Adams–Jefferson Letters, the Complete Correspondence Between Thomas Jefferson and Abigail and John Adams*. Chapel Hill: University of North Carolina Press, 1959, p. 279.

169. John Tebbel, *The Compact History of the American Newspaper*.

New York: Hawthorne Books, 1963, p. 70ff. *People* v. *Croswell*, 3 Johns. Cas. 307 (N.Y. Sup. Ct. 1804). Levy argues that not even the Alien and Sedition Act itself qualified the defense of truth the way *Croswell*'s case did by requiring "good motives and for justifiable ends."

170. Johns. Cas. 307, 350 (N.Y. Sup. Ct. 1804). See Kyu Ho Youm, *The Impact of* People v. Croswell *on Libel Law*, 113 Journ. Monographs 6 (June 1989).

171. Richard Robertson, *Defamation and the First Amendment: In Praise of* Gertz v. Robert Welch, Inc., 54 Tex. L. Rev. 199 (1976).

172. Bruce E. Fein, New York Times v. Sullivan: *An Obstacle to Enlightened Public Discourse and Government Responsiveness to the People*. Washington, D.C.: American Legal Foundation, 1984, p. 12.

173. Eric Barendt, *Freedom of Speech*. New York: Clarendon Press, Oxford, 1987, p. 176.

174. John R. Finnegan, Jr., *Defamation, Politics, and the Social Processes of Law in New York State, 1776–1860* (unpublished doctoral dissertation, University of Minnesota, 1985), p. 174.

175. Norman Rosenberg, *The Law of Political Libel and Freedom of Press in Nineteenth Century America: An Interpretation*, 17 Am. J. Legal Hist. 336 (1973).

176. Finnegan, *op. cit.*, p. 234.

177. *Ibid.*, pp. 164, 232, 293.

178. *Ibid.*, p. 338.

179. The most important precedent among these cases was *Cooper* v. *Stone*, 24 Wend. 434 (New York, 1840), standing for the proposition that criticism of literary work must not reach personal character.

180. Horace Greeley, *Recollections of a Busy Life*. New York: J. B. Ford and Co., 1868, p. 261. See also Ethel R. Outland, *The "Effingham" Libels on Cooper*. Madison: University of Wisconsin Press, 1929.

181. *New York Tribune*, Dec. 21, 1842. See series, "The Press and the Law of Libel," beginning Dec. 13, 1842. See also *Cooper* v. *Greeley*, 1 Denio 347 (1841).

182. 418 U.S. 323 (1974).

183. Stephen Botein, "Printers and the American Revolution," in Bernard Bailyn and John B. Hench (eds.), *The Press and the American Revolution*. Worcester: American Antiquarian Society, 1980, p. 49.

184. *Fry* v. *Bennett*, 28 N.Y. 324 (1863).

185. Hudson, *op. cit.*, p. 743. See also Alfred McClung Lee, *The Daily Newspaper in America*. New York: The Macmillan Company, 1937, p. 416.

186. George Spring Merriam, *The Life and Times of Samuel Bowles*, Vol. i,ii, New York: 1885, p. 88, quoted in Payne, *op. cit.*, p. 329.

187. Willard G. Bleyer, *Main Currents in the History of American Journalism*. Boston: Houghton Mifflin Company, 1927, p. 265.

188. Mott, *American Journalism*, *op. cit.*, pp. 451, 466.

189. Rosenberg, *Protecting the Best Men*, *op. cit.*, p. 197.

190. *Ibid.*, p. 286.

191. *Ibid.*, p. 156ff.

192. Edmund S. Morgan, "The Pleasures of Paine," a review of A. J. Ayer's *Thomas Paine* (Atheneum, 1989) in *The New York Review of Books*, April 13, 1989, p. 30.

193. *United States* v. *Press Publishing Company*, 219 U.S. 1 (1911).

194. *New York World*, January 4, 1911.

195. Mott, *American Journalism*, *op. cit.*, p. 608.

196. *City of Chicago* v. *Tribune Co.*, 139 N.E. 86 (Ill. 1923)

197. John D. Stevens, R. L. Bailey, J.F. Krueger, and John Mollwitz, *Criminal Libel as Seditious Libel, 1916–1925*, 43 Journ. Q. 110 (1966). See also Stevens, *Congressional History of the 1798 Sedition Law*, 43 Journ. Q. 247 (1966).

198. Clifton D Lawhorne, *Defamation and Public Officials; The Evolving Law of Libel*. Carbondale: Southern Illinois University Press, 1971, p. 65.

Chapter 4

199. Alfred H. Kelley, *Constitutional Liberty and the Law of Libel: A Historian's View*, 74 Amer. Hist. Rev. 429 (1968).

200. *Green* v. *Alton Telegraph Printing Co.*, 438 N.E.2d 203 (Ill. 1982). For a detailed account of the case, see Thomas B. Littlewood, *Coals of Fire: The Alton Telegraph Libel Case*. Carbondale: Southern Illinois University Press, 1986.

201. Littlewood, *op. cit.*, pp. xv–xvii, 196–197.

202. *Brief for the Petitioner*, Herbert Brownell and Herbert Wechsler in *The New York Times Company* v. *L. B. Sullivan*, p. 51.

203. *Commonwealth* v. *Clapp*, 4 Mass. 163, 169–70 (1808).

204. *White* v. *Nicholls*, 3 How. 266, 285 (U.S. 1845).

205. *Coleman* v. *MacLennan*, 98 P. 281 (Kan. 1908).

206. *Masses Publishing Co.* v. *Patten*, 244 F. 535 (S.D.N.Y. 1917).

207. 376 U.S. 254 (1964).

208. *Ibid.*, p. 292.

209. 274 U.S. 357, 377 (1927).

210. William Brennan, *The Supreme Court and the Meiklejohn Interpretation of the First Amendment*,, 79 Harv. L. Rev. 1. 13–14, quoting

Meiklejohn in *The First Amendment Is An Absolute*, 1961 Sup. Ct. Rev. 245, 257.

211. *Gertz* v. *Robert Welch, Inc.*, 418 U.S. 323 (1974).

212. Harry Kalven, Jr., *The New York Times Case: A Note on "The Central Meaning of the First Amendment*," 1964 Sup. Ct. Rev. 191, 221.

213. *King* v. *Root*, 4 Wendell 113 (N.Y. 1827).

214. F. Dennis Hale, *The Federalization of Libel by Two Supreme Courts*, 11 Communications and the Law, 19, 25 (Sept. 1989).

215. *New York Times Co.* v. *Sullivan*, 376 U.S. 254, 293–305 (1964).

216. Thomas I. Emerson, *The System of Freedom of Expression*. New York: Vintage Books, 1970, pp. 530–531, 538.

217. William Prosser, *Handbook of the Law of Torts*, 4th ed. St. Paul: West Publishing Co., 1971, p. 737.

218. Sheldon Siporin, *Documenting Defamation: What is Stated? What is Truth?* Independent (Nov. 1989), p. 13.

219. Laurence Tribe, *American Constitution Law*, 2d ed. Mineola: Foundation Press, Inc., 1988, p. 865ff.

220. Martin Shapiro, *Libel Regulatory Analysis*, 74 Calif. L. Rev. 883, 886 (1986), concludes that libel no longer depends on outcome or a product of publication. Rather, *New York Times* constitutes a "process" standard that in time will generate judicial standards for news gathering and writing.

221. Susan P. Shapiro, *Libel Lawyers as Risk Counselors: Prepublication and Pre-broadcast Review and the Social Construction of News*, 11 Law & Policy 281, 289–295 (July 1989).

222. Steve Weinberg, "The Anderson File," *Colum. Journ. Rev.*, November/December 1989, pp. 35, 39.

223. William W. Van Alstyne, *First Amendment Limitation on Recovery from the Press: An Extended Comment on "The Anderson Solution*," 25 Wm. & Mary L. Rev. 794,796 (1984).

224. *Dun & Bradstreet* v. *Greenmoss Builders*, 472 U.S. 749, (1985).

225. Norman L. Rosenberg, *Protecting the Best Men. op. cit.*, p. 252.

226. *Coughlin* v. *Westinghouse Broadcasting and Cable, Inc.*, 476 U.S. 1187–1188 (1986), Chief Justice Burger, joined by Justice Rehnquist, dissenting to a denial of certiorari. See White in *Dun & Bradstreet* v. *Greenmoss Builders*, 105 S.Ct. 2939, 2952, fn. 3 (1985).

227. Richard A. Epstein, "Was *New York Times* v. *Sullivan* Wrong? in Dennis and Noam (eds.) *The Cost of Libel*. New York: Columbia University Press, 1989, pp. 121, 134–135, 149.

Chapter 5

228. 5 Coke 125 (1605), 3 Coke's Reports (Fraser ed., 1826 254, part 5—125a.

229. MaryAnn Yodelis Smith and Gerald J. Baldasty, *Criticism of Public Officials and Government in the New Nation*, 4 Journ. of Communication Inquiry 53, 58–59 (Winter 1979).

230. Hay, *op. cit.*, fn. 104, Richmond reprint, 1803.

231. Levy, *Emergence of a Free Press*, *op. cit.*, p. 208.

232. *Independent Gazetteer*, April 13, 1782, p. 1.

233. *Commonwealth* v. *Morris*, 3 Va 176, 5 Am. Dec. 515 (1811).

234. Robert J. Taylor, *Massachusetts, Colony to Commonwealth*. Chapel Hill: University of North Carolina Press, 1961, p. 148, cited in Smith and Baldasty, *op. cit.*, pp. 61–62.

235. Jeffery A. Smith, *Printers and Press Freedom: The Ideology of Early American Journalism*. New York: Oxford University Press, 1988, p. 165.

236. *Ibid.*, p. 11.

237. Letter to A. Coray, Oct. 31, 1823 in Andrew A. Lipscomb and Albert E. Bergh, *The Writings of Thomas Jefferson*. Washington, D.C.; Thomas Jefferson Memorial Assoc., 1904–1905, Vol. 15, p. 489, cited in Smith, *op. cit.*, p. 89.

238. Ford, *Writings of Jefferson*, Vol. II (June 1776), p. 27.

239. 250 U.S. 616 (1919).

240. Levy, *Emergence*, *op. cit.*, p. 320

241. *Cato's Letters*, 4 Vols., London: Printed for W. Wilkins, T. Woodward, J. Walthoe and J. Peele, 1724, Vol. 3, pp. 243–244, cited in Smith, *op. cit.*, p. 63.

242. Cannon, ed., *Letters of Junius*, pp. 14–15, 34–35, 39, cited in Smith, *op. cit.*, p. 66.

243. Brutus, *Gazette of South Carolina*, Aug. 27, 1783, pp. 2–3.

244. Isaiah Thomas, *The History of Printing in America*. Worcester: Isaiah Thomas, Jun. Press, 1810, pp. 142, 144–145.

245. *Virgil* v. *Time Inc.*, 527 F.2d 1122 (9th Cir. 1975); *Restatement (Second) or Torts*, sec. 652D (1977).

246. 401 U.S. 265 (1971).

247. Hale, F. Dennis and Robert O. Scott, *Impact of the Minnesota News Council on Libel* (paper presented to the law Division of the Association for Education in Journalism and Mass Communication, Orlando, Florida, March 2, 1991).

Chapter 6

248. *Paul* v. *Davis*, 424 U.S. 693, 702, 707 (1976). See Justice Brennan's dissenting opinion, pp. 722–723. Brennan equates reputation with what Justice Potter Stewart called "private personality" in his concurring opinion in *Rosenblatt* v. *Baer*, 383 U.S. 75, 92 (1966), rights the protection of which, said Stewart, are left to the States by the Ninth and Tenth Amendments. Brennan found in an earlier case, *Jenkins* v. *McKeithen*, 395 U.S. 411 (1969), liberty and property interests in reputation sufficient to invoke the strictures of the Fourteenth Amendment.

249. *Rosenblatt* v. *Baer*, 383 U..S. 75, 92 (1966).

250. Thomas I Emerson, *The System of Freedom of Expression*, *op. cit.*, p. 530.

251. *Whitney* v. *California*, 274 U.S. 357 (1927).

252. Marc A. Franklin, *A Declaratory Judgment Alternative to Current Libel Law*, 74 Calif. L. Rev. 809, 826–827 (May 1986).

253. David Barrett, *Declaratory Judgments for Libel: A Better Alternative*, 74 Calif. L. Rev. 847 (May 1986).

254. Rodney A. Smolla, *Law of Defamation*. New York: Clark Boardman Company, Ltd., 1989, 9.13(3).

255. Pierre N. Leval, *The No-Money, No-Fault Libel Suit: Keeping Sullivan in Its Proper Place*, 101 Harv. L. Rev. 1287 (1988).

256. Rodney A. Smolla and Michael J. Gaertner, *The Annenberg Libel Reform Proposal: The Case for Enactment*. 31 Wm. & Mary L. Rev. 25, 54–55 (Fall 1989).

257. *Miami Herald Pub. Co.* v. *Tornillo*, *op. cit.* See Barron, *Access to the Press—A New First Amendment Right* 80 Harv. L. Rev. 1641 (1967).

258. Zechariah Chafee, *Government and Mass Communication*, Vol. I, Chicago: University of Chicago Press, 1947, pp. 172–195.

259. Anthony Lewis, *New York Times*, Jan. 31, 1985, A23.

260. Martin Mayer, *About Television*. New York: Harper & Row, 1972, p. 273.

261. Richard Winfield, "Legally Speaking: *New York Times* v. *Sullivan*, 25 Years Later," *New York Times*, April 22, 1989, C 62.

262. Laurence Tribe, *American Constitutional Law*, *op. cit.*, p. 885.

263. *Miami Herald Pub. Co.* v. *Tornillo*, 418 U.S. 241 (1974).

264. Henry R. Kaufman, Harry M. Johnston, III, and Arthur D. Sackler, *Tort Reform and Libel*, Communication and the Law, December 1988, pp. 31–32, 36, 38–39.

265. Lois G. Forer, *A Chilling Effect*. New York: W. W. Norton & Company, 1987, p. 25ff.

266. Alfred McClung Lee, *The Daily Newspaper in America, op. cit.*, p. 237.

267. *Ibid.*, p. 180.

268. Martin M. Shapiro, *Libel Regulatory Analysis*, 74 Calif. L. Rev. 883, 886–8B7 (May 1986).

269. *Dun & Bradstreet* v. *Greenmoss Builders*, 472 U.S. 749 (1985); *Philadelphia Newspapers* v. *Hepps*, 475 U.S. 767 (1986).

270. Donald Meiklejohn, *Public Speech and Libel Litigation; Are They Compatible?* 14 Hofstra L. Rev. 547, 559–563 (Spring 1986).

271. ACLU Policy #6. See also Gilbert Cranberg, "ACLU: Second Thoughts on Libel," *Col. J. Rev.*, January–February, 1983,. 42–43.

272. Arlen W. Langvardt, *Media Defendants, Public Concerns, and Public Plaintiffs: Toward Fashioning Order From Confusion in Defamation Law*, 49 U of Pittsburgh L. Rev. 91, 128–129 (Fall 1987).

273. *Garrison* v. *Louisiana*, 379 U.S. 64, 77 (1964).

274. Todd F. Simon, *Libel as Malpractice: News Media Ethics and the Standard of Care*, 53 Fordham L. Rev. 449 (1984). Hugh J. O'Halloran, *Journalistic Malpractice: The Need for a Professional Standard of Care in Defamation Cases*, 72 Marq. L. Rev. 63 (1988).

275. Paul LeBel, *Defamation and the First Amendment: The End of the Affair*, 25 Wm. & Mary L. Rev. 779, 788–790 (1984).

276. Seth Goodchild, *Media Counteractions: Restoring Balance to Modern Libel Law*, 75 Georgetown L. Rev. 315 (Oct. 1986).

277. Kaufman, Johnston, and Sackler, *op. cit.*, pp. 33, 39.

278. David A. Hollander, "The Economics of Libel Litigation," in Everette E. Dennis and Eli M. Noam (eds.), *The Cost of Libel*. New York: Columbia University Press, 1989, p. 257.

279. Franklyn Haiman, *Speech and Law in a Free Society*. Chicago: University of Chicago Press, 1981, pp. 57–60.

Chapter 7

280. John Rawls, *A Theory of Justice*. Cambridge: Belknap Press, 1971. See also Thomas Scanlon, "A Theory of Freedom of Expression," *Philosophy and Public Affairs*, 1:204 (1972). Rawls was answered by Robert Nozick's *Anarchy, State and Utopia*. New York: Basic Books, 1974, which appeared willing to tolerate inequality as long as liberty was protected. There was disagreement as to whether Nozick followed a traditional liberal line or represented the New Conservatism.

281. Ronald Dworkin, *Taking Rights Seriously*. Cambridge: Harvard University Press, 1978.

282. Roberto M. Unger, *The Critical Legal Studies Movement*. Cambridge: Harvard University Press, 1986. Jurgen Habermas, *The Theory of Communicative Action*, Vols. 1 & 2. Boston: Beacon Press, 1981 and 1987; and *The Structural Transformation of the Public Sphere*. Cambridge: MIT Press, 1989.

283. For example, see Walter Berns, *The First Amendment and the Future of American Democracy*. New York: Basic Books, 1976.

284. Robert McKay, *The Preference for Freedom*, 34 NYU L.Rev. 1182 (1959). For a spirited and widely circulated attack on this position and on the prodigious use of footnotes generally in law review articles, see the deconstructionist essay by J. M. Balkin, *The Footnote*, 83 NWU L.Rev. 275 (1989).

285. *United States* v. *Progressive, Inc.* 467 F.Supp. 990 (W.D. Wis. 1979, appeal dismissed 610 F.2d 819 [7th Cir.]). See also Bruce M. Swain, *"The Progressive, the Bomb, and the Papers,"* *Journalism Monographs* No. 76 (May 1982), and A. DeVolpi, G. E. Marsh, T.A. Postol, and G. S. Stanford, *Born Secret: The H-Bomb, the Progressive Case and National Security*. New York: Pergamon Press, 1981.

286. *Cable News Network Inc.* v. *Noriega* 111 S.Ct. 450, 451, 18 Med.L.Rprt. 1358 (1990).

287. New York: Random House, 1970.

288. Laurence Tribe, "Rights of Communication and Expression," in *American Constitutional Law*, Chapt. 12, 2d ed. Mineola: Foundation Press, 1988.

289. John Hart Ely, *Democracy and Distrust*. Cambridge: Harvard University Press, 1981.

290. 274 U.S. 357 (1927).

291. Vincent Blasi, *The Pathological Perspective and the First Amendment*, 85 Colum. L. Rev. 449, 463 (April 1985).

292. *Ibid.*, p. 377.

293. William W. Van Alstyne, *Interpretations of the First Amendment*. Durham: Duke University Press, 1984, pp. 22–24, notes the clarity and positiveness of the language of the First Amendment compared with other provisions of the Bill of Rights.

294. Martin Redish, *The Content Distinction in First Amendment Analysis*, 34 Harv. L. Rev. 113, 138 (1981).

295. Alexander Meiklejohn, *Free Speech and Its Relation to Self Government*. New York: Harper & Brothers, 1948, pp. 65–66.

296. Thomas I. Emerson, *The System of Freedom of Expression*. New York: Random House, 1970, p. 487. The heart of Emerson's system is the distinction he draws between conduct that consists of "expression" and conduct that consists of "action," the latter to be regulated by gov-

ernment, the former not to be. The speech/action model can deal with most cases, at least the easier cases. William Mayton in *Seditious Libel and the Lost Guarantee of Freedom of Expression*, 84 Colum. L. Rev. 91 (1984) traces the test back to Montesquieu's *The Spirit of the Laws* and to the writings of Spinoza, one of the first general theorists of freedom of expression.

297. Emerson *op cit.*, 543, 496. Alan E. Fuchs, *Further Steps Toward a General Theory of Freedom of Expression*, 18 Wm. & Mary L. Rev. 347, 353 (1976).

298. Vincent Blasi, *The Checking Value in First Amendment Theory*, 3 Am. Bar Found. J. 521 (1977). For a critique of this concept, see Anthony Lewis, *A Preferred Position for Journalism*? 7 Hofstra L. Rev. 595, 626 (1979). An argument anticipating Professor Blasi's idea of countervailing power is found in John Kenneth Galbraith's, *American Capitalism: The Concept of Countervailing Power*. Boston: Houghton Mifflin Company, 1962 (1952).

299. Timothy W. Gleason, *The Watchdog Concept*. Ames: Iowa State University Press, 1990, p. 59.

300. *Ibid.*, p. 100.

301. Ronald Dworkin, *Is the Press Losing the First Amendment*? N.Y. Rev. of Books, Dec. 4, 1980, p. 49. See also *Taking Rights Seriously*. Cambridge: Harvard University Press, 1978.

302. *Village of Skokie* v. *Nationalist Socialist Party*, 373 N.E.2d 21 (Ill. 1978).

303. 108 S.Ct. 876 (1988).

304. Eric Foner (ed.), *The Complete Works of Thomas Paine*. Vol. 2, p. 588 (1945).

305. *Cohen* v. *California*, 403 U.S. 15 (1971).

306. Robert C. Post, *The Social Foundation of Defamation Law; Reputation and the Constitution*, 74 Calif. L. Rev. 691, 736 (May 1986). There is much to admire in Post's article. He is trying to find a balance between constitutional autonomy for the individual, a value that in other articles he has identified as dominant in constitutional thinking, and the maintenance of community cohesion. See, for example, his article, *Pornography and the First Amendment* 76 Calif.L.Rev. 297, 334 in which he says, "It is hard for us to imagine a system of freedom of expression that does not ultimately embody the value 'of assuring individual self-fulfillment'." To find his balance, he distinguishes among reputation as property, honor, and dignity—his way of making sense out of the conceptual snarl that is libel. In a subsequent article Professor Post analyzes what he calls the "paradox of public discourse." First Amendment doctrine, he argues, suspends legal enforcement of the very norms that make rational delib-

eration possible. See *The Constitutional Concept of Public Discourse; Outrageous Opinion, Democratic Deliberation*, and Hustler Magazine v. Falwell, 103 Harv. L. Rev. 601 (Jan. 1990).

307. For a critical examination of presidential campaign TV advertising, see Kathleen Hall Jamieson, *Packaging the Presidency*. New York: Oxford University Press, 1984.

308. Lee C. Bollinger, *The Tolerant Society*. New York: Clarendon Press, 1986, p. 186.

309. *Ibid*.

310. Eric Barendt, *Freedom of Speech*. New York: Clarendon Press, 1987, p. 17.

311. 391 U.S. 367 (1968). In his opinion for the Court, Chief Justice Warren held that the amendment to the Universal Military and Training Act, prohibiting destruction of Selective Service certificates, was constitutional. When speech and nonspeech elements are combined in the course of the same conduct, he wrote, a sufficiently important governmental interest in regulating the nonspeech element can justify incidental limitations on First Amendment freedoms. On this theory, Professor Thomas Emerson wrote in rebuttal, so long as the government regulation does not directly deal with the "communicative element" it may prohibit or control all other other aspects of holding a meeting, marching or demonstrating, distributing literature, exhibiting a motion picture, publishing a newspaper, forming an association, and many other forms of "expression."

312. Frederick Schauer, *Codifying the First Amendment*: New York v. Ferber, 1982 Sup. Ct. Rev. 285, 298, 302, 308–309.

313. Title 50, U.S.C., App. sec. 462(a).

314. Emerson, *op. cit.*, p. 85, fn. 37. In the House debate, Congressman Bray refers to "a filthy, sleazy beatnik gang," "Communist stooges" who were "praising the Vietcong," "chanting and screaming vile epithets." 111 *Cong. Rec.* 19,871 (Aug. 10, 1965).

315. Schauer, *op. cit.*, p. 305. For another view see a close analysis of the *O'Brien* case by John Hart Ely, *Flag Desecration; A Case Study in the Roles of Categorization and Balancing in First Amendment Analysis*. 88 Harv. L. Rev. 1482 (1975). Ely believes that categorization and balancing need not be regarded as competing general theories of the First Amendment, but can be used in tandem to protect expression once a guiding principle is found to direct them.

316. Blasi, *The Pathological Perspective . . .* , *op. cit.*, p. 472.

317. *FCC* v. *Pacifica Foundation*, 438 U.S. 726 (1978).

318. *Lehman* v. *City of Shaker Heights*, 418 U.S. 298 (1974).

319. Mayton, *Seditious Libel and the Lost Guarantee of Freedom of Expression*, 84 Colum. L. Rev. 91, 141 (1984).

320. Robert B. McKay, *The Preference for Freedom*, 34 NYU L. Rev. 1182 (Nov. 1959).

321. Frederick Schauer, *The Role of the People in First Amendment Theory*, 74 Calif. L. Rev. 761, 786–787 (May 1986).

322. 314 U.S. 252, 270 (1941).

323. Edmond Cahn, *Justice Black and First Amendment "Absolutes": A Public Interview*. 37 NYU. L. Rev. 549, 554 (1962).

324. Thomas Jefferson, 1743–1826, *Democracy*. Selected and arranged with an introduction by Saul K. Padover, New York: Greenwood Press (1939), reprinted 1969, pp. 151–152.

325. John Rawls, *A Theory of Justice*. Cambridge: Belknap Press, 1971, p. 39. Rawls' theory is in part a logical argument for greater access to the major organs of public opinion.

326. Steve Shiffrin, *The First Amendment and Economic Regulation; Away From a General Theory of the First Amendment*, 78 NWU. L. Rev. 1212, 1254 (1983). In a recent work, *The First Amendment, Democracy and Romance*, Cambridge: Harvard University Press, 1991, Shiffrin makes an impressive appeal for First Amendment protection of dissent in whatever form it may appear.

327. C. Edwin Baker, *Scope of the First Amendment Freedom of Speech*, 25 UCLA L. Rev. 964 (1978). For an elaboration of Baker's theory, see *Human Liberty and Freedom of Speech*. New York: Oxford University Press, 1989. For a skillful analysis of Baker's published works, see Richard F. Hixson, *C. Edwin Baker: A Review Essay on Free Speech*, unpublished manuscript, Rutgers University, 1989.

328. Shiffrin, *The First Amendment*, *op. cit.*, p. 1250.

329. See, for example, Jerome A. Barron, *Freedom of the Press for Whom? The Right of Access to Mass Media*. Bloomington: Indiana University Press, 1973; Bruce M. Owen, *Economics and Freedom of Expression*. Cambridge: Ballinger Publishing Co., 1975.

330. Baker, *Scope of the First Amendment*, *op. cit.*, p. 966.

331. *Ibid.*, p. 1004ff.

332. *Ibid.*, p. 1030ff.

333. *Ibid.*, p. 1000.

334. *Ibid.*, p. 1028.

335. For example, see Thomas M. Scanlon, Jr., *Freedom of Expression and Categories of Expression*, 40 U. of Pittsburgh L. Rev. 519 (1979). Scanlon incorporates John Rawls' *A Theory of Justice*. Cambridge: Belknap Press, 1971, into his free speech theory. Rawls' idea of dis-

tributive justice (all primary social goods, liberty and opportunity among them, ought to be distributed equally unless an unequal distribution works to the advantage of the least favored) is an idea based on equality.

There are critical theorists, themselves socially advantaged, who see humankind preoccupied with issues of power, and they foresee a kind of peasants' revolt of the powerless seeking to alter their status. Critical theorists themselves are in large part members of the Academy and thereby bona fide bourgeoisie, their own worst enemies perhaps, but remindful of traditional movers of social revolutions.

336. C. Edwin Baker, *Commercial Speech: A Problem in the Theory of Freedom*, 62 Iowa L. Rev. 1, 3 (1976).

337. Baker, *Scope of the First Amendment*, *op. cit.*, p. 996, fn. 102.

338. Baker, *Human Liberty and Freedom of Speech*, *op. cit.*, p. 254.

339. *Minneapolis Star and Tribune Co.* v. *Minnesota Commissioner of Revenue*, 460 U.S. 575 (1983), can be read as prohibiting special treatment of any kind for the press because what government gives today it can take away tomorrow. The press nevertheless has used the political process to achieve benefits it thinks it needs or deserves.

340. See Neuborne, *A Rationale for Protecting and Regulating Commercial Speech*, 46 Brooklyn L.Rev. 437 (1980); a recent expression of this view by Neuborne was made at the Nov. 8 and 9, 1990, meeting of the Communication Law section of the Practising Law Institute in New York City. Haiman, *Speech and Law in a Free Society*, *op. cit.*

341. Blasi *Pathological Perspectives . . .* , *op. cit.*, p. 477.

342. *Ibid.*, p. 478.

343. *Ibid.*, p. 474. Seldom is evidence of social behavior used by lawyers in the construction of legal theories in the First Amendment area. Lawyers live by rules of evidence, but when prescribing broad social theories having to do with speech, no evidence seems necessary, or, if evidence is provided, it is used for advocacy purposes. Much First Amendment theory drifts in a social vacuum.

344. Martin Redish, *The Role of Pathology in First Amendment Theory; A Skeptical Examination*, 38 Case Western L. Rev. 618, 626 (1988), makes the same argument: "[R]efusal to extend the First Amendment's scope (what I am calling a 'contractionist' theory) may logically imply reduced protection in more traditional areas of coverage."

345. James Randall, *Constitutional Problems Under Lincoln*. Urbana: University of Illinois Press, rev. ed., 1951, p. 2, quoting Nicolay and Hay, *Complete Works of Abraham Lincoln*, VI, p. 304.

346. *Ibid.*

347. *Ibid.*, p. 488.

348. *Ibid.*, pp. 499–500.

349. Bernard Bailyn, *The Origins of American Politics.* New York: Alfred A. Knopf, 1968, pp. 95–109.

350. *Street* v. *New York*, 394 U.S. 576 (1969); *Texas* v. *Johnson*, 491 U.S. 397 (1989).

351. *Spence* v. *Washington*, 418 U.S. 405 (1974).

352. *United States* v. *O'Brien*, 391 U.S. 367 (1968).

353. *Tinker* v. *Des Moines Independent School District*, 393 U.S. 503 (1969).

354. *Bethel School District No. 403* v. *Fraser*, 478 U.S. 675 (1986).

355. 315 U.S. 568 (1942).

356. *Houston* v. *Hill*, 482 U.S. 451(1987).

357. Compare, *Feiner* v. *New York*, 340 U.S. 315 (1951) and *Terminiello* v. *Chicago*, 337 U.S. 1 (1949).

358. *Chaplinsky* v. *New Hampshire*, 315 U.S. 568, 573 (1942), construing *State* v. *Chaplinsky*, 18 A.2d 754 (N.H. 1941).

359. Robert Bork, *Neutral Principles and Some First Amendment Problems*, 47 Ind. L. J. 20 (1971).

360. Herbert Marcuse, "Repressive Tolerance" in Wolff, Moore, and Marcuse, *A Critique of Pure Tolerance*, 1965, p. 110.

361. Laurence H. Tribe, *Constitutional Choices.* Cambridge: Harvard University Press, 1985, p. 198.

362. In *Frisby* v. *Schultz*, 487 U.S. 474 (1988), the Court upheld a Brookfield, Wisc., ordinance banning picketing in front of a particular residence. Unwilling listeners, said the Court, are entitled to protection within their own homes. Justice Brennan dissented because he thought the ordinance banned more speech than necessary, for example, the lone, silent individual walking back and forth with a sign.

363. A classic example is *Wooley* v. *Maynard*, 430 U.S. 705 (1977) where the U. S. Supreme Court ruled that a citizen of New Hampshire was not required to show the state slogan, "Live Free or Die" on his automobile license plate.

364. Annals of Congress 1789–1790, 434.

365. Geoffrey R. Stone, *Flag Burning and the Constitution*, 75 Iowa L.Rev. 111, 124 (1989).

366. *John Doe* v. *University of Michigan*, 721 F. Supp. 852 (E.D. Mich. 1989).

367. Robert L. Bartley, "Accurate News Is Libel in Some Quarters." *ASNE Bulletin*, January/February 1991, pp. 23, 26.

368. Kalven, *A Worthy Tradition*, *op. cit.*, p. 63.

369. Leonard R. Sussman, "The Press 1990: Contrary Trends," *Freedom Review*, January–February 1991.

370. Tunis Wortman, *A Treatise Concerning Political Enquiry; and the Liberty of the Press*, Reprinted by Da Capo Press of New York, 1970, L. W. Levy (ed.).

371. *Ibid.*, from an extended extract in, "The New Libertarianism Produces a Political Theorist," in Leonard W. Levy (ed.), *Freedom of the Press from Zenger to Jefferson*. New York: The Bobbs-Merrill Company, Inc., 1966, pp. 244, 254.

372. *Ibid.*, p. 282. Similar views were expressed by St. George Tucker in his editing of *Blackstone Commentaries* and in Thomas Cooper's *A Treatise on the Law of Libel and the Liberty of the Press. op. cit.*, fn. 156.

373. *Rosenblatt* v. *Baer*, 383 U.S. 75, 92 (1966).

374. 388 U.S. 130 (1967).

375. Frederick Schauer, *Public Figures*, 25 Wm. & Mary L. Rev. 905, 910 (1984).

Chapter 8

376. F. Dostoevsky, *Crime and Punishment*. New York: Norton Critical ed., 1964, p. 193.

377. *Rosenbloom* v. *Metromedia*, 403 U.S. 29 (1971).

378. *Gertz* v. *Robert Welch, Inc.*, 418 U.S. 323 (1974).

379. David Anderson, *Libel and Press Self-Censorship*, 53 Tex. L. Rev. 422,480 (1975).

380. *Ibid.*, p. 454.

381. Judy Lynch, *Public Officials, the Press, and the Libel Remedy; Toward a Theory of Absolute Immunity*, 67 Ore. L. Rev. 611 (1988).

382. *Goldwater* v. *Ginzburg*, 414 F.2d 324 (2d Cir. 1969).

383. *Op. cit.*, Lynch, pp. 633–634.

384. *New York Times* v. *Sullivan*, 376 U.S. 254, 267 (1964).

385. Lynch, *op. cit.*, p. 635.

386. See fn. 298.

387. Lynch, *op. cit.*, p. 638.

388. Anthony Lewis, *Annals of Law; The Sullivan Case*, The New Yorker, 52, 87 (Nov. 5, 1984).

389. *Lynch, op. cit.*, pp. 638–639.

390. *Ibid.*, p. 643.

391. *McDonald* v. *Smith*, 472 U.S. 479 (1985).

392. *Ibid.*, at 487.

393. *Ibid.*, at 490.

394. Walter Lippmann, *The Public Philosophy*. New York: New American Library, Mentor Books, 1955, p. 27.

395. *Libel Suits; To Fight or Not to Fight*, Newsinc., April 1990, p. 21.

396. Marc Franklin, *Winner and Losers and Why; A Study of Defamation Litigation*, 1980 Am. Bar Found. Res. J., pp. 455–500.

397. *Milkovich* v. *Lorain Journal Co.*, 110 S.Ct. 2695, 17 Med.L.Rptr. 2009 (1990).

398. Marc Franklin, *Suing Media for Libel: A Litigational Study*, 1981 Am. Bar Found. Res. J. pp. 797–831. For example, Franklin found newspapers defendants in 62% of media cases, broadcasters in 15%, and periodicals (magazines) in 14%. Comparable figures in the Iowa study were 69.5%, 18.3%, and 11%. For an analysis of how different kinds of media have fared before the United States Supreme Court since 1791, see David A. Anderson, "Media Success in the Supreme Court," *op. cit.*, pp. 5–6.

399. Pearson's $R = 0.77154$, significant at the $p = 0.00001$ level, meaning that there is less than one chance in 10,000 that this relationship could have occurred by chance alone. An R squared of $+ 0.59528$ ($+ 0.77154$ squared) indicates how much variation in the number of cases is explained by state population. In other words, state population explains more than 59% (0.59528×100) of the variation in the number of libel cases.

400. *LaRouche* v. *NBC*, 11 Med.L.Rptr. 1655 (D.C.E. Va. 1985); 12 Med.L.Rptr. 1585 (4th Cir. 1986).

401. *Embrey* v. *Holly*, 442A.2d 966 (Md. 1982).

402. David Anderson, *Libel and Press Self-Censorship*, 53 Tex. L. Rev. 422, 437, 479 (1975).

403. *Ollman* v. *Evans*, 750 F.2d 970, 996 (D.C. Cir. 1984), cert. den., 471 U.S. 1127 (1985).

404. Brief for the Petitioner, Herbert Brownell and Herbert Wechsler in *The New York Times Company* v. *L. B. Sullivan*, p. 51 (footnotes omitted).

405. Marc Franklin, *Winners, Losers and Why: A Study of Defamation Litigation*, Am. Bar Found. Res. J, 455, 500 (1980).

406. Dan Burt, Phyllis W. Beck, and Norman Pearlstine, Responses to Professor Franklin (*Public Officials and Libel: In Defense of* New York Times Co. v. Sullivan), 5 Cardozo Arts and Entertainment L. J. 51, 79, 83. 85–86 (1986).

407. 388 U.S. 130, 163–164 (1967).

408. The references are to *Old Dominion Branch, 496, Nat'l Ass'n of Letter Carriers* v. *Austin*, 418 U.S. 264 (1974) and *Paul* v. *Davis*. 424 U.S. 693 (1976), and are part of a general discussion in Laurence H. Tribe, *American Constitutional Law*. Mineola: The Foundation Press, Inc., 1978, pp. 631–648.

409. Burt, Beck and Pearlstine, *op. cit.* p. 87.

Chapter 9

410. 418 U.S. 241 (1974).

411. Jerome A. Barron, *The Search for Media Accountability*, 19 Suffolk U. L. Rev. 789, 799 (Winter 1985).

412. *Ibid.*, p. 813.

413. *Rosenbloom* v. *Metromedia*, 403 U.S. 29 (1971).

414. *Ibid.*, p. 47

415. *Ibid.*, fn. 15.

416. 418 U.S. 241 (1974).

417. 418 U.S. 323 (1974), fn. 3; Note, *Vindication of the Reputation of a Public Official*, 80 Harv. L. Rev. 1730 (1967).

418. *Dun & Bradstreet* v. *Greenmoss Builders*, 472 U.S. 749 (1985).

419. These models are elaborated in Everette E. Dennis, Donald M. Gillmor, and Theodore L. Glasser (eds.), *Media Freedom and Accountability*. Westport: Greenwood Press, 1989.

420. *Ibid.*, p. 47. See "Self-Regulation: A Critical Role for Codes of Ethics," in Dennis, Gillmor, and Glasser, Chapt. 4.

421. Dennis, Gillmor, and Glasser, p. 39.

422. *Ibid.*

423. *Cohen* v. *Cowles Media Company*, 17 Med.L Rptr 2176, 457 N.W. 2d 199 (MN Sup. Ct. 1990).

424. *Cohen v. Cowles Media Co.*, 111 S.Ct. 2513, 18 Med.L.Rptr. 2273 (1991). Promissory estoppel is the legal rule that if a promise is acted upon the law will help the actor enforce the promise.

425. *Cohen* v. *Cowles Media Co.*, 16 Med.L.Rptr. 2209, 445 N.W. 2d 248 (MN Ct. of Appeals, 1989). Some observers predict that the Court's decision in *Cohen* and in the "quotations" case, *Masson* v. *The New Yorker Magazine*, 16 Med.L.Rptr. 2089, 895 F 2d 1535 (9th Cir. 1989); 18 Med.L.Rptr. 2241, 111 S.Ct. 2419 (1991), will determine the course of media law for the foreseeable future. The issue in *Masson* is whether quotations claimed to be "deliberately altered and fabricated" are covered by the *New York Times* doctrine concerning falsity and reckless disregard of truth if the meaning of what the interviewee said has not been changed. A number of journalism educators filed amicus briefs in support of psychiatrist Masson while news organziations did the same for writer Janet Malcolm. Again the High Court reversed and remanded to the circuit court of appeals so it could reconsider plaintiff's argument that the writer's fabrication of quotations constituted actual malice, a question for a jury to decide. One major concern in *Cohen,* from the press perspective at least, is that news sources will make all kinds of inferences from an interview with a reporter about how a story is to be played or how the

source is to be portrayed in the story. Such inferences, if they became legal claims, would "constitute an enormous intrusion into newsgathering activities." On the other side, it is argued that if promises are not kept, sources will dry up or the credibility of the press will be severely damaged.

426. Robert M. Veatch, *A Theory of Medical Ethics*. New York: Basic Books, 1981. See Glasser, "Three Views on Accountability," in Dennis, Gillmor, and Glasser, *op. cit.*, p. 184.

427. Theodore L. Glasser, "Press Responsibility and First Amendment Values," in Deni Elliott (ed.), *Responsible Journalism*. Beverly Hills: Sage Publications, 1986, pp. 81, 96.

428. An example is Edmund B. Lambeth, *Committed Journalism*. Bloomington: Indiana University Press, 2nd ed. 1992.

429. James C. Thomson, Jr., "Journalistic Ethics," in Bernard Rubin (ed.), *Questioning Media Ethics*. New York: Praeger Publishers, 1978, pp. 51, 53.

430. James Madison, 1799, *Writings of James Madison, 1790–1802* (G. Hunt, ed.), 1906, p. 336.

Chapter 10

431. *Milkovich* v. *News-Herald*, 473 N.E.2d 1191, 11 Med. L. Rptr. 1598 (1984).

432. *Scott* v. *News-Herald*, 496 N.E.2d 699, 13 Med. L. Rptr. 1241 (1986).

433. *Milkovich* v. *Lorain Journal Co.*, 110 S.Ct. 2695, 17 Med.L.Rptr. 2009 (1990).

434. Renas, Hartmann, and Walker, "An Empirical Analysis of the Chilling Effect" in Dennis and Noam (eds.) *The Cost of Libel*. New York: Columbia University Press, 1989, pp. 41, 55.

435. Hazel Dicken-Garcia, *Journalistic Standards in Nineteenth-Century America*. Madison: University of Wisconsin Press, 1989, p. 219.

436. "Reform the Libel Laws," *New York Tribune*, March 13, 1889, p. 6. Samuel Merrill, *Newspaper Libel*. Boston, 1888.

437. Commission on Freedom of the Press, *A Free and Responsible Press*. Chicago: University of Chicago Press, 1947, pp. 23–24.

Appendices

Appendix 1
Grounds Pleaded by Media Defendants and Considered in Judicial Process in Media-Related Libel Cases

	Privileged as Opinion	Privileged as Fair Report	True	Not Defamatory	Non-Identifiable Plaintiff	Innocent Construction	Libel-Proof Plaintiff	No Actual Malice	No Negligence	No Actual Injury	Remanded	*No Grounds Indicated
Media Defendant Wins, 496 Cases	100% (119)	95.8% (68)	93.5% (43)	98.4% (60)	89.5% (17)	100% (20)	100% (2)	94.9% (129)	100% (16)	100% (1)	23.8% (20)	2.9% (1)
Plaintiff Wins, 114 Cases	—	4.2% (3)	6.5% (3)	1.6% (1)	10.5% (2)	—	—	5.1% (7)	—	—	76.2% (64)	97.1% (34)
Percentage of Total Cases	19.5%	11.6%	7.5%	10%	3.1%	3.3%	.3%	22.3%	2.6%	.2%	13.8%	5.7%
Total Cases in Category	(119)	(71)	(46)	(61)	(19)	(20)	(2)	(136)	(16)	(1)	(84)	(35)

N = 610

*The authors were unable to determine the grounds for court success in these cases.

Appendix 2
Winners by Type of Injury Claimed by Plaintiff in Media-Related Libel Cases

	Reputation	Status	Business	Reputation & Status	Reputation & Business	Status & Business	Reputation, Status & Business	Type of Injury Not Specified
Media Defendant Wins, 251 Cases	78.6% (165)	90% (9)	77.3% (34)	64% (16)	64.7% (11)	100% (2)	100% (2)	85.7% (12)
Plaintiff Wins, 73 Cases	21.4% (45)	10% (1)	22.7% (10)	36% (9)	35.3% (6)	—	—	14.3% (2)
Percentage of Total Cases	64.8%	3.1%	13.6%	7.7%	5.2%	.6%	.6%	4.3%
Total Cases in Category	(210)	(10)	(44)	(25)	(17)	(2)	(2)	(14)

N = 324

Appendix 3
Winners by Public Life vs. Private Life in Media-Related Libel Cases

	Public Life	Private Life	Both
Media Defendant Wins, 491 Cases	82.3% (428)	76.6% (59)	57.1% (4)
Plaintiff Wins, 113 Cases	17.7% (92)	23.4% (18)	42.9% (3)
Percentage of Total Cases *Total Cases in Category*	86.1% (520)	12.7% (77)	1.2% (7)
	N = 604		

Appendix 4
Winners by Actual Malice in Media-Related Libel Cases

	Actual Malice Found	*Actual Malice Addressed But Not Found*
Media Defendant Wins, 297 Cases	19.4% (6)	94.5% (291)
Plaintiff Wins, 42 Cases	80.6% (25)	5.5% (17)
Percentage of Total Cases *Total Cases in Category*	9.1% (31)	90.9% (308)
	N = 339	

Appendix 5
Winners by Negligence in Media-Related Libel Cases

	Negligence Found	*Negligence Addressed But Not Found*
Media Defendant Wins, 64 Cases	25% (4)	95.2% (60)
Plaintiff Wins, 15 Cases	75% (12)	4.8% (3)
Percentage of Total Cases *Total Cases in Category*	20.3% (16)	79.7% (63)
	N = 79	

Appendix 6
Winners by Fact or Opinion in Media-Related Libel Cases

	Fact	Opinion
Media Defendant Wins,	77.2%	97%
410 Cases	(281)	(129)
Plaintiff Wins,	22.8%	3%
87 Cases	(83)	(4)
Percentage of Total Cases	73.2%	26.8%
Total Cases in Category	(364)	(133)
	N = 497	

Appendix 7
Winners by Truth or Falsehood in Media-Related Libel Cases

	Truth	Falsehood
Media Defendant Wins,	90.1%	76.2%
335 Cases	(82)	(253)
Plaintiff Wins,	9.9%	23.8%
88 Cases	(9)	(79)
Percentage of Total Cases	21.5%	78.5%
Total Cases in Category	(91)	(332)
	N = 423	

Appendix 8
Winners by High or Low Influence in Media-Related Libel Cases

	High Influence	Medium Influence	Low Influence
Media Defendant Wins, 495 Cases	77.9% (102)	78.9% (161)	84.7% (232)
Plaintiff Wins, 114 Cases	22.1% (29)	21.1% (43)	15.3% (42)
Percentage of Total Cases Total Cases in Category	21.5% (131)	33.5% (204)	45% (274)
	N = 609		

Winners by Access to Media in Media-Related Libel Cases

	High Access	Medium Access	Low Access
Media Defendant Wins, 495 Cases	77.6% (104)	77.9% (162)	85.8% (229)
Plaintiff Wins, 114 Cases	22.4% (30)	22.1% (46)	14.2% 38)
Percentage of Total Cases Total Cases in Category	22% (134)	34.2% (208)	43.8% (267)
	N = 609		

Appendix 9
Winners by Presence of Retraction in Media-Related Libel Cases

	Retraction Made	No Retraction Made
Media Defendant Wins, 495 Cases	58.8% (10)	81.9% (485)
Plaintiff Wins, 114 Cases	41.2% (7)	18.1% (107)
Percentage of Total Cases Total Cases in Category	2.8% (17)	97.2% (592)
	N = 609	

Appendix 10

Media	Audience	Size
Newspapers	Large	Circulation 100,000 +
	Medium	Circulation 50,000–100,000
	Small	Circulation less than 50,000
Television	Large	Network, Network affiliates
	Medium	Local TV, Fox, TBS, PBS
	Small	Cable TV
Magazines	Large	Nat'l reputation, popular
	Medium	Regional, state, trade
	Small	Local, geared to small audiences
Books	Size of audience determined by size of publishing house	
Radio	Arbitron rating used to determine market size of location	
Wire Services	AP and UPI coded as large media due to their large audience potential	
Journals and Pamphlets	Size estimated by group to which publication is geared	

Appendix 11
Winners by Media Audience Size in Media-Related Libel Cases

	Large	Medium	Small
Media Defendant Wins,	82.9%	74.5%	83.2%
493 Cases	(335)	(79)	(79)
Plaintiff Wins,	17.1%	25.5%	16.8%
112 Cases	(69)	(27)	(16)
Percentage of Total Cases	66.8%	17.5%	15.7%
Total Cases in Category	(404)	(106)	(95)
	N = 605		

Appendix 12
Winners by Type of Media in Media-Related Libel Cases

	Book Publisher	Wire Service	Newspaper	Pamphlet	Magazine	TV	Radio	Journal
Media Defendant Wins	92.6% (25)	88.2% (15)	84.8% (324)	83.3% (5)	75.9% (66)	72.6% (69)	64.7% (11)	33.3% (1)
Plaintiff Wins	7.4% (2)	11.8% (2)	15.2% (58)	16.7% (1)	24.1% (21)	27.4% (26)	35.3% (6)	66.7% (2)
Percentage of Total Cases Total Cases in Category	4.3% (27)	2.7% (17)	60.3% (382)	.9% (6)	13.7% (87)	15% (95)	2.7% (17)	.5% (3)

*N = 634

*In some cases a plaintiff sued more than one media defendant, therefore, the sample size is larger than 614.

Winners by Print or Broadcast Media in Media-Related Libel Cases

	Print Media	Broadcast Media
Media Defendant Wins, 486 Cases	83.4% (407)	71.8% (79)
Plaintiff Wins, 112 Cases	16.6% (81)	28.2% (31)
Percentage of Total Cases Total Cases in Category	81.6% (488)	18.4% (110)

N = 598

Appendix 13
Court and Author Designation of Libel Plaintiffs in Media-Related Libel Cases

	Public Official	Voluntary Public Figure	Involuntary Public Figure	All-Purpose Public Personality	Public Employee	Private Person	Plaintiff Not Designated by Court
Court Designation:							
Total Cases	139	230	7	1	4	166	67
Percentage of Total Cases	(22.6%)	(37.5%)	(1.1%)	(.2%)	(.7%)	(27%)	(10.9%)
Author Designation:							
Total Cases	164	254	14	44	21	117	—
Percentage of Total Cases	(26.7%)	(41.4%)	(2.3%)	(7.2%)	(3.4%)	(19.1%)	—

N = 614

Outcomes in Court- and Author-Designated Categories

Summary Judgment: granted in 333, or 54.2 percent of 614 cases, denied in 33, or 5.3 percent of 614 cases.

	Court-Designated (Granted/Denied)	Author-Designated (Granted/Denied)
Public Official	78/7	93/8
Voluntary Public Person	128/12	142/10
Involuntary Public Person	5/0	6/1
All-Purpose Public Personality	0/0	17/3
Public Employee	2/1	12/2
Private Person	85/12	63/9
Total	298/32	333/33

Motion to Dismiss: granted in 111, or 18 percent of 614 cases, denied in 12, or 1.9 percent of 614 cases.

	Court-Designated (Granted/Denied)	Author-Designated (Granted/Denied)
Public Official	17/3	19/3
Voluntary Public Person	42/3	53/3
Involuntary Public Person	1/0	4/0
All-Purpose Public Personality	0/0	11/2
Public Employee	0/0	2/0
Private Person	23/3	22/4
Undesignated	23/3	0/0
Total	106/12	111/12

Directed Verdicts: granted in 4, or .6 percent of 614 cases for plaintiff and 32, or 5.2 percent of 614 cases for defendant.

Initial Jury Trial Outcome: verdicts for plaintiff in 86, or only 14 percent of 614 cases.

	Court-Designated	Author-Designated
Public Official	23	28
Voluntary Public Person	31	30
Involuntary Public Person	0	2
All-Purpose Public Personality	1	11
Public Employee	0	2
Private Person	28	13
Undesignated	3	0
Total	86	86

Initial Dispositions:

	Public Officials	
	Court-Designated	*Author-Designated*
Defendants' Favor		
Summary Judgment granted	78	93
Motion to Dismiss granted	17	19
Directed Verdict denied	9	11
Plaintiffs' Favor		
Summary Judgment denied	7	8
Motion to Dismiss denied	3	3
Directed Verdict granted	1	1
Jury Verdict for Plaintiff	23	28
Total	138	163

	All-Purpose Public-Personality	
	Court-Designated	*Author-Designated*
Defendants' Favor		
Summary Judgment granted	0	17
Motion to Dismiss granted	0	11
Directed Verdict denied	0	0
Plaintiffs' Favor		
Summary Judgment denied	0	3
Motion to Dismiss denied	0	2
Directed Verdict granted	0	0
Jury Verdict for Plaintiff	1	11
Total	1	44

Final Jury Trial Outcome (including appeals): verdicts for plaintiff *34, or 5.5 percent of 614 cases.

	Court-Designated	*Author-Designated*
Public Official	6	9
Voluntary Public Person	12	10
Involuntary Public Person	0	2
All-Purpose Public Personality	1	6
Public Employee	0	1
Private Person	15	6
Total	34	34

*This number differs from the 33 cases reported in the text because in one case in which the jury awarded damages, no damages were subsequently paid for unexplained reasons.

213

Appeals
Appeal 1: 378 cases
Appeal 2: 54 cases
Appeal 3: 5 cases

Initial Monetary Award: 86 plaintiffs awarded money damages by jury; mean average award—$1,497,000.

Final Monetary Award: 33 plaintiffs awarded money damages by jury; mean award (**31 cases)—$504,000.

**No figures were reported for two cases.

Appendix 14
Time Taken to Reach Final Judgments in Media-Related Libel Cases

Years	Cases	Percentage
1	87	20.4
2	89	20.8
3	77	18.0
4	46	10.8
5	43	10.1
6	33	7.7
7	28	6.6
8	9	2.1
9	6	1.4
10	2	.5
11	3	.7
12	2	.5
13	2	.5
Total	427	100%

Appendix 15
Faring of Plaintiffs and Defendants in Federal vs. State Courts in Media-Related Libel Cases

	Federal Courts	*State Courts*
Media Defendant Wins, 495 Cases	78.5% (139)	82.4% (356)
Plaintiff Wins, 114 Cases	21.5% (38)	17.6% (76)
Percentage of Total Cases *Total Cases in Category*	29.1% (177)	70.9% (432)
	N = 609	

Index

America prides itself on its freedom of expression, and it has a reputation for tightly restricted libel law. Indeed, a study of more than 600 media-related suits in the 1980s found that ninety percent were won by the media or thrown out of court before even going to trial. However, even a case ending in summary judgment can cost the victorious defendant $25,000 or more, and the bill for a full trial can easily pass $100,000. The volume of libel suits has not diminished and many defendants settle out of court simply to avoid crippling costs. Clearly, writes Donald Gillmor, we are suffering a major crisis in libel law.

In *Power, Publicity, and the Abuse of Libel law*, Gillmor takes a revealing look at the state of libel law and offers a compelling agenda for change. He begins with a disturbing review of the abuses of libel in our times, examining both famous and little known cases. Wayne Newton, for example, won an initial $22.7 million jury award against NBC for an unflattering story—even though he went on to get a Nevada casino license, a $19 million loan, the Presidential Medal of Freedom, and was made grand marshal of an Independence Day parade in Washington, DC. "It was not clear," Gillmor writes, "for what NBC was being punished; the network obviously hadn't damaged Newton's reputation." Even tiny papers suffer crippling lawsuits. One 1,300-circulation publication was sued for $20 million; even though the case was dismissed, the defense cost $20,000. Such actions, Gillmor writes, dampen the fire of a free press.

Lively journalism has always been an American tradition—if anything, the press was far more reckless in the days of the framers of the constitution; they often suffered its